**To renew this** 
call 01823 334344 (automated)
or visit www.foursite.somerset.gov.uk

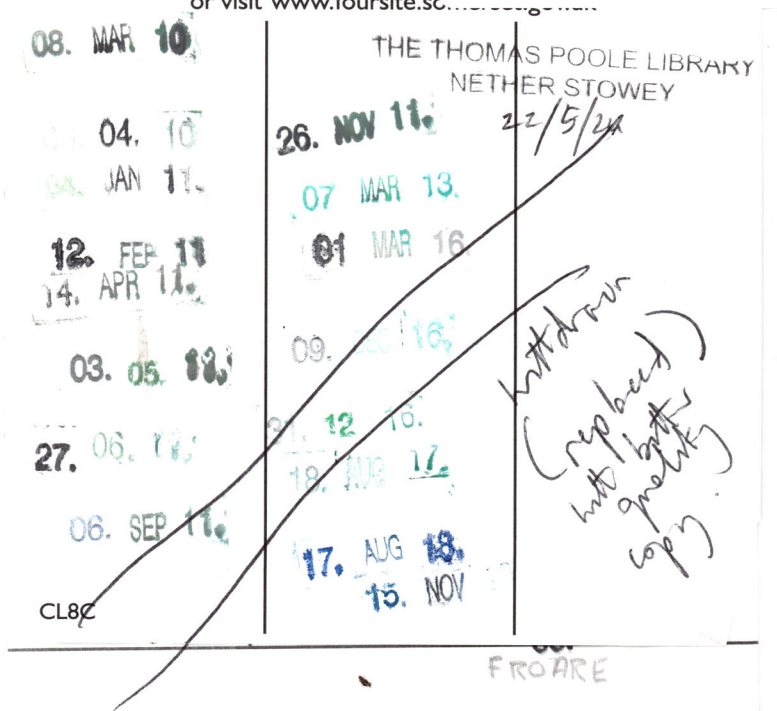

THE THOMAS POOLE LIBRARY
NETHER STOWEY

22/5/24

08. MAR 10
04. 10
JAN 11
12. FEB 11
14. APR 11
03. 05. 11
27. 06.
06. SEP 11
26. NOV 11
07 MAR 13
01 MAR 16
09.
12.
18. AUG 17
17. AUG 18
15. NOV

withdrawn
(replaced
with both
quality
copy)

CL8C

FROARE

Please return/renew this item by the last date shown.

*Somerset County Council*
LIBRARY SERVICE

# SOMERSET v HITLER

**Secret Operations in the Mendips 1939–1945**

## Donald Brown

COUNTRYSIDE BOOKS
NEWBURY, BERKSHIRE

First published 1999
© Donald Brown 1999

All rights reserved. No reproduction
permitted without the prior permission
of the publisher:

COUNTRYSIDE BOOKS
3 Catherine Road
Newbury, Berkshire

ISBN 1 85306 590 0

Cover design by Graham Whiteman

Produced through MRM Associates Ltd., Reading
Typeset by Techniset Typesetters, Merseyside
Printed by Woolnough Bookbinding Ltd., Irthlingborough

# CONTENTS

| | | |
|---|---|---|
| Introduction | | 5 |
| Area map | | 6 |
| 1 | Setting the Scene: 'There Will Come A Battle For Our Island' | 9 |
| 2 | Beating the Invader | 14 |
| 3 | Mendip Sea Watch | 22 |
| 4 | The Green Line | 32 |
| 5 | Mendip's Home Guard | 38 |
| 6 | The Weston Front | 46 |
| 7 | Wells on Watch | 53 |
| 8 | Ready to Resist | 64 |
| 9 | Underground Army | 75 |
| 10 | Arming the Auxiliary Units | 89 |
| 11 | Training to Defend Mendip | 99 |
| 12 | Secret Army | 112 |

| 13 | Wartime Life | 116 |
| 14 | Dig for Victory | 127 |
| 15 | Back to the Land | 138 |
| 16 | The Threat from the Air | 146 |
| 17 | Starfish Wars | 165 |
| 18 | Mendip Sky Watch | 178 |
| 19 | Yoxter | 189 |
| 20 | Turning the Tables: D-Day | 194 |
| 21 | For You The War Is Over | 204 |
| 22 | Peace Returns to Somerset | 208 |

| | |
|---|---|
| Appendix A: A Home Guard War Book | 216 |
| Appendix B: Mendip Auxiliary Units | 221 |
| Appendix C: Auxiliary Unit Operational Patrols | 229 |
| Appendix D: Auxiliary Unit Training Tests | 234 |
| Appendix E: Royal Observer Corps Posts | 238 |
| Acknowledgements | 240 |
| Bibliography | 242 |
| Index | 244 |

# INTRODUCTION

When invasion threatened in 1940, Somerset's Mendip Hills were beset by land, air and sea. Defenders looked south for invaders and bombers, while along the seaboard, convoys crept in, under the protection of the Mendip Sea Watch, carrying war materials to sustain a desperate defence.

In the face of these dangers, Mendip contained – and concealed – more wartime activity than even its own people suspected. Most of those people were engaged in their own unending war-work on the land, beating the even greater danger of starvation by blockade.

This book gathers together their memories of how they faced that war. Even if some memories are incomplete, or inexactly recalled, or perhaps polished by time, they are all valid. They represent the experience of every community. Set into a factual historical context, they recall and illustrate life in those perilous years.

Most of this Mendip story takes place on the high ground between Frome and Steep Holm, but a few episodes spread over into adjacent areas.

Donald Brown
1999

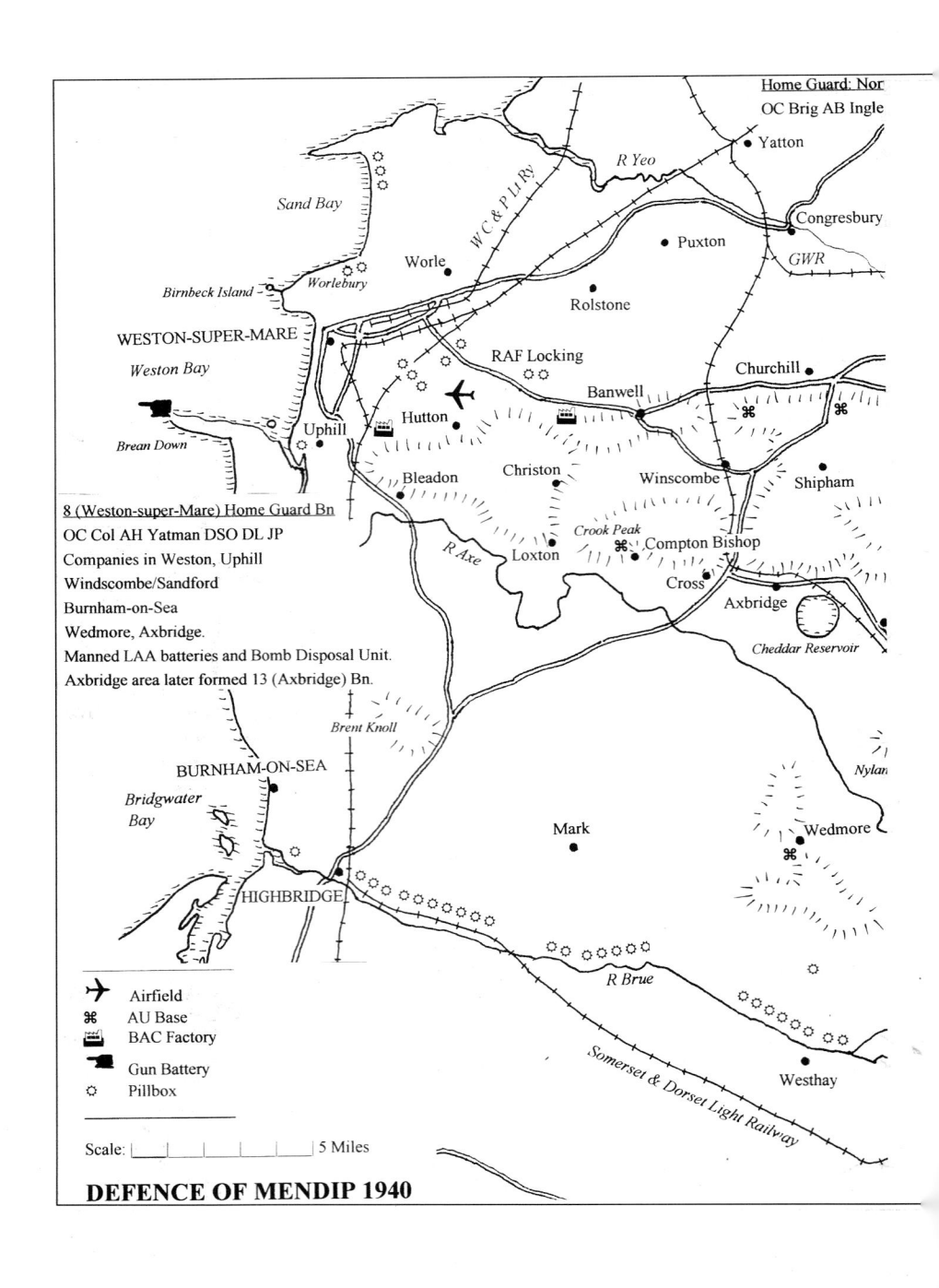

Home Guard: Nor
OC Brig AB Ingle

• Yatton

R Yeo

Sand Bay

Congresbury

WC & P L Ry

GWR

Worle
• Puxton

Birnbeck Island
Worlebury

• Rolstone

WESTON-SUPER-MARE

RAF Locking

Weston Bay

Churchill •

Banwell

Brean Down

Uphill
Hutton

Bleadon
Christon
Winscombe
Shipham

8 (Weston-super-Mare) Home Guard Bn
OC Col AH Yatman DSO DL JP
Companies in Weston, Uphill
Windscombe/Sandford
Burnham-on-Sea
Wedmore, Axbridge.
Manned LAA batteries and Bomb Disposal Unit.
Axbridge area later formed 13 (Axbridge) Bn.

Crook Peak
Compton Bishop
R Axe
Loxton
Cross
Axbridge
Cheddar Reservoir

Brent Knoll

BURNHAM-ON-SEA

Nylan

Bridgwater
Bay

• Mark
Wedmore

HIGHBRIDGE

R Brue

Westhay

Somerset & Dorset Light Railway

- ✈ Airfield
- ✵ AU Base
- 🏭 BAC Factory
- 🔫 Gun Battery
- ○ Pillbox

Scale: |___|___|___|___| 5 Miles

# DEFENCE OF MENDIP 1940

North Somerset Group
igledon Webber CMG DSO

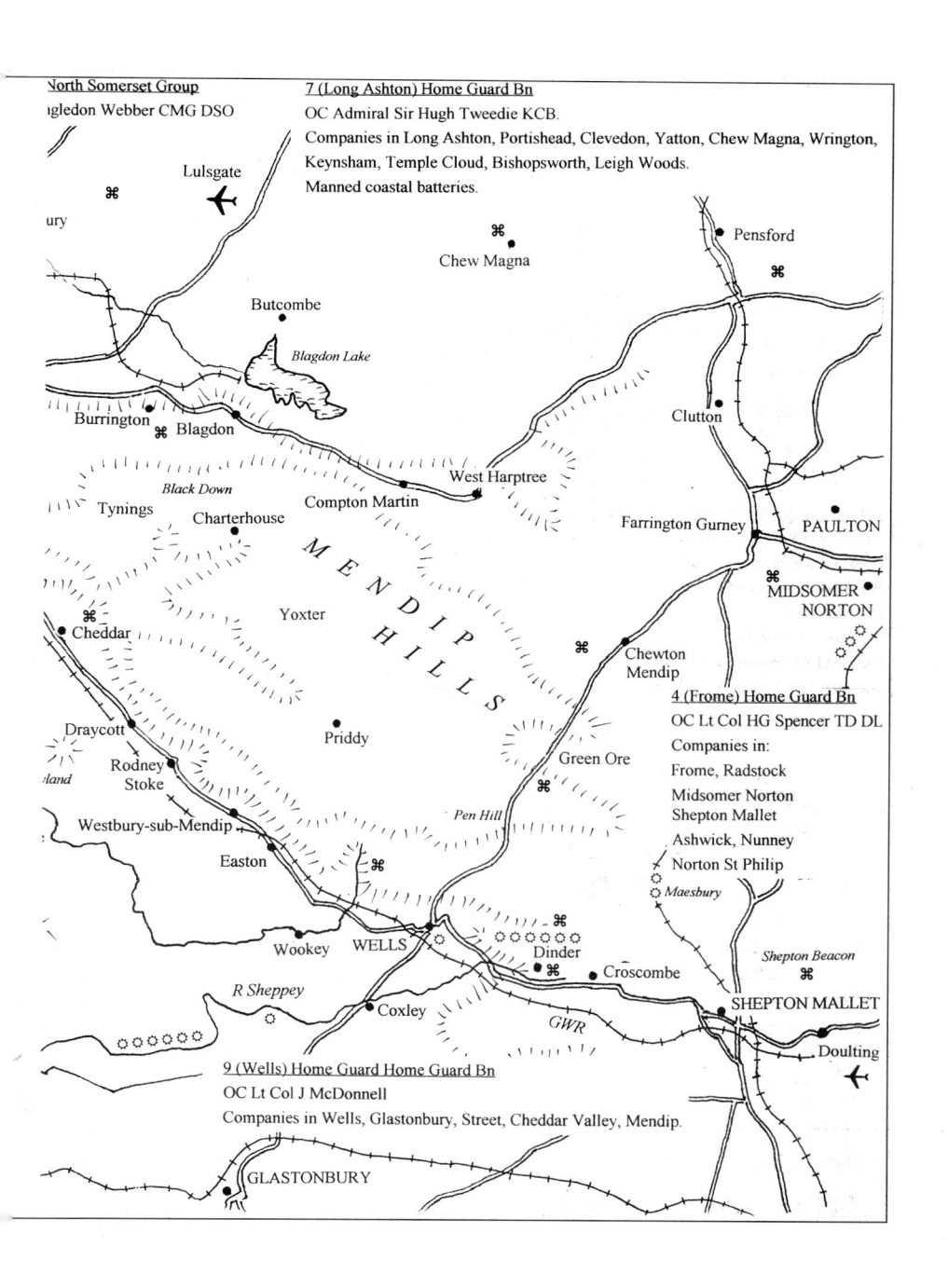

7 (Long Ashton) Home Guard Bn
OC Admiral Sir Hugh Tweedie KCB.
Companies in Long Ashton, Portishead, Clevedon, Yatton, Chew Magna, Wrington, Keynsham, Temple Cloud, Bishopsworth, Leigh Woods.
Manned coastal batteries.

Lulsgate

ury

Chew Magna

Pensford

Butcombe

Blagdon Lake

Burrington  Blagdon

Clutton

West Harptree

Black Down
Tynings  Charterhouse

Compton Martin

Farrington Gurney   PAULTON

MIDSOMER NORTON

Yoxter

Cheddar

MENDIP HILLS

Chewton Mendip

Priddy

Green Ore

4 (Frome) Home Guard Bn
OC Lt Col HG Spencer TD DL
Companies in:
Frome, Radstock
Midsomer Norton
Shepton Mallet
Ashwick, Nunney
Norton St Philip
Maesbury

Draycott
Rodney Stoke
land
Westbury-sub-Mendip

Pen Hill

Easton

Wookey  WELLS    Dinder
R Sheppey                 Croscombe

Shepton Beacon

SHEPTON MALLET

Coxley
GWR
Doulting

9 (Wells) Home Guard Home Guard Bn
OC Lt Col J McDonnell
Companies in Wells, Glastonbury, Street, Cheddar Valley, Mendip.

GLASTONBURY

*The author, Donald Brown, with tape measure at the ready. (Graham Max)*

# I
# SETTING THE SCENE

## 'There will come a battle for our island'

Mendip in the 1930s looked much as it had for centuries, though in its old churchyards, new memorials mourned villagers who had died in the Great War with Germany. Now, war was again in the air. Hitler's Germany had marched into Czechoslovakia, made a pact with Stalin's Soviet Union and, in 1939, invaded Poland.

In response Britain ordered general mobilisation and on September 3rd the people gathered round their wireless sets to listen to the Sunday morning broadcast by the Prime Minister, Neville Chamberlain, which explained that, as Herr Hitler had not responded to Britain's ultimatum to leave Poland, this country was once more at war with Germany. A few hours later, they heard King George VI call for 'calm, firm unity'.

Military strategists expected immediate German air strikes that would kill half a million and wound another million before the end of the year. In response to these forecasts, volunteers filled sandbags from Somerset's beaches to build blast barriers. In the streets, air-raid wardens kept watch to see that lights were blacked out to baffle enemy bombers. Householders criss-crossed windows with sticky paper tape to hold glass splintered in a bomb explosion. Pillar-box tops were painted a bilious yellow that would turn colour to indicate a poison gas attack. Newspapers ran articles on how to construct air-raid shelters in back gardens.

From bomb-threatened London, Somerset looked safe. Cooper's Company Secondary School left Stepney to find refuge in Frome Grammar School, while hundreds of children moved to Wells from London's Isle of Dogs. Sidcot School and Winscombe Woodborough Elementary School accommodated classes from Regent Polytechnic

Craft Day School, and evacuees displaced trippers from trains into Weston-super-Mare. Even little Ubley acquired an Evacuee Welfare Officer.

The Germans had conquered Poland in 26 days. The expected aerial bombardment did not come, as Britain experienced a period of inactivity that became known as the Phoney War, but in April 1940, Hitler seized Denmark and swept through Norway. In May, the Germans took just two weeks to rip through the Low Countries to the English Channel. With the British Expeditionary Force struggling home from the Dunkirk beaches, and the French Army in a state of collapse, German domination of continental Europe was complete and Britain stood alone.

For some British soldiers back from France, Shepton Mallet was the first place of refuge. Schoolboy Charles Wainwright watched:

> The first lot, poor devils, were literally lying on the ground asleep in Collet Park. They were so shattered and so worn out that all

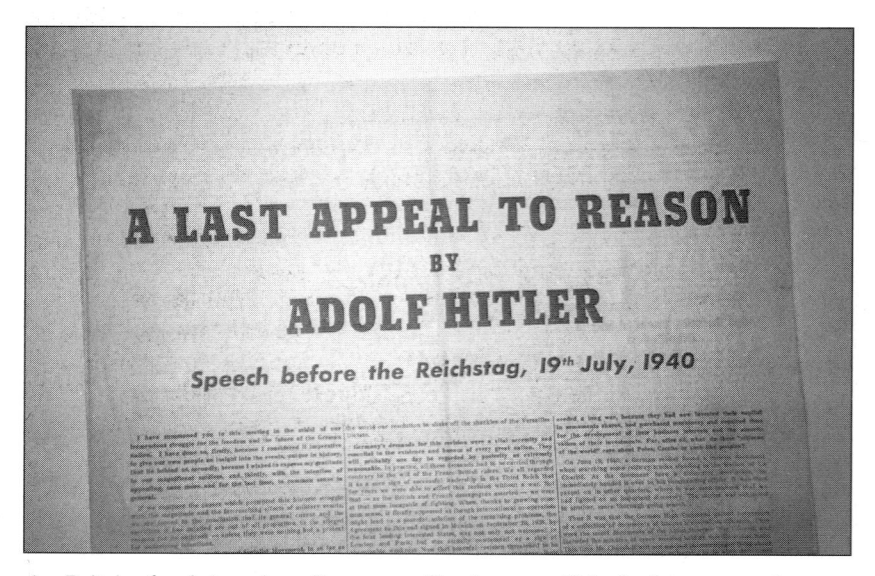

*As Britain faced invasion, Germany offered peace. This leaflet, scattered across Somerset, carried a translation of Hitler's latest speech to the Reichstag, demonstrating the justice of his cause. Most of these close-printed pages found their way into rural privies. (Robert King)*

they wanted was somewhere safe to get their heads down. Arthur Parsons remembers others at Cranmore:

They had some chaps come back from Dunkirk. They were plastered in mud, dried on them. You'd think they were prisoners of war, you wouldn't think they were our troops. But after about two days, they were back in shape, you wouldn't know them.

When he took over as Prime Minister in May, Winston Churchill forecast: 'There will come a battle for our island – that will be the struggle.' And on 16th July 1940, Hitler ordered his forces to prepare for *Seelöwe*, Operation Sea Lion, the invasion of Great Britain.

All the Germans needed was air supremacy. Hitler scheduled 12th August as *Adlertag*, Eagle Day, when the Luftwaffe would open its attack. On 1st August, German aircraft flew over the Mendips and elsewhere scattering leaflets headed 'Last Appeal to Reason' in a final attempt to justify Hitler's actions and achieve a negotiated peace. But with irrational confidence, the British people ignored Hitler, listening instead to Winston Churchill who looked into a grim future with the words, 'Hitler knows he will have to break us in this island or lose the war.'

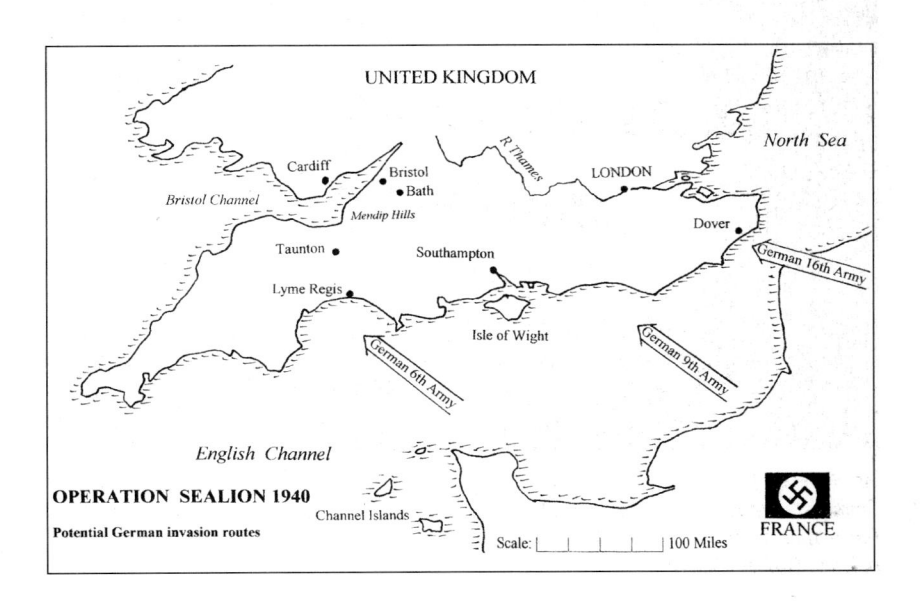

**OPERATION SEALION 1940**
**Potential German invasion routes**

*Home Guard sentries watched the skies for invading paratroopers dropping from Junkers Ju 52 troop-carrying aircraft. German airborne forces had spearheaded their blitzkrieg victories across Europe. (Author's collection)*

As he spoke, the German General Staff was deciding where to put its troops ashore. One of the options was Dorset. A landing at Lyme Regis would launch their Sixth Army northward through Somerset towards Bristol and then east along the Thames Valley to London.

As barges from Europe's canals and rivers massed in northern France to carry the invasion force to England, forecasts of tides and weather suggested 15th September 1940 as the best date. Throughout the summer, the Germans fostered fears of airborne attacks by dropping empty parachutes and bundles of military equipment across England. In Kent, men of the Somerset Light Infantry captured two real agents, landed by the Germans to be in place before the invasion.

Hoping to get home before the enemy came, Mrs Jelley, landlady of the Bunch of Grapes in Denmark Street, Bristol, cut short her last brief holiday in Mr and Mrs Beer's guest house on the southern slope of Crook Peak. Her son Harry remembers every detail of that journey:

> My mother was driving the family Ford 8, using her last petrol coupons. Her sister sat in the front passenger seat, with myself in

the back. Somewhere along the old A38, my mother stopped to give a soldier a lift.

We were daily expecting the invasion to begin and that at any time paratroops might descend. Furthermore, we believed these invaders could be disguised in British khaki, or even garbed as nuns.

Our wayside soldier was dressed in British khaki, wearing a greatcoat, with a rifle slung over his shoulder.

In the most guttural, incoherent English I had ever heard, he made us understand that he wished to go to Bristol. My mother did not have the nerve to leave him and refuse a lift, so he was seated in the back with me. As a young lad of ten years, convinced that we had just taken a German paratrooper on board, I was scared witless. I found out later that my mother and her sister were equally scared.

During that nightmare journey, I have no recollection of the turn of conversation. I don't think there was any, except that our passenger did tell us that he was from Czechoslovakia.

To crown it all, my mother stopped just beyond Star, where in those days there was a little vegetable shop. I was left alone at the mercy of our passenger until the two women returned. And then, in spite of our unallayed suspicions, my mother dropped this soldier off in the Tramways Centre.

Today, 57 years onwards, on the few occasions that I pass the site of that wartime vegetable shop, I still wonder, was that soldier really from Czechoslovakia?

# 2
# BEATING THE INVADER

In London, Churchill analysed the elements that had led to the disintegration of Western Europe's defences. The German *blitzkrieg*, or 'lightning war', had combined ruthless air-raids with rapid armoured thrusts. Panic-stricken refugees clogged the roads, preventing defensive military movement. Fear, rumour and indecision shattered civilian morale.

For Britain, the first lesson from this was to tell the people what to

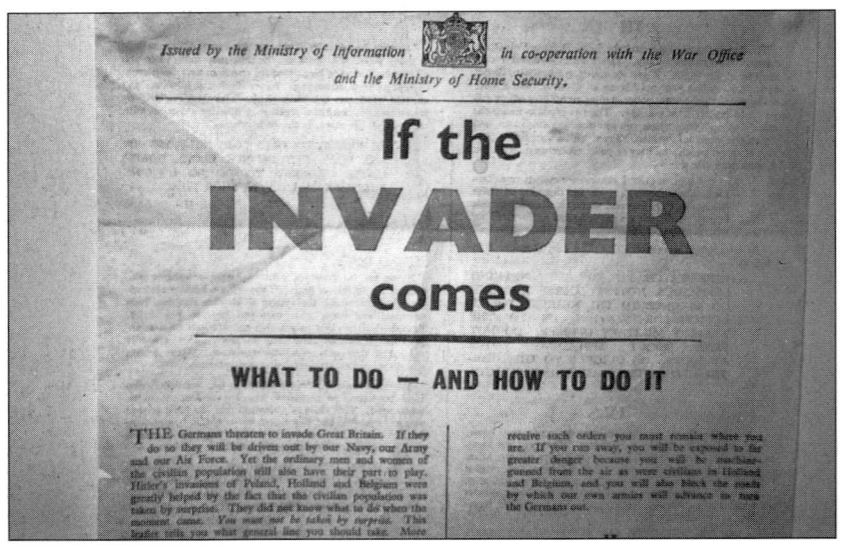

*British Government leaflets went to every household with terse instructions on how to face invasion. Top priority was to keep refugees off the road. (Bryan Green)*

expect. Leaflets went to every home, starkly headed 'If the Invader Comes'. They stressed: 'You must not be taken by surprise.'

The second lesson was to tell the people what to do. In another leaflet, headed 'Beating the Invader', Winston Churchill assigned two orders and duties to the nation: 'First, STAND FIRM, and then, after the battle, CARRY ON.'

The third lesson from the French experience was the need for strong local leadership. The War Cabinet ordered every community to set up an Invasion Committee to plan for the worst. Their powers would be almost total.

The Invasion Committees pulled together the various arms of local government, civil defence, police, ambulance and hospital services. Their first tasks were to stockpile building materials and organise the digging of defensive trenches. With the Women's Voluntary Service, they prepared to feed local defenders as well as the civilian population. In the aftermath of invasion or a devastating air attack, they would set about restoring essential services like telephone and power lines, the GPO, water and sewerage, transport and petrol. Bristol Waterworks Company, for instance, set up 280 Emergency Drinking Water Supply Units in the area, which they maintained until March 1945.

The Invasion Committees also planned how to cope with heavy casualties and how to dispose of the dead.

In Weston-super-Mare, the Committee advertised for helpers:

> Your Home is at stake!
> 600 Volunteers wanted
> ... The work will be vital – your very existence may depend
> on it. Protect your home, your family, your friends
> and your town.
> Enrol to aid Weston in times of stress.

The Committees were not secret but they did receive secret orders. And they were careful over their membership, as 18 year old Helen Boileau of Rackley discovered on a summer day in 1940, after she had cycled home from work. Her mother told her that Dr Scott of Axbridge had called. Giving no reason, he had asked if Helen would go to a meeting at Axbridge Police Station the following Sunday.

> When I got to Axbridge Police Station, a policeman was sitting inside the door. He must have been expecting me because he

# What do I do...

### if I hear news that Germans are trying to land, or have landed?

I remember that this is the moment to act like a soldier. I do *not* get panicky. I *stay put*. I say to myself: Our chaps will deal with them. I do *not* say: "I must get out of here." I remember that fighting men must have clear roads. I do *not* go on to the road on bicycle, in car or on foot. Whether I am at work or at home, I just *stay put*.

### Cut this out—and keep it!

*Issued by The Ministry of Information.*
*Space presented to the Nation by The Brewers' Society.*

Everyone looked for ways to help. Government ads in local papers directed and encouraged this patriotism. (Weston Mercury)

knew my name. He led me along a corridor, past a cell door and into a room. A group of men were sitting round a table. One was in army service dress.

He seemed to know all about my family, which ones had been in the army, and asked about my uncle who had been in the Somerset Light Infantry. Then he asked me to be their secretary.

They were called the MIC which stood for Military Information Committee. Colonel Yatman was in charge and sometimes another Home Guard colonel. Two of the men were army sergeants. I also remember two policemen and two ARP wardens. No women.

Colonel A. H. Yatman DSO DL came from Winscombe. He commanded the 8th (Weston) Home Guard Battalion which had a company in Axbridge.

Messengers were also an essential part of local defence communications, at a time when few homes and not many businesses had telephones. Most were women and boys, carrying instructions by hand. One of them, Connie Consford of Winterhead Farm, Shipham, eventually took over from Helen Boileau as Axbridge MIC secretary.

The Invasion Committees outlined their contingency plans in War Books, following a pattern laid down by the Home Office. Harry Matthews chaired the Committee covering Binegar, Emborough and Gurney Slade, with the Rev Warren of Binegar Rectory as his vice-chairman. Their War Book defined the military issues thus:

> 1. It may be expected the enemy's intention will be to make progress by advancing through the village or probably to enter and rest or feed his troops. It is the duty of the Home Guard to deny him such progress, and the first duty of this Committee is to assist the military in every way and also enlist the help of the public.
> 2. The possible enemy action in the locality is Airborne troops and dive-bombing.
> 3. The Home Guard plan is a defence scheme, the sites have been inspected and the whole scheme approved by the military.

To operate this defence scheme, they could muster 51 Home Guard soldiers and six army cadets commanded by 2/Lt G. Cobb of Chilcompton and Sgt R. Gill of Gurney Slade.

While local government officers at Shepton Mallet provided general administrative back-up, final responsibility fell to villagers. Mr W. Payne of Binegar Station, deputy chairman of the Invasion Committee, controlled food and water supplies. Mr Thorner, Gurney Slade's butcher, held eight days' emergency food stocks in his loft. The WVS set up a Rest and Feeding Centre at Binegar Schools, under Mrs Allen of Dalleston and Mrs Warren of Binegar Rectory. They could feed 35 at a time and sleep 70.

"... *right over the hill till you strike the main road, then turn to your left and straight on for two miles.*'

*Anything that could help an invader was taken away or locked up. Maps vanished from the shops; although the Germans had bought theirs before war broke out. (Reproduced with permission of Punch Ltd)*

## HITLER WILL SEND NO WARNING

### PRACTISE PUTTING ON YOUR GAS MASK

1. Hold your breath. (*To breathe in gas may be fatal.*)
2. Hold mask in front of face, thumbs inside straps.
3. Thrust chin well forward into mask. Pull straps as far over head as they will go.
4. Run finger round face-piece taking care head-straps are not twisted.

### MAKE SURE IT FITS

See that the rubber fits snugly at sides of jaw and under chin. The head-straps should be adjusted to hold the mask firmly. To test for fit, hold a piece of paper to end of mask and breathe in. The paper should stick.

*Arrows indicate points needing particular attention*

34—9999

*Gas masks were issued immediately and had to be carried at all times. (Author's collection)*

If the pumping station failed, water could be drawn from Emborough Pond, using Mr A. R. Emery's water cart and milk churns from Stone Edge Farm. The War Book notes the need to boil such water 'for a good ten minutes before being used for drinking purposes.' With other farmers, the same Mr Emery figured on the emergency transport list of 21 horses and carts.

The War Book anticipated no difficulty over sanitation, 'seeing there is no Sewerage at Binegar, Emborough & Gurney Slade.'

Prepared to counter the effects of any air attack were eight first-line and five second-line ARP Wardens under Head Warden Jack Matthews. The Book notes that, 'All wardens have been instructed to carry out the STAND FIRM policy.'

As the villages had no Fire Service unit, Jack Matthews supervised teams of Fire Guards who were also 'earmarked for use as an emergency labour force'. They would find 'ample supply of tools, picks, shovels etc' at the four local quarries.

Dr Finn of Oakhill was in charge of Casualty Services at Binegar Rectory where his staff comprised 'ten partly trained Red Cross members, two helpers for hospital and four stretcher bearers.' They had four beds and 24 blankets. Available supplies were listed as: 'Sterile Dressings, Bandages, Splints, Disinfectants, Cotton Wool and Lint Gauze. One ARP emergency Tin Box and one Red Cross box.'

In the event of gas attack – signalled with football rattles – a Housewives' Scheme offered 20 private houses for use as decontamination centres.

Phone numbers – all just two digits – were given for these emergency unit HQs, but the Committee backed up the telephone service with a team of cycle dispatch riders. In emergency, R. Ham would muster the seven girls, three boys and three Home Guard cadets at the Memorial Hall for deployment by Mrs H. Snook of Dalleston. The book notes that: 'All messengers can recognise in the dark their own cycles and know roads, lanes and paths in the locality.'

As well as providing an emergency food store in his butcher's shop, Mr Thorner found his slaughter-house designated as the Emergency Mortuary. The final entry in the War Book reads: 'Equipment for Mortuary – Nil.'

Even Charterhouse, remote on top of Mendip, had its plans. The school was designated an emergency feeding and catering centre, although it had no phone. First aid and anti-gas centres were in the 'Church Room' and the Casualty Clearing Station at 'the Hospital'. The

Church Room was in St Hugh's church while the hospital was Nordrach, then an isolation hospital, an extension of Ham Green.

Special Constable Wilf Saunders kept a special eye on Charterhouse, reporting back to Wilf Saint at Blagdon Police Station. One task was to watch for breaches of black-out regulations. As homes were still lit by oil-lamps and there were no street lights, this was not an onerous duty.

Where there was no electricity, accumulators powered the wireless sets that took Churchill's powerful oratory into every home:

> We shall defend our island whatever the cost may be. We shall fight on the beaches, we shall fight on the landing grounds, we shall fight in the fields and in the streets, we shall fight in the hills. We shall never surrender.

On July 14th 1940, Churchill broadcast: 'We are prepared to go to all extremities, and to endure all extremities, in defence of liberty.' And he later revealed that his final call to the people would have been: 'You can always take one with you.'

# 3
# MENDIP SEA WATCH

The Mendip Hills plunge into the Bristol Channel at Brean Down. Five miles out, they surface again as the hump-backed island of Steep Holm.

From those coastal extremities, big guns had covered the sea approaches for the last 30 years of the 19th century, ready in those days to repel the French. But the danger faded and the soldiers left, handing their Victorian barracks over to the sea-birds.

Soldiers came back in 1940, hastily repairing and updating the defences. Engineers metalled a military road along Brean Down to a new settlement of Nissen huts. They bricked up the old fort's big 19th-century windows to keep out 20th-century high-explosive blast. Alongside the abandoned but still elegant stonework of the original cannon platforms and powder magazines, they planted concrete gun-sites. With the installation of a pair of First World War 6" naval guns and a solitary Lewis gun for anti-aircraft cover, the Brean Down garrison settled down to keep watch over the sea-passage between the coast and Steep Holm island.

Looking across Weston Bay, their sentries could see the White Ensign flying over Birnbeck Island. Re-designated HMS *Birnbeck*, the island provided a secure base for the Admiralty's Department of Miscellaneous Weapons Development. The Department's official abbreviation to DMWD was soon scurrilously re-interpreted as the Department of Middle-aged Wheezers and Dodgers. Working among the abandoned relics of peace-time pier-end entertainment, their secret task was the development of wartime weaponry.

Inside its military perimeter, Brean Down provided DMWD with a useful testing-ground. First they tried out a rocket-fired device that successfully immobilised a tank by wrapping it in strands of wire. Then, at the end of 1942, their engineers built a short rail track at the

**MENDIP SEA WATCH**
Fixed Defences, Severn

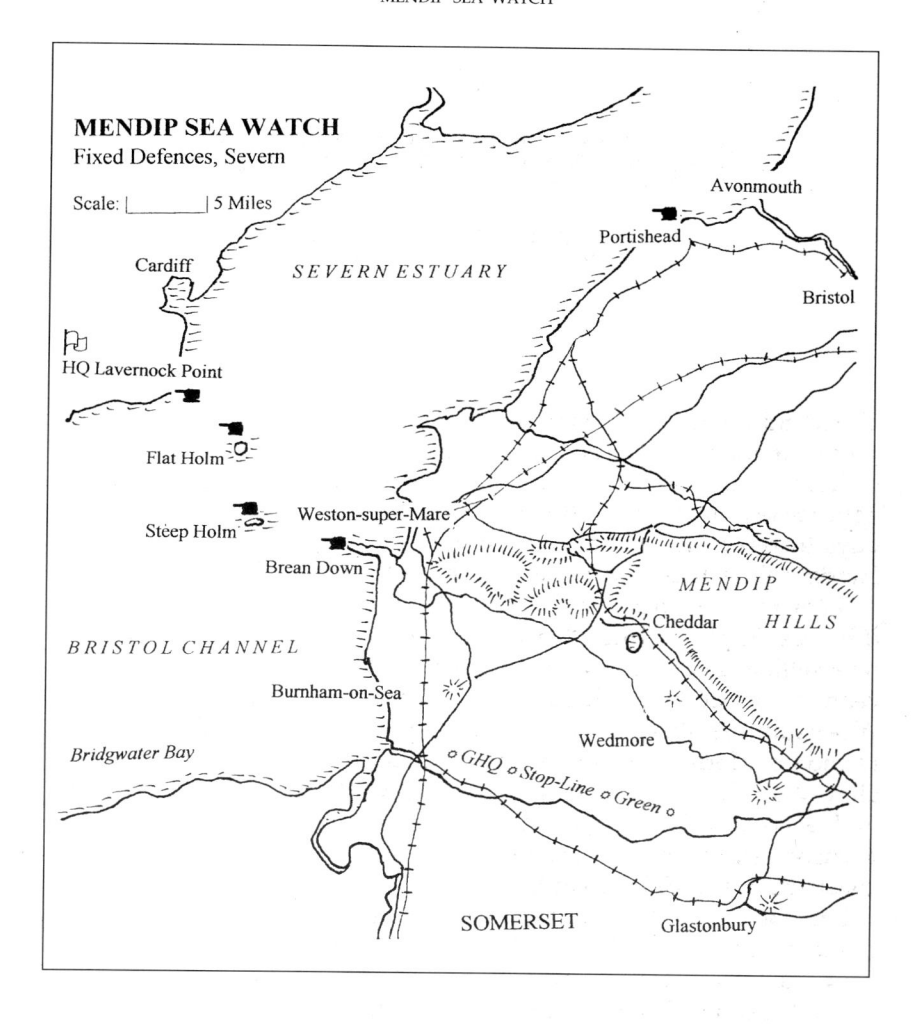

very tip of the peninsula. Along this, twelve 2" rockets propelled a trolley at high speed into a set of hydraulic buffers inside a concrete blast wall. The sudden stop was meant to hurl a missile across the waves, skimming towards its target like a Dambuster bouncing bomb.

The Brean Down gunners watched in awe as the rockets, wrapped in flame, roared over the track at enormous speed, projecting the entire experiment – trolley, missile, buffers and all – far out to sea.

Over on Steep Holm, responsibility for defence fell first to the

*Brean Down's fort was built to keep Napoleon's fleet out of Weston Bay. When Hitler threatened, naval guns replaced the cannon, covering the same fields of fire. (Author)*

Admiralty. They appointed the island's Warden, Harry Cox, as a coastguard at the record recruitment age of 70. He was joined in 1940 by a patrol of Local Defence Volunteers from Weston-super-Mare. Like many others they found the island not only desperately uncomfortable but undeniably spooky, and were relieved when their spell of overseas service ended.

In August 1940, the Army took the island over. Through 1941 and 1942, they re-fortified it, linking its fields of fire with batteries on Flat Holm, Brean Down, Lavernock Point and Portishead. Designated the Fixed Defences Severn Line, their guns covered the Bristol Channel, initially to stop invaders and later to protect incoming convoys.

The first problem on Steep Holm was hoisting guns and equipment up a vertiginously steep and narrow cliffside path to the top of the island. Old-fashioned muscle-power provided the solution: in July 1941, a contingent of the Royal Indian Army Service Corps arrived with their mules to provide the necessary brute force.

Concrete floor pads still mark where lines of Nissen huts accommodated the Sergeants' Mess and housed the men. Officers were billeted in the old Victorian barracks alongside the NAAFI and

*Far from prying eyes on the tip of Brean Down peninsula, and secure inside the fort's defences, boffins built a rocket-launcher designed to skim missiles across the waves. (Author)*

*Dominating the Bristol Channel, tiny Steep Holm island bristled with fortifications. (Author)*

*Concrete emplacements on Steep Holm island housed naval guns from World War I. (Author)*

*The dramatic outline of Steep Holm's coastline defences. (Author)*

*A series of six small gun emplacements covered Uphill beach from Brean Down. (Author's collection)*

HQ offices. Royal Engineers sappers provided some mod cons, improving the old rainwater catchment water supply and tapping searchlight generators to provide domestic electricity. They even built an ingenious food store, cool inside cork-lined walls.

Conditions on Steep Holm were harsh and dangerous. Every single item had to be brought in from the mainland through some of Britain's most testing tidal waters. After a case of typhoid, even water had to be shipped in from Wales on the barge *Peter Piper* and pumped up to storage tanks. Tank landing craft carried live sheep over to satisfy the dietary needs of the Indian Army troops.

Pioneers joined the Engineers to improve the primitive path that zig-zagged up the cliffs. Alongside it, they hacked out enough space to install a railway track with a diesel-engined winch-house at each of three zig-zags. Mules or diesel engines then powered the trucks along a line across the top of the island. The trucks and $1'11\frac{1}{2}''$ gauge track were German, seized at the end of the First World War.

The island's fire-power also dated back to the First World War, its four Mark VII 6" breech-loading guns coming from scrapped Royal Navy warships. Two emplacements housed two guns each. One, above the south-east corner, covered Bridgwater Bay. The other, on the north-

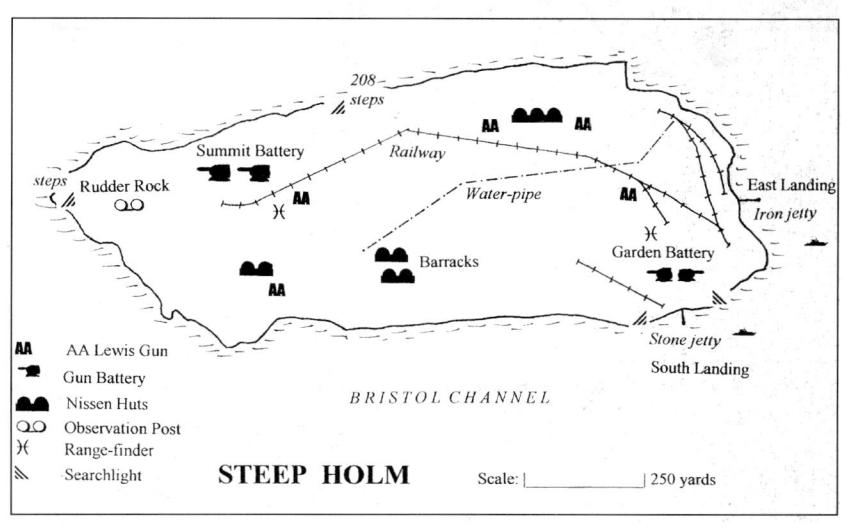

*Steep Holm. Very few people visit the island but it is mapped in specialist books on its history.*

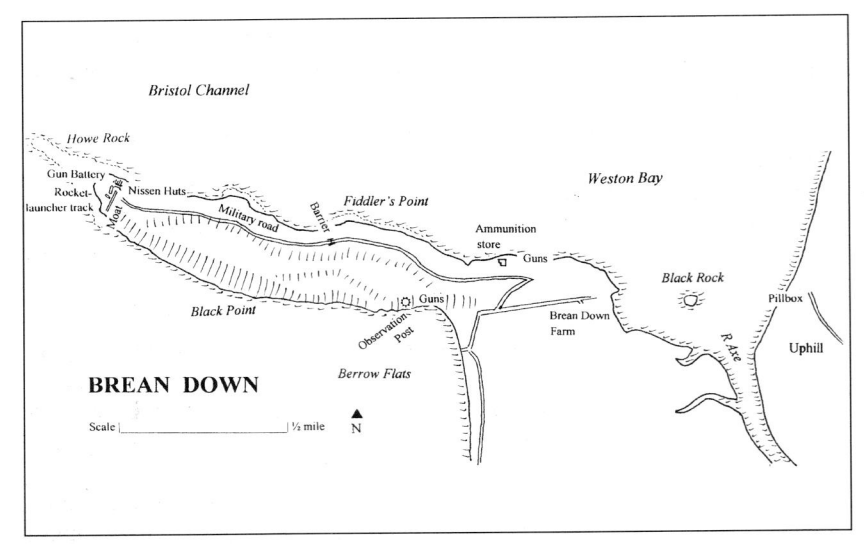

*Brean Down. No books about it, no maps, a popular spot to visit.*

*Gunners kept 24-hour watch from the battery observation post on Steep Holm island. (Author's collection)*

west corner, covered the Channel sea-lanes from Lavernock Point to Flat Holm. A floating wooden target towed by a steam tug provided firing practice.

The most likely form of surface attack on shipping would be from E-boats, fast motor vessels with crews accustomed to operating at night in tight coastal waters. To counter this threat, four searchlight posts low on the Steep Holm cliffs swept the water. Access to these posts was difficult and dangerous, down narrow concrete steps that arched out from the cliff face over the notorious tidal races of the Bristol Channel.

Protection against air attack was provided by half a dozen Lewis guns on the high ground. In case they proved inadequate, sappers covered the installations with plates of 'plastic' roof armour made of pebbles embedded in tar on an iron base. Although untested by enemy attack, the armour did resist unofficial tests by the garrison using their own rifles.

A multi-core submarine telegraph cable eventually linked Steep Holm, Brean Down and the other batteries of the Fixed Defences Severn Line with their HQ at Barry. The cable still lies on the sea-bed, made useless after the war by salvage-hunters who chopped out the few feet that ran on the surface. A few strands remain, protruding from the pebbles on Steep Holm's East Landing.

Having reached a peak strength of five officers and 130 men in 1943, the Steep Holm base closed at the end of 1944 and the sea-birds returned to an island of concrete and corrugated iron.

# 4
# THE GREEN LINE

German invasion planning had started with pre-war shopping. British Ordnance Survey maps, bought openly in London, were overprinted in German to show military objectives. Extra detail came from the 1937 AA Handbook.

From this material, the Germans prepared a series of 20 map-books for issue to invading troops. Entitled *Militärgeographische Angaben über England*, they included aerial photographs of possible invasion beaches from Dover to the West Country as well as pictures of the landscape inland. The aerial photographs were taken from civil airliners in the 1930s, the landscapes from picture postcards of scenic views on sale in the shops.

The Gestapo compiled their own handbooks, *Informationsheft GB* and *Sonderfahndungsliste GB*. Planning an HQ in Bristol, they determined to arrest all Jews, Freemasons, socialists, communists and refugees from Europe. In Weston-super-Mare they targeted the Rt Hon Albert Victor Alexander, First Lord of the Admiralty. But first they had to get here.

The British boldly abandoned the fortress mentality that had failed so dismally in France. Should the invasion come, the Home Guard were to stand fast on their own home ground and fight where they stood. They may not last long, but their actions would free trained troops to move to points of greatest need.

German airborne forces were expected to spearhead the invasion. Stakes dotted Brean beach to deny it to troop-carrying gliders. Tides still occasionally scour the sand from remnants of stone piles that blocked Weston's shore. In 1940, the Bristol Waterworks Company moored rafts of tree-thinnings on their reservoirs at Blagdon and Cheddar to stop seaplanes from touching down.

Mary Small grew up on Tynings Farm:

> I can remember in the summer of 1940, turf mounds across Blackdown and stone cairns on all the large fields to prevent

enemy aircraft landing. Bus loads of volunteers came out from Bristol on Sundays to build the cairns. They travelled up on Clifton Greys coaches.

They were promised refreshments, but when the mobile canteen ran out, they came to the farmhouse. Mother had a catering licence but obviously could not find food for large numbers. But we could always provide cups of tea.

Local people joined the work force: fireman George Wilson from Blagdon was one, schoolboy Hugh Tyson of Cheddar another. The construction work was contracted out to specialist Bristol companies: builders William Cowlin and Colston Electrical Company. Mary continued:

Cowlins were paid 4s 6d to build each tump and 5s 6d each when the time came to take them down. They took dressed stone from old lime kilns and pig-sties and then quarried more from where

*Signposts, place names, milestones, all vanished in a plan to baffle the invader. The effect was to baffle our own soldiers looking for camps in remote parts of the country. (Author)*

*Tank trap sockets still survive at Dinder. (Author)*

*Defenders of Brent Knoll's Iron Age fort could see from Brean Down to Minehead, from Steep Holm to Glastonbury Tor. Saxons sheltered there from Viking raiders. Elizabethans prepared an Armada beacon on the 450 foot summit. In 1940, the Home Guard dug their trenches round the fort's perimeter. (Author)*

the racing stadium now stands. My father, Gilbert Small, used his horse and cart to help haul it up there.

In many villages, bent railway lines lay ready to be stuck into slots in the road to stop armoured vehicles. Thanks to a leisurely road-maintenance programme, such slots survive at Dinder.

People loyally obeyed Government instructions not to give directions to anyone no matter how official they seemed. Place-name boards vanished from towns, villages and railway stations. On Congresbury bridge, a stone bearing the village name was reversed. The national network of milestones was removed and signposts disappeared from road-junctions. In a stable-door exercise, the sale of maps was prohibited.

On his way to Wells Cathedral School, Charles Wainwright remembers showing his Identity Card to suspicious sentries at their road-block on the bend of the Wells Road between Shepton and Croscombe. At cross-roads on and around the Mendips, portable

*Clusters of concrete blocks, cast on the spot like these at Sharcombe Park, Dinder, kept enemy tanks where defenders could see and hit them. Attempts to ride over the obstacles exposed their under-sides to fire. (Author)*

barbed-wire barriers lay ready to be rolled out by Home Guards who stood duty there every night. Faint roadside indentations remain from slit trenches below Dulcote Hill, while a series of trenches still clearly cover the approach from the sea between Uphill, Purn Hill and Brent Knoll.

But it wasn't all slit trenches. As France was falling, the War Office was already designing 'stop-lines' to protect threatened areas. One of these areas comprised Dorset and Somerset, the path of the expected German thrust north to Avonmouth and Bristol from Lyme Regis.

Three defence-lines boxed in this potential invasion area. Two ran north from the English Channel on each side of Lyme Regis: GHQ Stop-line Yellow closed off the east flank as far north as Bath, while the Taunton Stop-Line hemmed in the west flank from Seaton to Burnham. Pushing north between these two lines, German tanks would splash into the rhynes and rivers of the low-lying Somerset levels, south of

*Hundreds of pillboxes still dot Somerset. Most made up continuous defence lines. Others, like this one at Locking airfield, were part of local defences. They were six-sided, of concrete and brick, with a thick concrete roof. A low tunnel protected the entrance from blast. Pillboxes were not permanently occupied but stood ready for use if the enemy approached. (Author)*

Mendip. Along these waterways ran GHQ Stop-line Green, facing south between Burnham and Bath.

As a schoolgirl, Mrs Valerie Alderton lived for a year with her uncle, Mr R. O. Stiles, an architect in Wells. By 1940, as Captain Stiles, her uncle had joined the Royal Engineers staff at Salisbury. Despite a medical grade of C3, he spent the entire war in uniform, living in his own house, a billeting record perhaps. Working from an office above the Bekynton Cafe in Wells Market Square, his task was to build the Green Line, also known as the Bristol Outer Defence Line.

Captain Stiles made good tactical use of the soggy Somerset levels. He placed over a hundred pillboxes along the River Brue from Burnham to Westhay. His line then followed Division Rhyne to Godney, turning north and east to Coxley. Running out of rhynes, his men dug an anti-tank ditch round Wells and Dinder. Circling Maesbury Ring, the defences followed the Somerset & Dorset railway through the Somerset coalfield to Freshford just south of Bath.

A work-force of Irish labourers was controlled by Mr Bell and Jock Bissett from an office above the old printing works at the back of Clare's in Wells. Also in the squad were Mr Noble and Alfy Stratt from London. One of Gunnings Garages' drivers, Mr Lane of Wookey Hole, drove the workers out to Westhay, Bason Bridge, Burnham, Godney and Chilcompton. Having already camouflaged the County Hall buildings at Trowbridge, the team used their skills to merge their pillboxes into the landscape.

As a boy, John Nurse lived on Wick Farm, Coxley, the family farm since the 19th century. He watched bungalows sprout in their fields, concealing pillboxes. Another on a neighbouring farm looked like a haystack. And a concrete 'cottage' on Constitution Hill outside Wells has proved its strength by resisting all attempts to destroy it.

Although the pillboxes were built quickly, many have survived half a century of neglect. A solid roof sat on thick concrete walls behind external brick shuttering, while wires stretched between iron eyelets, holding nets or foliage as camouflage. With elbows on a concrete shelf, defenders fired through loopholes that pierced five of the six sides. Behind them, a central trefoil wall absorbed ricochets from any incoming fire. Access was through the sixth wall, facing what was hoped would be the rear, using natural cover to conceal movement in and out.

By October 1940, Mendip's Green Line was ready for the assault.

# 5
# MENDIP'S HOME GUARD

'We cannot tell when they will try to come. A full-scale invasion is being prepared and may be launched at any time. If this invasion is to be tried at all, it cannot be long delayed.'

As Churchill's stark warning was reinforced by advice to every man and woman to prepare themselves for the battle ahead, there was no lack of Ministry guidance. The leaflet 'If the Invader Comes' was widely distributed in Somerset as elsewhere and set out a series of rules in block letters:

1. IF THE GERMANS COME ... YOU MUST REMAIN WHERE YOU ARE. THE ORDER IS 'STAY PUT'.
2. DO NOT BELIEVE RUMOURS.
3. KEEP WATCH. GO QUICKLY TO THE NEAREST AUTHORITY AND GIVE HIM THE FACTS.
4. DO NOT GIVE ANY GERMAN ANYTHING. DO NOT TELL HIM ANYTHING.
5. BE READY TO HELP THE MILITARY IN ANY WAY. BUT DO NOT BLOCK ROADS UNTIL ORDERED TO DO SO.
6. IN FACTORIES AND SHOPS, ORGANISE SOME SYSTEM NOW BY WHICH A SUDDEN ATTACK CAN BE RESISTED.
7. THINK BEFORE YOU ACT. BUT THINK ALWAYS OF YOUR COUNTRY BEFORE YOU THINK OF YOURSELF.

There was soon overwhelming evidence that people were indeed thinking of their country. Expecting the seemingly unstoppable *blitzkrieg* to sweep unchecked across the Channel, Foreign Secretary Anthony Eden broadcast a call on 14th May 1940 for men between the ages of 17 and 65 to offer their services as Local Defence Volunteers, the

*Home Guard HQ at Burnham-on-Sea. The Company was part of 13 (Axbridge) Battalion. (Roddy Southwell)*

LDV. He thought about 150,000 would respond. But even before the broadcast ended, men were arriving at police stations to volunteer. Next day a quarter of a million joined. That number doubled in a fortnight. Next month, another million came in.

Medical requirements were minimal: recruits had to be 'of reasonable fitness and capable of free movement.' Some volunteers were awaiting call-up though most were men in 'reserved' occupations like farming. Many were retired, sporting First World War medals, and there was a fair sprinkling of boys trying hard to look 17 years old.

Whatever their military capability, the mere existence of the LDV demonstrated that this population would not be terrorised into chaotic submission as in France. It ensured some sort of instant defence in depth across the whole country. And, most important, it established firm local systems of control.

Somerset's LDV, dubbed 'parashots' by the press, took up nightly guard duties on road junctions, railway stations, bridges and tunnels, airfields, factories, fuel depots, reservoirs and mines, gasworks and power stations. Young farmer Bryan Green was one of them:

Four of us stood guard every night. Two at a time, two hours on and two hours off, from 10 at night to 6 in the morning. Then we went back to work.

We were the ever-open eye.

Although the British Government embodied the LDV as part of the Crown's armed forces and subject to military law, there was no doubt about the Nazi attitude to the new units. They dubbed them 'Churchill's murder squads, contrary to all the rules of international law', and accused them therefore of operating outside the Geneva Convention. A German Army Order promised the death penalty for armed opposition, violence or sabotage, for keeping firearms, using radio transmitters, even for posting hostile notices. Further, as the bridgehead expanded, they intended arresting all able-bodied males aged 17 to 45 and deporting them to camps in France.

Unaware of their threatened fate, the Volunteers kept on working and patrolling. Between times, they fitted in training sessions in fieldcraft and weapon handling while learning new approaches to their local terrain. LDV, they said, stood for Look, Duck and Vanish. The joke concealed good guerrilla tactics.

Desperately short of weapons and ammunition, some Somerset men used their own .22 rifles and shotguns, augmented by others handed over by the public in exchange for receipts. As well as converting 12-bore cartridges to solid shot, the Volunteers learned to make petrol bombs – 'Molotov cocktails' – for use against tanks. And there was always the good old pitchfork.

In July 1940, the LDV was renamed the Home Guard and 80,000 rifles were issued with the promise of more. Local units were officially affiliated to the Somerset Light Infantry. Instead of an LDV arm-band, they wore khaki denim battledress with a Home Guard shoulder flash and forage caps with the Somerset badge. Leather boots proved a popular issue in the countryside, while gas-capes resisted even Mendip's penetrating rain. Harold Lane remembers how it began in Wells:

Mr McDonnell was manager of Wilts United Dairies. He'd been an army captain in the first war. He was given the job of calling a unit up in Wells and volunteers were asked to meet in the Market Place, I think at the end of May. At that time I was 29. I was a printer and they were exempted from call-up for the time being.

*All members wore the Home Guard shoulder flash. The numeral indicated the battalion, in this case 9 (Wells) Battalion, and SOM stood for Somerset. (Bryan Green)*

I went to that first meeting and we formed a unit with headquarters in the stables of the last house at the end of Burcott Road. We had about 24 members. Tommy Webster was in that first parade. He had been an army man and still had his uniform. He lived near Charlie Clark up on top of Milton Hill. Charlie joined as well.

During that period we had no weapons whatsoever. All we had was an arm band. Some had a few shotguns they'd scrounged from farmers. Old Dr Mullins from up New Street, he was a collector of antique weapons. He lent us some long pikes. Eventually we received some rifles from Canada in boxes, six to a box. They were covered in grease. We had six rifles each to clean and that took a while.

Postal staff joined the 15th Gloucestershire (Post Office) Battalion to guard GPO installations. They had platoons in Shepton Mallet, Weston-super-Mare and Bath. Although they wore Gloucestershire cap badges, they operated as part of the Somerset Home Guard.

Bristol Water Company also ran a private army from 1940 to 1942, enlisting all employees at reservoirs in their own Home Guard units. Rumours persist of secret Government equipment stores in the company's many underground installations, including lines of Green Goddess fire-engines garaged beneath a reservoir.

In June, the government ordered church bells to be used as a national signal that the Germans had landed. Until then, they were to remain silent. They did not ring again until 1943.

Everyone expected the invasion to be spearheaded by airborne forces. Once on the ground, however, these would become no more than lightly armed infantrymen, far from any supply base. Part of the

*There was never much transport available for the Home Guard. Driving permits carried a brief description of the authorised driver, in this case '6ft. Eyes blue.' (Bryan Green)*

defence plan, therefore, concentrated on stopping the invaders from seizing transport. The Home Guard were authorised to commandeer private vehicles and seize or destroy petrol stations. Drivers of the few vehicles that survived rigorous petrol rationing were ordered to leave them locked and immobilised by removing the rotor arms.

Home Guard transport was limited to privately-owned cars and motor-bikes for which petrol coupons were issued. It was not until February 1944 that Somerset Home Guard set up its own Motor Transport Column, based in Wells at 23 High Street, commanded by Lt Col N. S. M. Durnford.

By the summer of 1942, Germany's Russian campaign made invasion unlikely; but the Home Guard remained necessary to resist enemy commando raids. And if Russia collapsed, a full-scale invasion could still be mounted – there could be no relaxation of contingency plans yet.

In February 1943, Col McDonnell, commander of the 9th (Wells) Battalion, Home Guard, produced this bitter-sweet definition of their function.

> Members of the unpaid, unfed, unthanked, part-time, part-town, sockless, shirtless army known as the Home Guard, are supposed in the first place, to be crack shots with a rifle, bayonet fighters and expert throwers of hand grenades. They are supposed to know the weight and length of the rifle and all its parts. The weight, characteristics, contents, parts and destructive power of several kinds of grenades or bombs, and all are supposed to be tommy-gunners. There are many other weapons they are supposed to use too, but as only 1,700,000 men know about them, they are too secret to be mentioned here.
>
> Apart from this, they are supposed to know the exact position of local post and telegraph offices, railway stations and petrol filling stations, the distances and routes to neighbouring villages and towns, and the telephone systems and the position of available instruments.
>
> They are supposed to know the names of their section, platoon and company commanders, to recognise by sight their Colonel, whom they have probably never seen, and know the name of their Zone Commander, they have often never heard of. They are supposed to know the address, location and nearest route to platoon, company, battalion and zone headquarters, which are

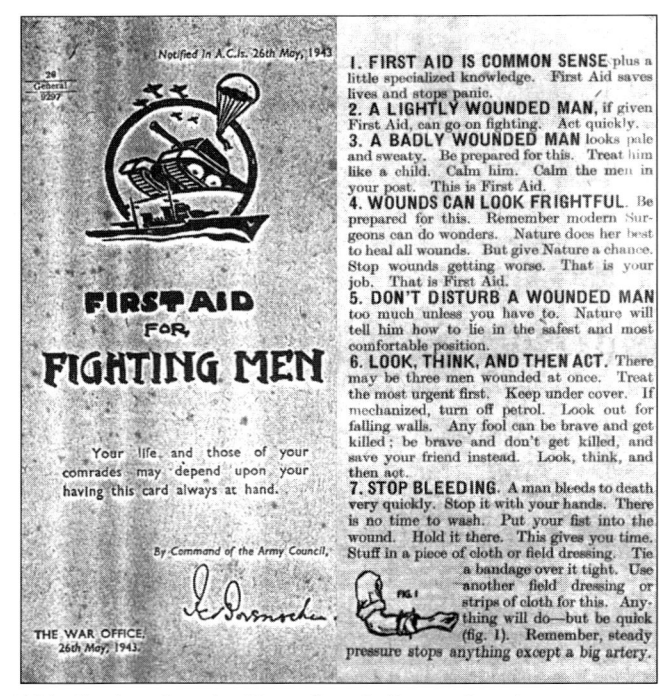

*A First Aid leaflet issued to the Home Guard. (Bryan Green)*

sometimes changed overnight without their knowledge, and to be experts on fieldcraft, street-fighting, map-reading and defence in depth.

They must know how to deal with paratroops, how to camouflage their positions from air observation, how to use natural cover, how to move unseen and unheard, how to crawl on a middle-aged tummy through undergrowth and how to convert themselves from a clerk or businessman who wouldn't hurt a fly in the daytime, into an assassin with a dagger at night. They are supposed to know how to destroy tanks and erect road-blocks, how to deal with all known gases, and how to provide for themselves an iron ration, without points.

Incidentally, they are supposed to earn their living and mount a 12 hour guard at least once a week, for which they are paid 54 whole pennies to spend on whatever luxuries they can find.

And now all Home Guards must attend first-aid lectures. This means they should have a working knowledge of pressure points, bandaging, splinting, artificial respiration and should be able to treat cases of poisoning, concussion, fainting fits and shock. They must be able to drive W.D. vehicles and private cars, motor cycles, and ride bicycles.

Not one of us will be surprised if we are expected to take a course in midwifery in our spare time – to prepare us to give a hand in an emergency!

An unattributed song, *McDonnell's Own*, put it another way:

> When his country stood at bay
> And the peril seemed at hand
> Brave McDonnell rose to slay
> Th'invader of this cherished land,
> Gathering round him all alike,
> Drawn from office, pub and farm,
> Armed with shotgun, fork or pike,
> Ready for the dire alarm.
>
> *Chorus*: McDonnell's Own, McDonnell's Own,
> Boys of the Old Brigade!
> Now shall the foe be overthrown
> Now shall the low be laid!
> Rushing ahead with their Blackers,
> Spigotting all they see,
> Ripping away their knackers
> And chucking 'em back to the Spree!

Training continued until 6th September 1944 when the Home Guard stood down. Parades and dinners marked the end of a remarkable four years when nearly 3,000 Somerset men formed part of a national army of 2,500,000. On 3rd December 1944, the King took the salute as the Home Guard Commander-in-Chief at a final Stand Down Parade in London.

Charles Graves summed up their achievement in the opening words of his book *The Home Guard of Britain*: 'The Home Guard is the most fantastic force ever raised. History can provide no parallel to its speed of recruitment, enthusiasm and numbers.'

# 6
# THE WESTON FRONT

The *Dad's Army* image dies hard. But if the average age of the Home Guard was high, so was its military experience.

Lt-Col A. H. Yatman DSO DL exemplified this. A regular soldier in the Somerset Light Infantry, he had first fought in the South African War. After service in India, he went in 1914 to France, where he was wounded. He ended that war commanding a battalion in the Balkans, winning a DSO and the Greek Military Cross. Back with the Somersets, he confronted the IRA in Ireland before retiring to Winscombe in 1922.

Colonel Yatman commanded the 8th (Weston) Home Guard Battalion from Langford Road Drill Hall with an administrative HQ at Salisbury Terrace. His eight infantry companies covered Mendip's seaward approaches.

They faced heavy bombardment during the air-raids on Weston, in which five men were killed. Private Philip Herbert Masters died aged 19 on the night of 4th January 1941. Colour Sergeant S. F. Hook was killed in the air-raid of 28th June 1942, as were brothers Arthur and Reginald Charles Owens, aged 14 and 16 respectively. Private L. C. Addicott died in the raid of 27th March 1944.

Bravest of all, the Home Guard Bomb Disposal Unit made safe 78 unexploded bombs (UXBs) on the Bristol Aircraft Shadow Factory at Oldmixon.

From 1942, the Home Guard were able to fight back when they replaced regular soldiers on Light Anti-Aircraft guns round Weston. But throughout the raids, the Home Guard still stood watch and trained for their primary defence mission. From Weston Golf Club's 5th hole, they practised lobbing grenades over the sea-wall onto the beach between Slimeridge Farm and the ferry. On the next hole, they built up the tee as butts for their own .303 range. Another sporting grenade

## 8th & 13th Bn. Somerset Home Guard

This Folio records that a **Silver Salver** was presented to **Colonel A.M. Yatman, D.S.O., D.L., J.P.,** to mark the occasion of his relinquishing command of the Battalions which he formed and commanded, and to show the appreciation of all ranks.

1940 — 1944

*Col Yatman's service with the Home Guard was remembered in 1945. (Mrs H.B.S. Gunn)*

*The Home Guard suffered its casualties, in training as well as at the hands of the enemy in air-raids. The six named on Uphill War Memorial ranged in age from 14 to 59. (Author)*

range provided throwing practice beyond the furthest boundary of the Cricket Club on the edge of Uphill Great Rhyne.

Three died in accidents on firing ranges. Private Jack Raines was killed at Worle on 18th September 1940, CSM F. Atkins in Uphill Quarry on 20th February 1943 and Private M. T. Wills at Rowberrow on 2nd May 1943. Henry Trego was a boy in Worle at the time:

> I remember one Home Guard killed at Worle Observatory. He was called Raines and he lived up Lawrence Road at Worle. The men used to stand on top of the tower as look-out. Two were going up the stairs and one must have had one up the spout. It went off and shot the man in front.
>
> I used to play with the Atkins children. They lived by the Woolpack. Their father was shot in the head during the First World War and he had a steel plate there. Then in the Home Guard he was a sergeant-major. He was killed on the range.

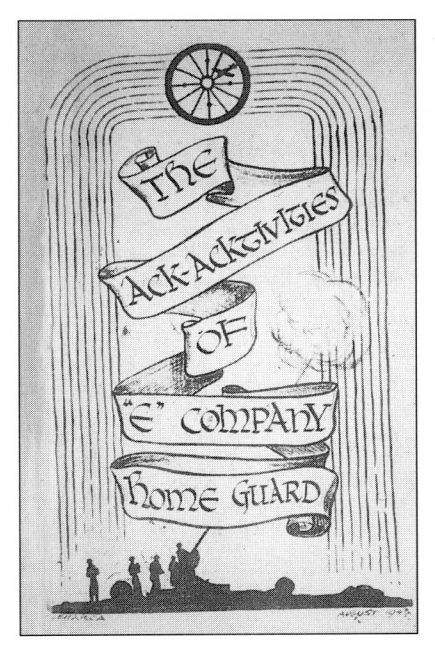

*The Home Guard saw action as anti-aircraft gunners, manning sites between Bristol and Weston. Artist Lewis E. Heath was one of them, recording his impressions in a book of cartoons. (Author's collection)*

Verdon Besley lived at Hill Farm cottage, on Col Yatman's estate. He was 16 when he joined Winscombe Home Guard:

> We used to go down to the Drill Hall, just behind where the pub is now. We did drill and a few exercises and weapon training. There were quite a few guard duties especially when they expected trouble. I remember guarding the railway bridge down the A38, all night long. We never got paid.

When Anthony Eden made his appeal, every member of Churchill British Legion volunteered for the LDV. They paraded in the Drill Hall which then stood in the south-east angle of Churchill cross-roads. In 1914, Territorial Frank Gilling had fired on the .22 range there when he left Burrington to fight in the First World War. In 1940, his son Sam fired on the same range when he joined the Home Guard.

Other ghosts of past conflicts watched the defensive preparations round Churchill. One Home Guard soldier, Albert Frost, grew up on Grange Farm, reputed to have been used as a jail for 17th century Mendip rebels captured at Sedgemoor. In 1940, Albert dug slit trenches at Burrington Combe, where, in the Napoleonic Wars, a thousand local volunteers had formed the East Mendip Legion to fight the French.

Dolebury's Iron Age fort provided a look-out point, linked with Churchill Platoon HQ by a field telephone. The platoon commander, Lt Jones, was not local, having moved from his bombed-out shop in Bristol. To help him find his way up Dolebury in the dark, the men kindly whitewashed big stones at intervals. But the RAF protested about this pattern of white dots across the landscape and the Churchill men had wearily to turn all the stones over, white side down.

If a German landing force had appeared off Brean or Weston, Churchill Platoon's mission was to join Wrington Company as reinforcements for the troops on Brean Down. Part of their training was to attack Blagdon Home Guard one Sunday – and repel Blagdon's attacks the next Sunday. They revived old military skills, including flag-signalling, taught by 2nd Lieutenant Ricketts. He cycled over from Weston, although 70 years old.

More up to date was the Blacker Bombard mounted on the Batch, covering Churchill cross-roads where a mobile barrier lay ready to be wheeled out. The Blacker Bombard, or spigot mortar, was too heavy to move around and inaccurate. But it did fire 14lb anti-personnel or 20lb anti-tank bombs, adding explosive power to an ambush.

John Poulsford of Winterhead Hill Farm commanded Shipham Home Guard with one of his farm-workers, Ken Watts, as corporal. Their task was to patrol the hillside above the village. In the winter of 1941, they had to run a dance to raise funds to heat their headquarters and pay for transport to Yoxter range.

By May 1943, Home Guard strengths were enough for Axbridge to separate from Weston as the 13th Somerset Battalion. Over the A38 at Cross, concrete blocks lay ready to bar the bridge in Old Coach Road. The Cross Home Guard section paraded in the former village brewery, now part of Brewers Farm. Although disused as a brewery for many years, a strong beery smell persisted in the building where a special Victory Brew had celebrated the 1918 Armistice. On their way back from training in the quarry, the men would often rest on benches in the big old porch of Cleeve Head House. Fire Guards sat in the same oak seats when watching for incendiaries.

*Bomb damage provides the backdrop to one of Weston's Home Guard platoons in 1941. The diagonal shoulder-strap held the gas respirator which had to be carried at all times. Several men wear 1914–18 medal ribbons and the central officer is in his Great War riding-breeches. (Bristol Evening Post)*

Helen Boileau saw them sitting there as she walked to Axbridge from Compton Bishop. Already recruited into Axbridge Invasion Committee, she now joined the Home Guard as a Woman Auxiliary and trained as a signaller. She went into Axbridge at night to be taught the Morse Code by a Home Guard milkman from Burnham. Wireless transmitters were then barely portable, their valves and heavy batteries being contained in an unwieldy metal case. But despite the size, transmission range was very limited, just about reaching the old Axbridge council offices from the town's outskirts.

Though women had always lent an unofficial hand with Home Guard activities, in 1943 they were allowed to enlist as Auxiliary Home Guard signallers and clerks. No uniforms were issued, but many women remodelled male battledress and joined in weapon training, firing rifles on the ranges. Helen Boileau still has her Home Guard badge and a membership certificate, serial 753, signed by Col G. H. Rogers DL, OC North Somerset Sector, Home Guard.

*The old porch of Cleeve Head House, convenient for Home Guardsmen and fire watchers. (Author)*

# 7
# WELLS ON WATCH

As the men of south-east Mendip fell in to join the LDV, their commander, Lt Col J. McDonnell, prepared for action. On 15th May 1940, just one day after their formation, he put out 20 two-man patrols, armed with whatever weapons they could find.

Jim Loxton was a founder member of the Easton-Westbury platoon:

> We did the very first guard at the Hollybrook Post. We only had an armband with LDV on it, a twelve-bore shotgun and a broomstick. We couldn't have stopped anything.

His brother Tony joined with him. He remembers the gun well:

> I think we were called "parashots" when we started off, the first night. We went up with this gun with this bloody great cartridge with ball-bearings stuck in the end. I'm sure if we'd fired this thing he'd have blown to pieces.
>
> Brother Jim, he was there with Boxer Carver. We'd had a meeting about 8 o'clock to start it all off and at 10 o'clock we were up there on this hill. We had sandwiches and this old gun with this cartridge thing in.
>
> Lo and behold, Mr McDonnell come along in his car and stopped down along the road and walked up through to us.
>
> Well of course, we'd only started an hour or two before but when he come up, he cussed Jim and Boxer Carver cause they never saluted him.
>
> Boxer Carver, he said, "Next bloody time he do come up 'ere, I'll bloody 'ave 'e."

Less exciting, if safer, broom handles replaced the doctored twelve-bore until the official Home Guard weapons arrived.

Sergeant the Reverend Cecil Buckingham, Vicar of Easton, com-

*Village rivalries emerged when a commander was needed for the platoon drawn from Westbury-sub-Mendip and Easton. Col McDonnell firmly appointed an outsider, Arthur Packer from Wookey Hole, who proved an effective and popular leader. (John Sealy)*

manded the village platoon. Schoolboy John Sealy and Scorcher Shepherd were on unarmed sentry duty on the Beacon above Westbury. Following his colonel's example, the Rev Buckingham crept through the darkness to test their alertness. From out of the night, Scorcher challenged him: 'Halt! ... before I shoot thee with this brush-handle.'

His place secure in local legend, the vicar enlisted as an Army padre.

Well aware of the platoon's ruffled pride, Col McDonnell personally selected its next commander. Sergeant Arthur Packer lived in Wookey Hole and worked at St Cuthbert's paper mill. He was commissioned and remained a popular and respected commander of the platoon for the rest of the war.

Another vicar, the Rev Hubert Lawrence Walker of Wookey, commanded Cheddar Valley Company. In Cheddar itself, the village platoon had two officers, Mr Butcher and Mr Baker.

Arthur Parsons and Jack Chew were two of 30 men who paraded with them in Cheddar's old mill where they installed a .22 range. Platoon Sergeant Edson proved to be a skilled weapon handler. When the new Sten gun arrived with no instructions, he stripped it down, put it back together again and issued the warning, 'Watch that spring': a perceptive comment, as any Sten gun user will appreciate.

From 1942, the British-made Sten machine-carbine became a standard Home Guard weapon. Costing under £2, it was the only weapon originally devised for the Home Guard that went into regular service. It eventually armed most of Europe's resistance movements.

'Cromwell' was the British code-word to signal the imminence of invasion. On hearing it, the appropriate Army Command HQs were to take up battle stations. On Saturday 7th September 1940, the code-word 'Cromwell' went out to some HQs in the south and east. The usual 'copy for information' went to other Commands where leaks became rumours, rapidly picked up by the Home Guard. The more vigorous battalions mobilised, rang their church bells and manned their road blocks.

This over-enthusiastic 'Cromwell' signal reached Cheddar where Jack Chew responded to it:

> When we had the invasion scare, Arthur Parsons had to come down to call me out. My wife went to the door. It was pitch dark and she could just see the silhouette of him. It frightened her. We had to go in the paper mill, on sentry, so we spent the rest of the night marching up and down in front. We really thought the invasion was coming.

With companies at Wells, Glastonbury, Street, Cheddar Valley and Mendip, Col McDonnell's 9th (Wells) Battalion Home Guard manned the central sector of the Green Line. A few months after formation, they were issued with rifles, Lewis guns, Browning automatic rifles and Mills 36 grenades. Men did two and a half hours training on one evening a week. On Sundays they trained for three hours, on ranges, manning road blocks or fighting mock battles.

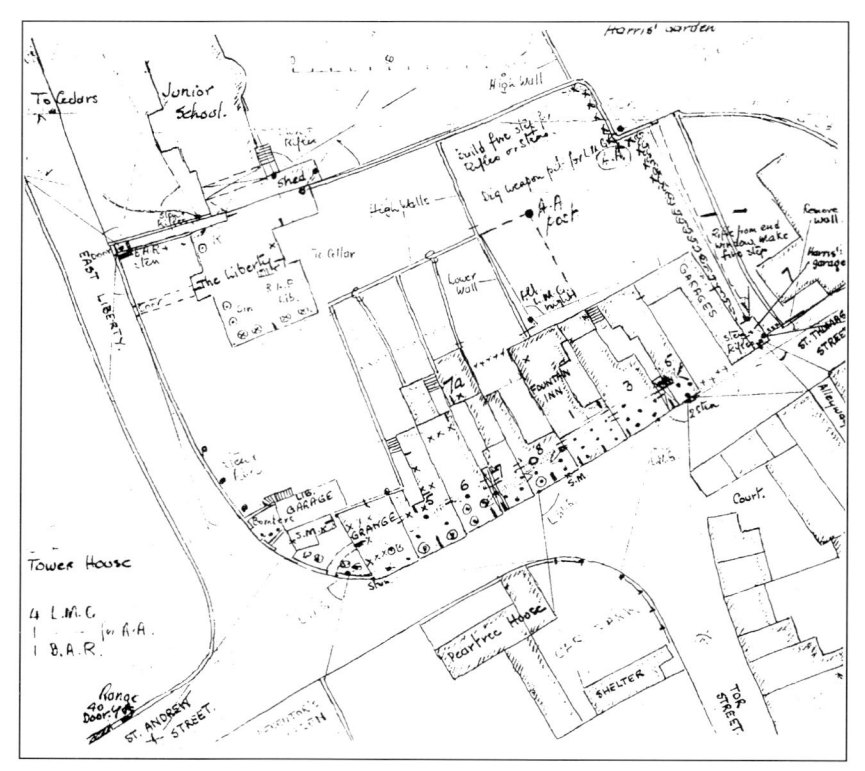

*Wells Home Guard Company planned a street-by-street defence of the city in meticulous detail. (Mrs Enid Smith)*

Jim Loxton heard echoes of earlier wars:

> At Ben Knowle, near Worth, one of the fields is called Targets. That's because during the First World War the soldiers had target practice there. We went there again in the Second World War and we had very improvised butts as you can imagine. We could fire at a hundred yards but to get 200 yards we had to cross over the road and fire from another field, across the road. Somebody had to be on duty to see no traffic came through.

The Charterhouse Platoon drew most of its men from farms and Springfields Refinery. Locally known as the 'fat factory', Springfields

*"I grant you it MIGHT be a bit awkward if the invasion came up Cherry Lane instead of the High Street."*

However hard the Home Guard tried, its best efforts remained a joke to most observers. (Reproduced with permission of Punch Ltd)

rendered down fat from slaughterhouses, producing a formidable smell reputedly reaching as far away as Blagdon. The platoon sergeant, Cecil Mainwaring 'Lofty' Upton, was factory manager and son of the owner. Volunteers included Fred Villis, Harry Stubbs, Bill Pole and Ted

Targett. Still suffering from front-line experiences in the first war, Percy Walters, husband of the Charterhouse school teacher, could only watch them parade in the school playground.

The men kept rifles and ammunition at home, but machine-guns were in short supply. When the platoon received a Vickers machine-gun – described by Fred Villis as 'our pride and joy' – Sgt Upton made a special lightweight tripod for it and stored it in an armoury at the factory. A hand-drawn map survives, detailing the platoon plan to defend Charterhouse cross-roads, drawing 'necklet' mines across the roads as tanks passed.

The platoon had a section at Blagdon and, in emergency, an RAF squad at Beacon Batch came under their command. Muster points and ammunition stocks were in Charterhouse School, Tynings Farm and at Bleak House. The platoon was also on call as Mendip Company's mobile reserve. They were certainly eager. Whenever there was a raid on Bristol, one First World War veteran donned his greatcoat and patrolled the Charterhouse area with a round up the spout, ready for any eventuality.

At its peak, the Charterhouse unit mustered an officer and 36 soldiers, armed with a Bren gun, nine Stens, 21 rifles and two EY grenade launchers. Dating from 1917, the Number 68 Rifle Grenade was often called the EY, after its inventor Edgar Yule whose initials were cast into the casing. Fired from a discharger cup on the end of a rifle barrel, it could prove more dangerous to the firer than to the target.

Bryan Green tells of a training tragedy:

> Jack Hillier commanded Oakhill Home Guard. Down in Gurney Slade quarry they were demonstrating firing a grenade from a rifle. You pulled the pin out and dropped the grenade into a cup screwed on the end of the rifle. The cup was the same size as the grenade and the pressure kept the lever in. You fired a blank cartridge and that threw the bomb. The landlord of the Horse and Jockey, Sergeant Carter, was holding the rifle. Jack Hillier was doing the demonstration and he put the bomb in upside down so there was no pressure and the bomb just dropped out. Jack went to dive on it and throw it away but it exploded and killed him. His name's on the war memorial.

Mendip Company was commanded by Captain Reynolds, a retired

*Adjacent to the Cathedral, inside the 15th century stone Bishop's Barn, Wells Home Guard not only drilled, but fired on a .22 range. (Mrs M Lees)*

*By 1941, every Home Guard platoon had its own Northover Projector. Costing under £10 each, this weapon propelled a grenade in a forward direction for about 150 yards, except when it was raining. (Author's collection)*

bank manager living at Green Ore. His son, Bob, drove the company truck. His Company War Book (see Appendix A) defined their intention as: 'To deny the enemy use of road Wells-Bristol and Burnt Wood to Miners' Arms, in vicinity of Cross Roads.'

Around their 'Fighting Base' in Green Ore Farm, they deployed '7 Officers and 132 men, 57 Rifles, 17 EY, 45 Sten, 1 Bren Machine-Gun, 3 Browning Automatic Rifles, 3 Lewis, 4 Northovers, 3 Spigots.'

The Northover Projector, a metal tube on a cast-iron tripod, cost under £10. A cap ignited its gunpowder charge to propel a grenade in a great cloud of white smoke that instantly betrayed the location of the weapon. But it was an ideal Home Guard weapon, requiring no training for its crew of three. Eight thousand were produced and eventually every platoon had one. Later models fired almost any available grenade that would fit the barrel.

The platoons at Horrington and Nedge had an international flavour. A White Russian named De Cremer commanded Horrington, based in

*Wells Battalion Home Guard on parade on the Recreation Ground. (John Sealy)*

the Old Chapel. The Nedge platoon officer was Lt Douglas who had escaped from his farm in France by the skin of his teeth. Hence, the Nedge men were known as 'the Free French'. Just inside the trees at Nedge, they kept their kit in an old van, part of a steam waggon built by the Mendip Motor Company. Larger weapons were stored by Chewton Hill platoon in the Men's Club Reading Room.

The Wells Battalion paraded through the city on Sunday 16th May 1943 to mark the Home Guard's third anniversary. By now, they were well trained and equipped with a wide range of effective weapons. Col McDonnell organised an exercise to test how well his units could mobilise and stand to. It was to be a wide-ranging scheme, involving Red Cross and civilian 'casualties', one of them a psychiatric case.

Captain Reynolds of Mendip Company knew the day of the exercise but not the timing of events. He detailed Lt Cecil Stevens to put Chewton Hill platoon in a defensive location on the village cross-roads, covering the northern approach to Company HQ in Green Ore Farm. They also manned an Observation Post on Nedge Hill.

Newly-commissioned Bryan Green suddenly found himself second-in-command to Lt Stevens. His job was to draw field sketches of both

*In addition to their steel helmets, this Home Guard platoon in Wells wore '37 webbing, unusual for the Home Guard at that time, and carried American .300 rifles. (Roddy Southwell)*

locations for use in planning. His youngest brother Harold was cast as the psychiatric patient.

When the day arrived, orders came in by phone and went out by tractor, driven by Claude, another Green brother. Lt Stevens positioned his men and set up a camp table and field telephone as platoon HQ, manned by 2/Lt Green. All seemed set when three private soldiers turned up, late from work but willing to join in. Bryan Green remembers it well:

> Stevens said, "Righto, Bryan. Let's walk round and see where to put these three."
>
> As we got on the main road, his hands went up and he went down and that was him. Heart attack. He was dead.
>
> He was on duty, so he's on the war memorial down at Chewton Mendip. It shows his date of death as 11/4/43.
>
> I sent a message down to Headquarters, but they thought it was part of the exercise and wouldn't believe anything I said.

Down at the road junction, my brother had gone mad as planned. He's about 6'2" and he jumped out from the conker tree, waving this great stick about. A little Special Policeman, Walter St John, was trying to arrest him just as the big brass came marching up the hill to see how well the exercise was progressing.

Captain Reynolds with his monocle came over to me. "What the hell is going on up here? Why aren't you under cover?"

So I told him.

"Well you take charge," he said. "You're second-in-command."

I never felt such an idiot in my life. The sergeant wasn't there, he was at work down the mine. None of us knew anything about the scheme, but we carried on for the rest of the day.

# 8
# READY TO RESIST

While the Home Guard were the public face of armed civil defence, Britain's Secret Intelligence Service (MI6) was already running a rather thin covert agency known as Section D which aimed, 'to investigate every possibility of attacking potential enemies by means other than the operations of military forces' – in other words, sabotage.

The British have always enjoyed stories of how their gentlemanly amateurs overcome the hard professionals of other breeds. But in 1940, Winston Churchill was having no truck with wishful romantic thinking. Until the army had recovered from Dunkirk, the people would have to fight. Amateur they may be, but there would be nothing gentlemanly about their methods.

Churchill now beefed up Section D into a 'D for Destruction' unit under Major Colin Gubbins. An unorthodox soldier, Gubbins was soon running subversive operations in Poland and Norway. Section D was absorbed into Special Operations Executive (SOE), with the brief to 'Set Europe ablaze'.

It was a task that attracted soldiers from military backgrounds that were unusual to say the least. They included men who had operated in the desert alongside Lawrence, on the Indian North-West Frontier, in Russia with White Russian guerrillas against the Bolsheviks, or underground against nationalist groups in Palestine and Ireland. To this active experience they added studies of guerrilla campaigns in South Africa, China and Spain.

Through that first wartime winter, they also watched Finland, a small isolated country, doggedly resisting a massive Russian invasion. They noted how small squads operated swiftly, silently and unpredictably behind Russian lines, destroying dumps and convoys before vanishing again. If the Finns could do it, so could the British.

The scene was set for one of the most remarkable missions ever undertaken by civilian volunteers, the creation of a guerrilla network across the United Kingdom. By September 1940, a British Resistance

*With Headquarters in Francis Banwell's cider cellar, Wedmore AU patrol trained every night. From left to right: Sgt Arthur Duckett, not wearing his stripes, but with the AU Battalion number 203 visible on his sleeve; Stanley Clarke who farmed at Theale; Capt H. Radford, Axbridge wine-merchant; Jack Morgan, engineer with the Electricity Board; Andrew Higgs, Theale farmer; Charles Binning, baker; Ernest Bethell; George Turner, by then in the Army; Cpl Francis Banwell, also with no stripes, Oldwood Farm, Sand, dispenser of the cider. (Keith Salter)*

Organisation lay ready, prepared to strike at an occupying army. Within a year, over a hundred highly trained patrols, fully equipped and armed, were operational. According to the SAS magazine Mars and Minerva, the patrols mustered 3,000 volunteers between them.

Their sole mission was sabotage. Frontal battle remained the task of the army and the Home Guard. The resistance squads would operate only in enemy-occupied territory, attacking dumps, communications, airfields and headquarters.

Gubbins concealed the true purpose of his British Resistance Organisation behind the meaningless title of Auxiliary Units or AUs. But it was sufficiently important for a weekly Progress Report to go to the Commander-in-Chief, Field Marshal Ironside, with a copy to the Prime Minister. As a young officer, Ironside had himself carried out clandestine missions inside Boer territory.

Secret orders went to selected Invasion Committees requiring support for the AU sabotage squads. Gubbins sent out Intelligence

*Capt Ian Fenwick KRRC (driver) came to Somerset in 1940 to set up a network of secret sabotage units. In 1944 he joined the SAS and parachuted into France to do the same behind German lines. (Author's collection)*

Officers to establish Auxiliary Units in a 30-mile wide coastal strip from Cape Wrath clockwise to Pembroke. One was Alan Crick who went on to serve as military intelligence officer to Montgomery and Eisenhower. His obituary in *The Times* of 9th November 1995 noted that in 1940 he 'spent some time in Dorset and Somerset, organising auxiliary forces to form a resistance movement in the event of a successful German invasion of this country.'

Captain Ian Fenwick of the King's Royal Rifle Corps was the Intelligence Officer directly in charge of Somerset's Auxiliary Units. He worked from an HQ in Bridgwater. Fenwick had always enjoyed the less conventional aspects of his career. Winchester College knew him best as a demon bowler. From Cambridge University he went to pre-war Berlin as an honorary attaché at the British Embassy where, alongside undefined diplomatic activities, he studied art. Back in London, Ian Fenwick worked as a book illustrator, but preferred drawing cartoons for humorous magazines. By 1939 he was in North America where one Somerset legend placed him in the Canadian Mounties. Hurrying home to join the colours, he went into the elite 60th Rifles, the King's Royal Rifle Corps but on 30th June 1940, only three weeks after Dunkirk, 2/Lt Fenwick's entry in the Army List noted his transfer to a 'specialist appointment'.

This was in Somerset, where one of his sergeants, Freddy Chapman, commented, 'Nobody argued with Fenwick. He could get anything done.' Arthur Parsons of Cheddar remembered him as 'a mad bugger. Used to chuck live explosives around to make you move.' Off duty, Ian Fenwick billeted himself and his wife with one of his Auxiliary Units' officers, Mortimer White, at Nerrols Farm, near Taunton.

Based in the stables of Southill House, Cranmore, Lt John McCue, Wiltshire Regiment, established Units in Mendip and the north of the county. Twelve men from the Welch Regiment under Sgt Ron Garnham made up his training team. In 1941, Lt Keith Salter came from 6th Battalion Somerset Light Infantry to replace Lt McCue, while Freddy Chapman and Tommy Webster were promoted to sergeant.

Between them, they built up Somerset to become the second largest resistance organisation in the country. At its peak, nearly 300 men formed nine groups of 44 patrols operating out of 50 secret bases. Mendip was rapidly ringed with Auxiliary Units, from Compton Bishop, round through Cheddar, Wedmore, Ebbor Gorge, Green Ore, Chewton Mendip, Dinder, Shepton Beacon, Pensford, Blagdon and Sandford. Each patrol was self-sufficient and members – known as

*Auxiliary Units wore ordinary Home Guard uniform and flashes, except for the battalion number, 203. (John Sealy)*

'Auxiliers' – were sworn to secrecy.

Captain Fenwick's first task was to create cells of half a dozen men each. He relied on personal contacts to ensure the absolute reliability of his recruits. He needed men who knew the land and could merge into it, who could live rough and survive, who could fight rough and kill; and who could accept the almost certain prospect of being killed.

Their cover was to appear in public as ordinary Home Guard soldiers. This ruled out women as members, as they were not yet allowed to join the Home Guard. Age limits were pretty wide, ranging from 16-year olds awaiting call-up, to men in their seventies. Estimates of their life expectancy should invasion come were narrower, put between ten and fourteen days. The volunteers understood that they would never return home or see their families again.

Farmers were an obvious choice as they knew every inch of their land. So did gamekeepers and poachers – and they knew it at night. People like vets, postmen, builders and lorry drivers were familiar with the whole area. Every recruit was checked through the Police, although they were not told the reason for the check. Once enrolled, recruits were asked to suggest other likely members. The result was a closely-knit unit of like-minded local men, most of whom knew each other.

As many had already volunteered for other organisations, Intelligence Officers had the authority to extract anybody from existing commitments such as the Home Guard. They also saw to it that their carefully selected and trained men were not snatched away by the national call-up. A member of the Pensford patrol, Jim Hooper spent two days at Chepstow race-course as an Ordnance Corps conscript before being told he could have his discharge papers whenever he wanted.

> I thought, Now I'm in, I'm not sure I want to go home. But after a week, I didn't care for the sergeant, so I went back.
> Much later, my officer told me I was released because I was in the Auxiliary Units.

With sabotage in mind, Arthur Walton stood out as an Auxiliary Units recruit. Arthur worked underground at Welton in the Norton Hill colliery where he carried the powder box for blasting. Shortly after joining the Home Guard, he was invited to a 'special meeting'. There, Captain Malcolm Shackell, a farmer from Swainswick, invited Arthur to use his explosive expertise as a member of Midsomer Norton Auxiliary Unit.

Two other members worked in the Standard Check Book Company at Welton and persuaded the manager to let them have a room as an 'office'. What the manager didn't know was that the room also served as an explosives arsenal.

Charlie Lanning mysteriously left Midsomer Norton Home Guard 'to do something else', nobody knew what. Although naturally a talkative man, Charlie never said that he was now a corporal in the Auxiliary Unit. Known as a bit of a lad, he nearly blew his house up one day, reputedly while making bombs on the kitchen table.

Farm-worker Sam Gilling was an early volunteer in Shipham Home Guard. His old friend Ken Watts wore a Home Guard corporal's uniform, but never appeared on parade. When Sam ribbed him about this, Ken said, 'Come and find out, we could do with a bloke like you.' Sam says,

> I think I was replacing somebody. I was 18 when the war started. When I signed up with Sandford Auxiliary Unit, I had to go to their head office in Exeter to sign secrecy papers. It was probably late '41.

Verdon Besley was recruited when older men were leaving the Units and younger men were brought in:

> I must have been 16 or 17. It was Spring because I'd been helping Father with sheep-shearing. Father stopped in the New Inn at Cross on the way home and I waited outside as I wasn't old enough to go in.
> Cliff Banner came out of the pub. He had a market garden near Winscombe and was a friend of Father's. I was already in the Home Guard and Cliff approached me to join this secret army. I had to sign this secret form. Not even my parents knew. They thought it was just the Home Guard.

Like Verdon and many others, Tony Loxton started his service in the Home Guard. He still has his old LDV pass No. 298, identifying him as LOXTON CW, signed by J. McDonnell for Platoon Commander (Captain). Captain McDonnell soon became Lieutenant Colonel McDonnell, commanding the Wells Home Guard Battalion. Tony remembers:

> We had Easton Farm, 300 acres, going right from Easton up over Deer Leap to Felton Drove. Jack Lunnon was my best mate. He was a captain or a lieutenant. He invited me into the Ebbor Unit. I think Jack got on to me because he thought I'd know all the fields and where we were at night-time as well. I would be about 20 then. Jack would have been older. I expect I was the youngest of our six. I stayed to the end.

After Harold Lane had been in Wells Home Guard for some months, he saw a decline in the original enthusiasm of some of his fellow volunteers. He says:

> One of the officers, Lieutenant Harrison, asked me, "How are you getting on, Harold?"
> I knew Mr Harrison. He was teaching my son at the Blue School. I told him, "OK I suppose. I don't want to give it up but some of these youngsters aren't doing their duty properly. It's understandable – they might as well have a good time while it lasts."
> Harrison said, "Meet me outside the Mermaid on Sunday

morning. We'll talk about it then. You'll be picked up."

There were three or four of us waiting at the Mermaid. Jack Lunnon was there. We were all the same age group. Along comes this black Daimler or something driven by a young lady in uniform with two young lads – captains – in the back.

They took us to Chewton Mendip. Mr Harrison had told us we were to form a new signalling corps but we then found out something different. It meant leaving the Home Guard. We were told it had to be secret.

Over in Chewton Mendip, Bryan Green had been in the Home Guard for some weeks:

Captain Reynolds said to me, "Look, there's a meeting down at Wells and we've got to send a representative. Will you go down?"

Somewhen after that we went to Bishop's Barn in Wells. Captain Fenwick was there. And Lieutenant Harrison who was my old Geography master at Blue School.

They said it was completely hush-hush. Would I join their unit and recruit a couple more from our area, which I did.

Jim Hooper, on the other hand, was an AU recruit who never served in the Home Guard:

I lived in Bristol but I'd been courting out in Wellard. I knew the captain and he asked me to join Pensford Unit. He was Captain Trussler, the gamekeeper. They were just digging out their base in the estate woods. I was a builder so I was useful to them.

There were about a dozen in the Unit. All the men were in their late 20s, early 30s. I was one of the younger ones, only 17 at the time. We were not in the Home Guard. We had to sit tight, do nothing, get overrun, until they were past us. Then we had to emerge and do whatever we could to slow them down. There was no suggestion that we were going to stop any attack.

Like all the men in Blagdon Auxiliary Unit, Eion Fraser was born and bred in the village:

Four of us younger ones in the Home Guard were invited to join

*Membership of the British Resistance Organisation relied on the local 'old boy net' ... literally, in John Sealy's case. As he left Wells Blue School Sixth Form, he was recruited by his former schoolmaster Mr E.A. Harrison. When not teaching geography, Lt Harrison co-ordinated the activities of secret units round Wells. (John Sealy)*

the Unit in 1940 or '41. I was 18, one of the youngest. I think Mr Light asked us, from the post office. He was one of the men in charge of the Home Guard. Our boss was called Radford. He was the wine merchant in the Square in Axbridge. He was a captain. He'd come up perhaps once a week to see us. And Pike, he worked for Willets the millers at Sandford. He had one or two pips.

Francis Stott and John Sealy of Westbury joined the LDV on the same day and transferred into the same AU at the same time. Francis recalls:

Percy Reid came out to Westbury. He was friendly with John Sealy's family. They went down to Sealy's, then they came up over to see me. That's how it was done. It had to be word of mouth.

My old schoolmaster, Lieutenant Harrison, ran it. He was the only one who could control us at school. He'd done a bit of boxing in his time and he wasn't averse to giving me a dig in the ribs.

Another of Lt Harrison's recruits from Wells Blue School was Horace Godfrey, born at Pen Hill Farm in 1912, then farming at Coombe House, North Wootton:

I controlled the resistance group based on Dulcote Hill above the old quarry. Sidney Down was a farmer in Dinder and Percy Hull was the son of the postmistress in Dinder. He worked on Somerville's Estate. Charlie Clark came from Keward and Fred Shatwell was an evacuee schoolmaster from London. Youngest was Clifford Taylor of Poulsam, Coxley Wick. He was 21.

In Cheddar, Home Guard Lieutenant Butcher from Battscombe quarry, asked for volunteers for special duties. Arthur Parsons went along:

We were all transferred to Mr Radford in Axbridge. He was our captain. The first meeting we had was in Art Pavey's woodwork place where he used to make his doors and that.

Jack Chew went with him:

We joined the Home Guard and then we had to go to the Cliff Hotel for a meeting and they asked for volunteers for this special, secret thing. Of course, young and stupid, we put our hand up, me and my mate Arthur Parsons, Arthur Pavey and about half a dozen of us, Phil Leigh and John Hewlett.

Arthur Pavey was our sergeant and I was the corporal.

# 9
# UNDERGROUND ARMY

To be successful guerrilla fighters, the men of the Auxiliary Units must come out of nowhere, make an unseen attack and vanish again.

The British Resistance Organisation therefore prepared to vanish into a network of secret underground Operational Bases (OBs). Just off Mendip at Southill House, Cranmore, Lt John McCue's training team built theirs. Freddy Chapman worked on it:

> We dug our OB in Cranmore Woods. From it we ran a field telephone line to two underground Observation posts, each just large enough to take two men.

Field telephones linked Observer OBs with main Unit OBs. Lines had to be buried, crossing roads or streams under bridges or culverts and instructions were clear.

> The wire should not leave or enter the ground at the OBs, but a small tunnel should be bored some five yards away, so that an enemy who may have picked up the wire will come to an abrupt halt a short distance away from the OB. The tugging of the wire will be noticeable and necessary drastic action taken at short range without delay.
>
> A recess should be constructed in the Observer's OB to take the telephone. This recess should be covered so that it remains hidden – a board on a hinge is not good enough.
>
> In case the enemy discover the telephone, a password should precede the conversation.

Observer OBs operated on these lines in Cranmore Woods, Ebbor Gorge and Cheddar Gorge.

Most Mendip Units adapted existing caves or mines as hide-outs. Some dug their own base, with assistance from Cranmore, excavating a chamber measuring about twelve feet by ten feet with six to eight feet of earth on top. Fittings included seats, a table and half a dozen bunks made of wood and chicken wire. Ventilation pipes did little to counter condensation, especially when an oil-stove was used for heating or cooking. A narrow escape tunnel led away from the main room to a concealed exit. Stocks of arms and explosives were stacked on shelves, sometimes in a second chamber or another base nearby. A wooden box held food rations for 14 days and a sealed keg of rum was hidden away until needed for operational purposes.

All the equipment and stores had to be moved with as little fuss as possible. The Boileau family moved into Rackley Lane outside Compton Bishop in 1938 and Helen was in her teens when war broke out:

> The postman was called Lew Croker. He was an old soldier from the 1914–18 war and still walked with a straight back. One day he asked my father if he could deliver a load of larch poles to the house. He asked us to keep them out of sight. They arrived at night and a few nights later, Lew and some men took them away.

Up the hill, the village Auxiliary Unit needed the poles to set up their Operational Base in Denny's Hole, a large cave.

> Lew Croker came back and asked my mother if she would store tins of food for them. A smart Army soldier turned up with a lorry, at night again, and delivered three big metal containers. They had no writing or markings on them. We kept them in our larder all through the war.
>
> Yet we were new in the area, with a foreign name. They must have checked our background.
>
> When I walked the spaniel up the hill with my sister, we saw men in uniform throwing clumps of earth into bushes. They warned us they would be doing some blasting. It was underground and it shook the house.

A metal threshold still crosses the entrance to a tunnel out of the large main chamber. That tunnel opens into a deeper cave used as the

Operational Base. It also concealed the spoil dug out to enlarge the entrance. Access is steep and slippery; climbing out is impossible without a rope.

Some auxiliers worked on a hide-out at Chewton Mendip. A Waldegrave estate worker, Charlie Ford, remembered an old mineshaft in the woods. Bryan Green went with him to dig it out:

> We had a huge rock in the way. I was digging and this ruddy rock fell on me. I managed to pull my leg out but I tore my trousers off. We were doing this on Sunday morning and I had to get right the way across Chewton Mendip to get home, which I did holding my trousers round me. I've suffered a bit since with that knee.
>
> We were working with four or five regular army men from Cranmore. They got fed up and they blew the rock out. They made the entrance straight down and then horizontal. They put duck boards down and started putting shelving in, but it was very damp.

John Sealy was based near Green Ore:

> The Army dug in a Nissen hut in one day. It was right in the middle of the wood. You pulled a trapdoor down behind you when you went down the shaft. You'd never find it.

This was essential. Details of AU hide-outs were revealed in papers that emerged in the 1990s from a garden shed where they outlasted wartime secrecy requirements. Marked SECRET, a paper on 'The Camouflage of OB Doors' commented:

> Undoubtedly the weakest thing about our OBs is the camouflage of the doors. The first step in perfecting the camouflage is to choose one camouflage artist and provide him with all he wants in the way of tools, paint and bird-lime or sticky varnish.
>
> A door should always be judged when it has been opened and shut and not subsequently touched from outside. It is good enough if it would pass the following test: – Suppose an Auxilier who did not know it, were told that if he walked straight ahead for a hundred yards he would pass within five yards of it. Would he see it?

*Where there were no caves or mines, the Auxiliary Units dug their own bunkers, burying 'elephant shelters', a cross between an Anderson shelter and a Nissen hut. Lost in woodland, this base survived the 20th century. (Author)*

When the OB is deserted for a week or more, additional leaves should be scattered over it as a safeguard against local children.

A door should never be so sited that it might get trodden on. It is simple to arrange an overhanging branch or bush so that anyone will instinctively make a detour instead of passing right over it.

Francis Stott confirms the concealment at Green Ore:

The base was so camouflaged you didn't know where it was. We planted grass and brambles on top and let that grow. You couldn't even see the joint. It was an elephant shelter, made of steel. We dug an escape tunnel into a big ditch outside that ran right down through the wood so we could get out. When they cut the wood down they didn't even find it then.

We built bunks into the hide-out and had food in tins. We dug holes outside for phosphorus bottles, stored in crates like beer crates.

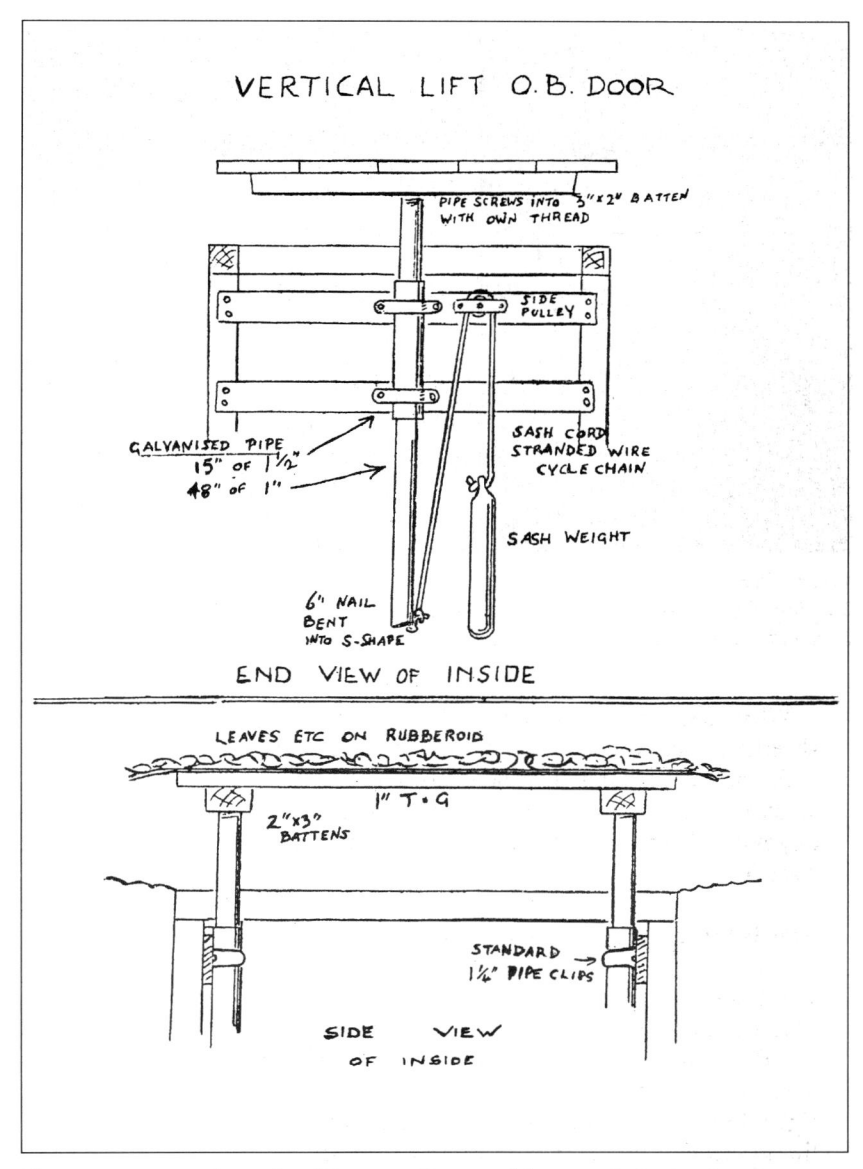

*The entrance to an Operational Base was like something out of a boy's adventure story: a concealed trapdoor. This sketch showed how to build it from everyday materials. (Mrs Nora Trego)*

'Elephant shelter' and 'Nissen hut' referred to a circular-section structure of corrugated-iron, some twelve feet in diameter, buried in the ground. With a flat earthen floor, this provided a quickly installed base.

When Harold Lane transferred into the Auxiliary Units from Wells Home Guard, he joined the Ebbor Unit:

> Our base was in Ebbor Gorge on the north side of Primrose Valley. The first thing we did was blow out a big ash tree because that gave us a big hole. But you couldn't leave the tree and the soil around the hole. We took it away in bags and disposed of it. We had to do it in the dark, so it took a long time.
>
> We dug a vertical shaft down 20 feet and built a 15 to 20-rung ladder. Then we buried this elephant shelter which came in sections. It was curved corrugated sheets, about 18 by 10 foot. In here we stored our explosives, ammunition and hard rations and supplies for three weeks for six men. We also built four wooden bunks along one wall, and a table. There was a hurricane lamp. No latrine. No stove.
>
> Once that was done we had to dig a horizontal tunnel about 20 feet long. Three of us worked together in a line. The one in front used half a pick and passed the earth back between his legs. The second one passed it back to the third who had to take it away and get rid of it.
>
> Of course the trouble with that place was that it was always soaking wet with condensation. Six blokes in there for twelve hours, especially when we were digging that tunnel. We didn't use the tunnel. It was to get out if needed.
>
> We made a cover on the top, a tray three inches deep, covered with soil. We planted flowers in there and put wire netting on. You could stand on the ladder and lift the cover up from inside and look out.
>
> I remember one Saturday afternoon when we were in the shelter and we heard voices. I lifted the cover about three inches and we found a mother and her children picnicking almost on the cover and we had to wait for them to finish and go away.
>
> We laid a telephone line underground across the valley up to the edge of the wood. We found a rock face with a split which was wide enough for two blokes to get in. We made it big enough for three. This was our observation post. These places were never

found by anyone until we were finished with them.

Tony Loxton joined the same Ebbor Unit.

> It was a marvellous hide-out. Jack Lunnon took me there. He went over this fence and about ten yards into the wood. "See if you can find it," he said.
>
> It was all covered with grass and flowers. I walked round, but I couldn't see anywhere at all. There was an old bush hanging down and that was on top of the entrance. You could lift it all up and the bush went up with it. You'd just slide in. When you pulled it down, you ruffled the leaves to cover it up. The lid was weighted.
>
> If we kept going to the dugout we made a trail, so we stayed away. We had a covered caravan like a gypsy caravan and we used to sleep in that.

On the other side of Wells, Dinder Unit based itself in Dulcote Hill above the old railway where the quarrymen used to load stone. Horace Godfrey organised AU training exercises in the worked-out GWR quarry, now Wells tip:

> We could fire our weapons there and set off grenades out of the way. Up over the quarry on the north side of the hill there was a split in the rock with a badger's sett. It opened out into a cavern with branches off. One led to the quarry face. We could crawl along and look out southward. It was a natural cave system in the hill. We enlarged it by blasting rocks out and made it quite comfortable as a base.
>
> We also dug a great hole in Lyatt Wood up above Wells golf course. We dug up a fir tree and sank a Nissen hut into the ground and put the tree back on top. We could sleep twenty-four men.

Dennis Dyke worked on that bunker:

> The army finished it for us, but we started it. It had two rooms. We stored tins of food, ammunition and explosives. We made bunk beds out of wire netting on a frame and built a trapdoor. There was a two-stage drop down but no ladder. It was right in

*A hidden trapdoor once concealed this entrance to Sandford Levvy where AU men stored their explosives. (Author)*

*A long mining tunnel inside Sandford Levvy led to the secret Operational Base. (Author)*

the Somerville Estate but the woods have since been felled and replanted.

In Cheddar, Arthur Parsons says,

> This cave, Great Oone's, marvellous place, just what we wanted. We built the front of the cave up with stones and ivy and a trapdoor with grass on, to lift up. We did it ourselves at nights. We built some bunks in there with wire netting and made a cupboard with galvanised iron for airing wet clothes.
>
> Then we planned what would happen if we got cut off, how we would live. We'd go up on the hill, get some swedes and turnips, catch a few rabbits and have a stew-up like. We had an oil stove and an oven like a biscuit tin for to go on top of the stove.
>
> We went up every night, usually two of us, to make sure everything was all right, and probably stay the night and the next night somebody else would go up. Once a week all the lot would stay. We had a telephone from inside the cave and buried the wire all up onto the top of the gorge and in case of emergency we did send a man up on top.
>
> Our orders were, when the church bells started ringing we had to disappear. No code-word. You didn't go home, you went straight to the base.

That was Cheddar's second attempt to find a hide-out, as Jack Chew remembers:

> When we started, we had to find a place for a base. We tried a cave on the hill by Axbridge but it wasn't very successful. The first night we were there, some kids turned up to watch, so that was out.
>
> Then we got a place up the gorge, Great Oone's Hole. It's all grown over now, but then there was only a few trees on the top. You had to go up and then over this ledge to get into the cave.
>
> Arthur Pavey fixed up a tank for us, made a frame to put it on and catch the drips from the ceiling and he had a pipe coming down with a tap on.

William Stanton found it all still there when he started his Mendip caving career after the war. And for decades, cavers passed the remnants of old bunks in Foxes Hole, a cave at the top of Burrington Combe on the north side of Mendip.

That had been Blagdon Auxiliary Unit's base. One member of the Unit, Eion Fraser, worked at BAC, the Bristol Aircraft Company's shadow factory at Banwell. As well as building Beaufighters for the RAF, BAC unwittingly helped build Blagdon's base. Eion confesses:

> We pinched a long hinge from BAC for the door. I put it down my overalls and walked stiff-legged out to my car. We made the door but didn't lock it. We took our weapons home and stored our explosives in the cave. We had some Army rations up there in case we got cut off. There were two compartments in this cave. The door opened into a first chamber and then there was a chamber down below that we were just able to go down. We made an airing cupboard down there for wet clothes.

Blagdon's saboteurs were not the first to find refuge in Foxes Hole. The cave has also been known as Plumley's Den since Lord of the Manor John Plumley went to earth there after the battle of Sedgemoor.

Years after the war, Ken Banwell was working for his father, Francis, on Old Wood Farm in Wedmore, south of Mendip on the Somerset levels. When a retaining bank round a pond collapsed, it revealed the remains of big old barrels. Francis explained that these had contained ammunition and explosives, buried there by the Wedmore Auxiliary Unit. Francis Banwell had been a corporal in the Unit, which located its HQ in his cider cellar. The men met there for a drink at the start of their duty and returned for another afterwards.

On the northern side of the Mendips, a few miles east of Weston-super-Mare, says Sam Gilling,

> We had our hide-out in Sandford Levvy, an old mine many feet underground. We blocked up the main entrance and made a new entrance some distance off. We had a lift-door on pulleys with shrubs and rubbish all over it. It looked just like a gruffy hole of which there are hundreds on Mendip. We only used to go there in the dark, never in daylight and never the same way twice. Inside we had sleeping quarters, hard tack rations, explosives and special equipment.

Of course, had the invasion come the men would have been active at

*Mendip mines and caves provided ready-made Operational Bases for the Auxiliary Units. In Sandford Levvy, Cecil Trego sat beside young Ken Weymouth while Cpl Watts examined a beer bottle. Lt Cliff Coombs leant against the bunk (made of chicken wire). Ammunition boxes were stacked alongside. (Mrs Nora Trego)*

*Crouched inside their base in Sandford Levvy, the AU patrol planned its programme of sabotage. Cpl Watts sat beside an oil-drum while Lt Coombs (who ran a shoe business) set high standards of boot polish in the foreground. (Mrs Nora Trego)*

night and resting in the OBs by day. A suggested daily routine summed it all up:

## 24 HOURS OF AN AUXILIER'S LIFE (WINTER)

| | |
|---|---|
| 1430 | Reveille. |
| 1515 | Meal – hot tea – cold food. |
| 1600–1700 | Clean OB, wash up, make up beds. Inspect weapons, stores, equipment. |
| 1700–1800 | Stand easy – smoking allowed for 15 minutes. |
| 1800–1900 | Meal – hot tea – cold food. Smoking 15 minutes. |
| 1900–2030 | Prepare for night patrol. |
| 2030–2045 | Emerge and rest in open air. |
| 2045–0545 | Patrol. During absence, hot meal is cooked by next day's Observer. |

0600          Hot meal – after which Observer moves to his task.
0700          Lights Out.

In 1945, the Royal Engineers were detailed to blow in the OBs. But as there were no records of their location, and no files of personnel, the sappers didn't always know where to look or whom to ask.

The war being over, they just didn't bother, leaving some British Resistance bases still to be found.

# 10
# ARMING THE AUXILIARY UNITS

Unlike the delays in equipping which dogged the Home Guard, weapons and war materials rapidly reached the Auxiliary Units. Ken Cleary explains:

> After Dunkirk, there was no hope of getting anything from the Army. But Churchill cut through bureaucracy to supply the Units. He sounded out the British Embassy in Washington. One of their contacts knew that the FBI still had a warehouse full of revolvers and Thompson sub-machine guns seized from gangsters in the Thirties. As the Americans didn't want them, indeed were glad to get rid of them, they discreetly sent the weapons to Britain where they were issued to the Auxiliary Units.
>
> Observant small boys couldn't understand why men in humble Home Guard uniforms were suddenly walking round armed with Tommy guns and pistols.

Advice came from Captain Radford of Axbridge in *A few notes for a member of an Auxiliary Unit*. 'Each man need not have a Rifle, but should carry TWO Hand Grenades, Knife and Wire Cutters, Cord or Garotting Weapon, Compass and Revolver complete with 12 rounds.' Soft shoes or rubber boots were to be worn and faces and hands blacked or covered. As for explosives, a training paper explained that, 'Each man should be a complete demolition unit in himself.'

Midsomer Norton miner Arthur Walton augmented his Canadian Ross rifle with a 6-chamber Colt revolver in a holster. Stuck in his rubber boot was 'a gurt flat dirk', the Fairbairn fighting knife. Both boots and knives were otherwise issued only to the new commando units. His patrol stored some explosives in their Operational Base near

> Returns. Personal
> Pistol & 36 Rounds ✓
> Denims, 1 suit ✓
> Ground Sheet ✓
> Gloves ✓
> Haversack ✓
> Cleaning Rod or ~~Brush~~
> Holster ✓
> Belt ✓
> Field Dressing ✓
> Face Veil ✓
> Lanyard ✓
> Mess Tin ✓
> Fighting Knife ✓
> Table Knife. Fork & Spoon ✓
> Steel Helmet ✓
> 2 Rifles, Pullthroughs & Oil Bottles. 200 rds
> 2 Slings, 2 Pieces gauze,
> 1 .22 Rifle, Cleaning rod & Set )
> 1 Telescopic Sight, & 1 Sound Moderator
> 1 Sten, 8 Mags, 1 Filler, Pull Through, 200 rds
> Oil Bottle, 1 Sling, 500 rounds.

*Auxiliary Units amassed amazing personal armouries. Sgt Trego lists a pistol, fighting knife, .303 rifles and a Sten gun with a total of nearly 1,000 rounds of assorted ammunition. His .22 rifle was fitted with telescopic sights and a silencer. (Mrs Nora Trego)*

# DELAY MECHANISMS

## I. THE TIME PENCIL

**Recognition.**

A Time Pencil looks rather like a propelling pencil. One end is copper and the other brass. They are packed in flat tins, which will open at either end.

**Properties.**

The coloured bands round the Time Pencil tell you how long a delay there is between the squashing of the copper tube and the firing of the cap. In the latest pattern the colour is shown on the safety strip only, hence this must not be left on the site. (See Fig. XVII.)

|        | Summer | Winter |
|--------|--------|--------|
| Red    | $\frac{1}{2}$ hour | $\frac{3}{4}$ hour |
| White  | $1\frac{1}{2}$ hours | $2\frac{1}{4}$ hours |
| Green  | 5 ,, | 6 ,, |
| Yellow | 10 ,, | 18 ,, |
| Blue   | 20 ,, | 30 ,, |
| Black  | 10 mins. (issued for training only) | |

Notice the difference in delays for summer and winter. This is because the acid works more slowly when it is cold.

The cap of the Time Pencil will fire Safety Fuze, Orange Line or a detonator. It will *not* fire Cordtex.

**Practical Points in Using.**

Stick to the following order and you won't have any failures.
1. Select *two* Time Pencils of the required delay for each charge.
2. Test to see that the sight hole is clear—either by eye or with a match stick. If it is blocked, the striker has come down and the pencil is useless.
3. Examine the cap. It should be dry and pink inside. If it is brown it is damp and will not work.
4. Crimp on the detonator or fit fuze inside adaptor.
5. Squeeze the copper tube until you hear the capsule break. Don't bend it. The pencil is now set.

Squash it             Don't bend it

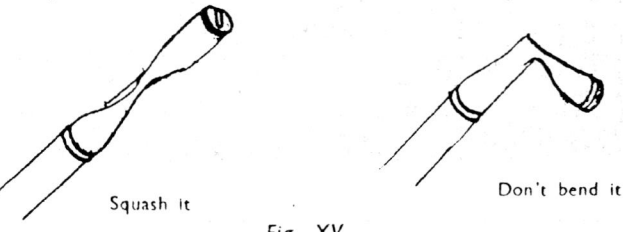

Fig. XV.

*This fuse, the time-pencil, became a standard fuse for Auxiliary Units. A coloured band indicated the time delay before the 'pencil' detonated the main charge, allowing the saboteur to get well away. (Bill Bent)*

Old Mills, and some in their 'office' at the Standard Check Book Company:

> We had all sorts. Guncotton, gelignite, explosive cord – that was Cordtex – and stuff for use under water. The timing pencil, that was the best of the lot. The colour showed the timing – half an hour, two hours, a day or two days. We had a book which showed which it was. I memorised that.

Time-pencils were gadgets picked up by Gubbins in Poland during a clandestine operation in 1939. Squeezing the soft copper end of a metal tube released acid inside. This ate through a copper wire, releasing a striker onto the detonator at a pre-determined time. A coloured ring on the fuse indicated the time delay. Being silent in operation, the time-pencil was ideal for saboteurs.

Safe storage of such materials was a problem, as Horace Godfrey found:

> I had a box full of stuff, explosives and booby traps, all in my garden cellar. There was plastic, like Semtex. And 808, the explosive out of hand grenades that smells like marzipan. And gelignite – that sweats a lot. Mostly we used a fuse ¼" thick that burned two foot per minute. We clamped it onto a detonator and pushed that into the plastic explosive. We also had a thinner, grey, instantaneous fuse which we used to set off half a dozen charges at once.
>
> Sticky bombs had a long arm and an adhesive head. We held it by the arm and threw it at a vehicle where it stuck and exploded.

The sticky bomb was officially the Number 74 ST Grenade. Military experts advised against it, but Churchill knew the troops would like it and sent out one of his famous terse orders: 'Sticky Bomb. Make one million. WSC.'

Made of glass, filled with nitro-glycerine, and covered with adhesive-coated fabric, it would, in theory, stick to the side of an enemy vehicle. In practice the sticky bomb was simply not sticky enough, falling off wet or muddy surfaces. But Churchill was right. Old Home Guards still talk proudly of their sticky bombs.

Jack Chew admits:

ARMING THE AUXILIARY UNITS

*Auxiliary Units worked with an array of detonating switches to suit every need. (Author)*

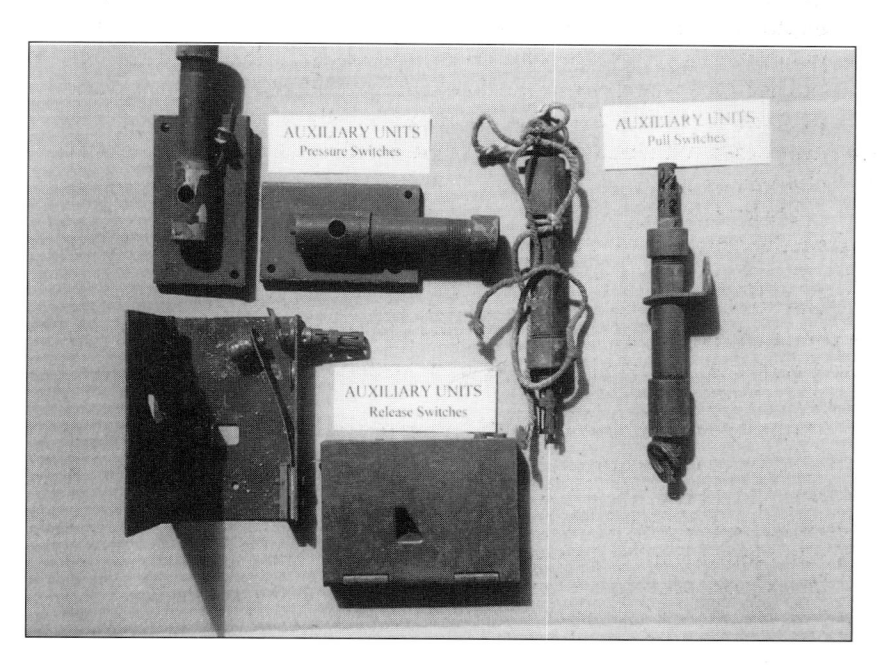

I had enough ammunition and stuff under my bed to blow up Cheddar. I had a knife and knuckle-dusters, two boxes of phosphorus bombs, a box of hand grenades and an ammunition box of .303 bullets and I had a rifle. That was before we found a base.

Phosphorus bombs were a mass-produced replacement for the Molotov Cocktail. Properly known as Number 76 (Self-Igniting Phosphorus) Grenades, they were half-pint bottles filled with combustible liquid. When thrown, the glass broke and a phosphorus fluid ignited the contents.

I always kept my revolver and its ammunition at home. The knuckle-dusters, they were deadly things. They had spikes on, sticking out. If you'd hit someone, you'd have tore his face off.

Another thing we had was booby-trap switches. We learned all about these booby switches and practised setting them off just with little caps in. We had an evacuee living with us. She worked down at Weston. We had the jerry under the bed in them days, or you had to go down the garden. One night I put one of these switches with a cap in under the jerry and she lifted it up and, oh dear, it nearly frightened her to death. Did my wife go for me.

John Sealy still has an old biscuit tin:

I've got some of the fuses here in this tin. They're all dismantled and safe now. That's the trip-wire we used, which was put across the roadway and attached to one of these pull-switches. Here's a pressure switch. It goes off when you step on it. All this was stored in the underground bunker.

Jim Hooper used Bickford fuses:

They are slow-burning. We didn't have guncotton or Molotov cocktails. That explosive stuff we worked with, you daren't rub your brow, it would give you an atrocious headache. And we had high-velocity .22 rifles with telescopic sights from the Army.

The .22 rifles were fitted with sound-reducers and telescopic sights. Unseen and unheard, firing high-velocity rounds, AU marksmen claimed they could kill tracker dogs at a mile. Or, as they add cheerfully, a German officer.

Or, more grimly, a collaborator. Bryan Green recalls a remark from one of his instructors:

> We were warned that there were "untrustworthy" people in the area. If the Germans invaded, we would be told who these people were and what to do with them.

Tony Loxton appreciated his personal weapons:

> I was issued with a beautiful knife, a thin one. We were taught how to hold it and use it. It only had to go in three inches and that was the end of him.
>
> I had a revolver, a .38 revolver, which was my pride and joy. I thought it was American. Some of them had a shorter barrel, mine was longer. If I could pull back the hammer, I could hit anything but if I'd got to pull the trigger, then the barrel lifted up a bit. I was pretty reasonable because I was used to guns. I would love to have kept my little pistol but we had to hand it all in.

Sam Gilling had a 'cheese-cutter': 'They were handy, a length of piano wire with wooden handles on each end. You strangled sentries with them.'

Transport was never adequate, as Francis Stott says:

> The unit had no transport, but the Government issued a G licence to let us use private vehicles for this job – so you didn't pay tax. Percy Reid, the sergeant, had a G licence and Reg Rose ran his Triumph on one. Big long bonnet, sports job, green one.

Sandford patrol had two vehicles, Ken Watts' Austin 7 and Cliff Coombs' Morris. The Morris towed a trailer with a rounded canvas top. Some men sat in the car, some in the trailer. Sergeant Trego moved independently on his Raleigh motor-bike, carrying stores in the side-car.

Although supplies were plentiful for the Units, delivering them had to be as secret as all their operations. Group Commanders controlled this aspect of the work. In Cheddar, that meant a message from Captain H. Radford, the wine merchant in Axbridge Town Square, to

*Invented by the Finns to destroy Russian tanks, the Molotov Cocktail was a favourite weapon with Auxiliary Units. At first home-made, the fire-bombs were later mass-produced and delivered in crates. (Author's collection)*

the patrol leader, Sergeant Pavey, in his builder's yard. Arthur Parsons remembers how it happened:

> Art Pavey would say, "We've got a delivery tomorrow tonight," and we'd go there about 7 o'clock and carry it up. The hardest work I think was climbing up over to the cave. The Army brought it up from Taunton. Always at night. We had gelignite and time-pencils and pull-switches. Molotov cocktails, like bottles of milk, they were the phosphorus ones. And we had sticky bombs.
>
> We buried all that stuff underneath the rocks, on the side of the hide-out. The gelignite was moved out and back about once in three weeks to a month, to help it stop getting sweaty.

When the war ended, Army sappers collected all the explosives and arms they could trace. But many AU men still treasure rubber truncheons and a few managed to keep their knives. Sam Gilling recalls:

> All we were told to do when the war was over was to get rid of our spare ammunition. No instructions on how to do it. I remember going up on Dolebury Warren and trying to hit rabbits with a Sten gun.

John Sealy's patrol was left with a huge stock of explosives:

> We asked what to do with it and they said we had to burn it. So we put a great heap outside in the wood and I thought, if they set that off, it'll blow up Wells. But do you know, we had a job to burn that stuff. It's the detonators that do the damage.

Horace Godfrey made good use of his:

> Quite a lot was left over. Once I wanted to cut up a car back-axle to make a farm-trailer. I warmed some plastic and made it nice and thin to spread round the axle. I stuck the detonator in and it cut the axle straight off.

AU dumps still turn up. Some time in the 1970s, an acquaintance approached Ron Hicks who was a keen dinghy sailor and asked him to dump some wartime goods in deep water. He produced a box holding

300 rounds of .300 ammunition and nearly a hundred 9mm Sten rounds, as well as books and maps of West Country railway lines and bridges. Ron tactfully explained that he couldn't do it as he was sailing on reservoirs and couldn't risk polluting the water.

> But, there was an arms amnesty at the time, so we handed the box in at Staple Hill police station. The police said it probably came from a special Home Guard unit.

For years after the war, a tin trunk stood in the cellar of Old Wood Farm, Wedmore. The sticks of explosive in it somehow didn't get sent back and were used for blowing tree stumps out. But some remained. In 1953, a group of old AU friends planned to mark Coronation Day by awakening the village at dawn. Drawing on their military training, they synchronised watches and stationed themselves on hill-tops on each side of Wedmore. At daybreak they set off their charges simultaneously.

Maintaining traditional AU secrecy, they told no one of this plan. But Ken Banwell remembers it:

> I was walking through the village to ring the church bells at daybreak, when this explosion woke the entire village up.

Their patriotic exercise revealed that the explosives were ominously sweating. They took advantage of another fortuitous amnesty and notified the police. A bomb disposal team blew up the rest in one of the fields.

# 11
# TRAINING TO DEFEND MENDIP

'The local Home Guard didn't know what we were doing. We'd go out training and making explosions. They'd come tearing up looking for us, but they never found us.' Farmer Dennis Dyke still relishes outwitting the official defenders of Dinder.

Because they did not turn out on ordinary Home Guard parades and duties, many Auxiliary Units members were derided as idle if not actually cowardly. Like the Home Guard, they trained after work, at week-ends and through the week, unpaid. But, unlike the Home Guard, their work had to be unseen and unrecognised. Tony Loxton remembers the problem:

> We practised up there in Ebbor Gorge on Sundays, throwing hand grenades. It was difficult. You're supposed to be secret, but you also got to practise.

At week-ends they vanished into deep woodland and disused quarries. Arthur Parsons:

> The Cheddar men used to train in Crowcatchpole Quarry, Shipham Hill, Cheddar Gorge and Dolebury Warren, all explosives and that. We enjoyed it. We used to get tired mind.

Farmer Horace Godfrey elaborates:

> We worked by day and were out on duty or training till 2 or 3 in the morning. After a couple of hours sleep, we'd be up for milking at 7. By 4 o'clock we could go to sleep walking about. We were worn out all the time.

*With Churchill's approval, Auxiliary Units were armed to the teeth. Cpl Watts, Lt Coombs, Pte Weymouth and Pte Trego displayed their new weapons in Sandford quarry. (Mrs Nora Trego)*

   Sergeant Tommy Webster trained us. He became a Wells councillor after the war. He showed us how to use the Tommy gun, revolvers, sticky bombs and grenades.
   Most of the training was in explosives. We carried the plastic explosive in our pocket to keep it warm. We learned how to fell a tree across the road and how to damage railway lines. You put the plastic on the inside of the rail joint. That forces the line out and derails the train. It's best on an embankment.

Jack Chew also learned the power of explosives:

Our Cheddar Unit practised with explosives on the hill. It's a wonder we hadn't been killed. There was a big pile of boulders up behind Maskall's Wood. Arthur Pavey said, "Let's put some plastic under there."

So we put it in and tamped it all down and put the fuse on and got back a bit. Do you know, it went up nearly as high as the trees. There was rocks that big, coming down all round us and you couldn't run for fear you run into 'em.

We used to go up Winscombe Quarry. 'Twasn't working. They had some rails for the drams they used to carry the stones. Mr Radford showed us the way to put the plastic under the rail, on the sleeper. Then we had to light the fuse and walk away, not run. We walked away and we got up on this bank. The thing went off and a piece of that rail whizzed up over our heads, bzzzzz. If we'd been a bit higher we'd have had our heads cut off.

John Sealy confesses:

Of course we shouldn't have done it, but we wanted something to practise on with our explosives. We put a charge in the middle of this pond, right in the bottom. It cleaned the pond out all right. The water went up in the air about 40 feet.

Using his miner's skills, Arthur Walton took a professional interest in demolition:

We practised on oil drums up the old quarry. We put a bit of oil in, wrapped the Cordex round and blew them up.

One of our tasks was to assess how to destroy railway lines and depots. We went down to look at the arches on the viaduct at Radstock. That was a bit of a job and the instructors decided it would take too much explosive. They'd sooner blow the line than the arches. One night we went down to Chilcompton to consider how to blow up the LMS railway line.

We found the best places where we could get the clay for clobbing, that's tamping the charge in. We used to carry a bag of that about for practice.

Just out of school, Verdon Besley learned some new lessons.

Down at Cliff Banner's place, he'd be practising blowing down his trees. I remember him giving me this explosive, it was like plasticine. We had fuses, red, green, yellow and blue, timed from instantaneous up to so many seconds or minutes. It was all stored

*The Auxiliary Units trained in disused quarries where their explosives and live firing attracted less attention. This abandoned lorry served as a target for (left to right) Ken Weymouth, Cecil Trego, Lt Cliff Coombs and Cpl Ken Watts. (Mrs Nora Trego)*

in Cliff's house. He took us to Sandford Quarry to throw Molotov Cocktails. We made our own with petrol in bottles.

As well as practising sabotage techniques, auxiliers had to be able to find their way over their whole area, silently, at night, carrying weapons and explosives. Tony Loxton recalled:

Some nights, we'd get taken up to Wellington Farm. They'd have regulars up there and you had to get to their base. They had trip wires down and you were taught how to hold something in front of you to feel for them.

Although their primary role was silent sabotage, the AU men also had to prepare for direct combat. Bryan Green:

Two regular army men were attached to the Unit. We were at the Keeper's Cottage where you come up out of Wells. They gave us the baptism of fire, being fired at with live ammunition just over our head. We had to walk through while they were shooting over us.

Tony Loxton enjoyed target practice:

Being a farmer I used to love shooting. I was all right, because all my young days I was up on Mendip, shooting rabbits between the bushes. I enjoyed going to Yoxter range because I could always pick up my money on competitions. We had a shilling or sixpence on it.

I was there with Francis Stott one day. He dived down and when he fired, the rifle split straight up through the middle. Frightened us to death.

Not surprisingly, Francis Stott remembers it well:

We were snap-shooting at Yoxter. You run forward and drop down and shoot at little targets in a split second.

The rifle just blew up. [Francis raises an arm.] I couldn't feel that hand for a week and that shoulder went all black.

I had to go to a Court of Enquiry at Radford's Wine Cellars with Regulars from Coleshill. The armourer eventually put it down to a weak charge in the previous cartridge, so the bullet didn't clear the barrel. Then the next one split it open. It disintegrated.

Arthur Parsons also went to Yoxter:

The Home Guard officer there, he were stood behind us. Old Phil were next to me. Phil had a rifle, 303. Bang! And he tore the turf up about fifteen yards down the range. So he tried again, went a bit farther, tore the turf up. The old officer put his foot on his back, cause we were laid out you know.

"Young man," he said, "do you know there's such a thing as double pressure?"

Phil says, "Yessir."

"Well, why the hell don't you use it man?"

Phil said, "I am sir."

"Get up," he said. "Watch me."

Phil got up. The officer had the rifle, stood up like this. Bang! He got nowhere near the target. He tore the turf up as well.

"Give him another rifle, sergeant," he said. "This damn thing's no good."

But it wasn't always the rifle that was to blame. Arthur took his turn in the trench beneath the targets, hoisting them as required and observing the strike of the bullets:

> We were up there marking at the back of the butts. We had the man-shaped targets up with numbers on boards above them. Mine was number 3. I could hear this whack behind me and I thought to myself, "What the hell's that?" and I looked round. And Bang! again.
>
> The number 3 board had three or four holes in it, all close together, on the number. He were firing at the number. One of the old Home Guard from Cheddar. He didn't know he had a target to fire at below the number.

Mendip's auxiliers soon learned that survival depended on silent movement and silent killing, but some of their training was distinctly noisy. Francis Stott remembers a training centre where:

> They had loudspeakers in the trees. They said, "Hurry, hurry, hurry on! Get that Hun! He killed your pal! Hurry, hurry, hurry on!"

Tony Loxton went to the same place, meeting men from Westbury and Dinder.

> Den Dyke was with me. Regulars did the training and I soon got told off: "You in the back with the glasses. That was a bloody lazy movement."
>
> It was all live ammo. We used to throw hand grenades in the pits. If one didn't go off, Jack Lunnon was the unfortunate man who had to go out and blow it.
>
> The army were rehearsing for something and these Dakotas had come in over. The sky was black with them. They had thousands of parachutists coming down. Every tree was covered in parachutes.
>
> I come across this great gun. They said it was a PIAT. It had come down on a parachute and I was in two minds whether we

# THE COUNTRYMAN'S DIARY - - - 1939

## HIGHWORTH'S FERTILISERS

### DO THEIR STUFF UNSEEN
### UNTIL YOU SEE

## RESULTS!

*With the Compliments of*
**HIGHWORTH & CO.**

**YOU WILL FIND THE NAME HIGHWORTH
WHEREVER QUICK RESULTS
ARE REQUIRED**

*Sabotage training manuals had to be as well camouflaged as the saboteurs themselves. (Bill Bent)*

could take it for our own armoury, but it was damaged.

The place had a huge house. I can't remember where it was.

The place was Coleshill House, at Highworth on the Wiltshire-Berkshire border, north-east of Swindon. Colin Gubbins, now a colonel, set it up as a training centre for the Auxiliary Units.

The Coleshill instructors were volunteers, fit and tough individualists with the will, skill and experience to survive. In addition to Guards officers, some came from the Lovat Scouts, already renowned for an unorthodox and audacious approach to military problems. Even the spoof title of their training manual, 'Countryman's Diary', carried a witty bit of extra deception on the cover which advertised 'Highworth's Fertilisers — do their stuff unseen until you see RESULTS!' They were very clear in their expectations of an AU operational patrol: 'Your task is either to destroy by incendiarism, demolition or ambush, enemy stores, aeroplanes and vehicles, or to overpower isolated sentries, stragglers' etc (see Appendix C). The quality of unarmed combat instruction is characterised by the title 'Thuggery' on training notes.

The dull buff cover of 'The Countryman's Diary for 1939' actually concealed contents which ranged from the domestic manufacture of bombs to serious sabotage on a professional level. It also explained the different ways of using explosive against particular targets: railway lines, vehicle fuel tanks, parked aircraft, ammunition dumps and armoured vehicles. Instruction on how to make booby traps and anti-personnel mines included the advice: 'Kill with splinters, not blast.'

In Somerset, the training team at Cranmore, known as a Scout Section, instructed AUs on their own ground. The lieutenant had a little Austin convertible as a scout car, Driver Townley RASC drove a Ford truck and the men got around on heavy army-issue push-bikes, with back-pedal brakes. Freddy Chapman recalls:

> We were asked one day who could ride a motor-bike. I said I'd sat on one, so they said, "Go up to Highworth. There's a motor-bike to be picked up." So I went up there and got on this motor-bike. The man said, "Are you capable of riding this bike?" I said, "Once I get it into gear." So he said, "Right, off you go then." And I fetched it back down to Cranmore.

Fresh from a Coleshill course on explosives, Lt Keith Salter took a

*The Army Scout Section at Southill House, Cranmore, trained Auxiliary Units in subversive warfare. Off-duty, they put on their best uniforms for pub skittles. Lt Keith Salter is in service dress alongside the tall figure of Sgt Freddy Chapman. (Keith Salter)*

Mendip patrol into Shipham Quarry to display his skills.

> I found an old lorry dumped at the back and blew bits out of it to show all the different ways of immobilising vehicles. Some weeks later I was hauled up to HQ. They'd had a complaint from the quarry-owner that a valuable vehicle had been wantonly vandalised. Did I know anything about it? I had to go down to the quarry office to apologise.

The Cranmore Scout Section ran training courses at Southill House. Eion Fraser recalls going to Cranmore for week-end training with different weapons, and Harold Lane remembers on one patrol, calling at Colonel Spencer's house near Cranmore at about 2 am. One of the soldiers in the stables they came to know later as Mr Chapman, a hotel-owner in Wells. Sergeant Chapman met the colonel himself.

We occupied the servants' quarters and old Colonel Spencer got very inquisitive about what we were doing. The lieutenant got our HQ to come down and tell him to keep to himself. He had to sign the Official Secrets Act.

Jack Chew says,

An Army captain was giving us a lecture. How to creep up behind a sentry and pull his German helmet back and break his neck. I said to Arthur after, "Say you get a fellow six feet tall? Do you ask him to just bend down a bit so's you can reach his helmet?"

The Cranmore team also visited Units in their own locality. Ken Banwell recounts a story told him by his father, Francis.

These soldiers came down to inspect the Wedmore Unit and the hide-out but they got on our cider.

About 8 o'clock at night, father still hadn't done the milking and he thought we've got to get rid of them somehow. So he said to Harry, "You go on down and do the milking and I'll take them to the New Inn."

Off they went down to the New Inn and imbibed a little longer like. Then one of the soldiers said they'd got to set off back up. They sat the other chap, who'd had too much to drink, in the passenger seat, slammed the door shut and off they went.

When they got back they found his fingers still shut in the door. He was so anaesthetised by the cider that he didn't feel it at all.

Lieutenant Keith Salter confirms the story. As the intemperate victim, he remembers the occasion better now than he did the next day.

As well as practising the Units in their black arts, and devising competitions to test their efficiency (see Appendix D), the Scout Section tested them against the defences of more conventional soldiers. The Ebbor and Dinder Units attacked the Coldstream camp in Marston Park between Nunney and Frome. Horace Godfrey remembers it clearly:

There was quite a contingent there, billeted in huts. They had a

*Demonstrating the best way to stop a tank. (Bryan Green)*

seven or eight foot high wall along the road but thank goodness we didn't have to go over that. There were six of us and we had to attack overnight from three areas.

Percy Hull and I had to come up across parkland from Marston Bigott. We didn't start until about 11 at night. It was pitch black. We got up to within a couple of hundred yards of the Coldstream huts and reached the edge of a cinder track. It was very noisy. We were about to roll across it when two Guardsmen came along the track. We stopped where we were and just lay there. Blow me, one stopped and did a leak right down in front of my face, splashing up from the cinders. I moved a bit and rolled away and that made a noise. He called out and the other fellow came back. They had torches and found both of us.

Jack Chew describes another exercise:

Us Cheddar men were supposed to be German parachutists, dropped in Lympsham. We had to get through to blow up the railway, the signal box it was, at Bleadon station. We had orders to do it before 5 o'clock in the morning. It was in the middle of the night, really dark. We made our way up across Bleadon by the village, over Purn Hill, down by the railway. We put chalk marks on to show what we'd blown up.

We got away but out comes about four or five blokes with rifles. Of course they saw we had our faces blackened so they took us in. I remember they give us great big jugs of cocoa.

We had to go in for an interview with the captain. He asked Art, "What outfit are you?"

But we weren't allowed to say, so Art said, "I'm a market gardener, sir."

Art – Arthur Parsons – continues:

The Home Guard marched us off to The Grange in Hutton. We were stood there, waiting for the officer to come and interview us. Bert Painter had some thunderflashes in his battledress and he asked if it was all right to smoke. They said yes and when he got out the cigarette, he took the thunderflash out as well and managed to drop it out the window. They all dived out to see what it were and we went out the back door and got away.

Jack Chew resumes:

After that, I said to Arthur Pavey, our sergeant, "Why don't we get a scheme up on our own? This one was all fixed. They knew beforehand that we were coming and what was going to happen. What about going to see if we can capture Cheddar reservoir from the Home Guard?"

So we went down to the reservoir and got in past the fence. The Home Guard were patrolling backwards and forwards on the bank. We could see 'em easy. We were crawling along underneath in the ditches and that. When we got to their hut, we threw stones onto the roof to make believe it was hand grenades.

Jim Hooper turned out nearly every week-end with the Pensford patrol:

We were several cuts above the Home Guard. We were all keen and well versed in training and explosives. We knew how to get around the countryside, all round the area.

We had great fun at times. We were attacking the Guards in Keynsham. We ran out of thunderflashes and finished up with throwing sticks of 808 over the wall.

It was an early finish that night, about half ten or eleven. There was a dance going on in Keynsham Town Hall so we all piled in with our blackened faces. They thought they were being invaded.

Another time, Units from the whole area attacked Locking airport. Each one had to capture a particular hut. Ours was the WAAF sleeping quarters.

Sam Gilling remembers that attack:

We had to get into Locking airport. One of the lads in the Wrington Wood Unit, Steve Fairhurst, was injured there. He had the thumb and side of his hand blown off with a detonator. A bit careless.

Arthur Parsons recalls more detail:

This chap put detonators in potatoes. You know these big doors on the aircraft places down at Locking there, he went to put one in between these doors and it went off and he lost a couple of fingers.

Bryan Green tells how,

We had to get through that long wood above Dinder with the Home Guard stationed all through. Before the wood, we had to cross three fields. It was full moon, calm as anything, the worst night to try to get through. There were three hedges and I thought they'd be guarding them, so I said, "Come on, we'll try to make it up the middle of the field."

We crawled right across the field, completely silent, the two of us, and all at once we found ourselves crawling across a harrow.

"Who goes there?" we heard.

So we just froze for a while, on top of the harrow. Nothing happened so we started again.

"Who goes there? ... Yer, Bill, is there any more I oughter say?"

We didn't get through. They caught us.

# 12
# SECRET ARMY

As was impressed on the men time and again, this was a secret army. No invader could find a way into the British Resistance Organisation just by reading the files. There were none.

Auxiliary Units were assigned to special Home Guard Battalions designated 201 (Scotland), 202 (N England), 203 (Wales and South). But these battalions appeared on no Home Guard records and the men were named on no Home Guard nominal rolls.

As the organisation developed, some patrols were grouped together under Group Commanders who wore the rank of Home Guard captains. But they were not gazetted as officers.

Bill Bent served as a second lieutenant near Wellington. A year after the war ended, a terse typed note arrived from Berkshire Territorial Association:

> According to instructions received from Headquarters Southern Command I have to inform you that you have been granted the Honorary Rank of 2/Lieut (H.G.).

Even their Intelligence Officers slipped away from Regimental records, being posted to 'specialist duties'.

Somerset's saboteurs dressed in ordinary army uniform, with the Somerset Light Infantry cap-badge and a Home Guard shoulder flash. On the arm, some wore the local Home Guard battalion number and SOM for Somerset. Others displayed the number 203 in black or blue on khaki. Patrol leaders had sergeant's stripes. Jim Hooper adds,

'We were allowed to wear civvies if we wanted.'

As civilians, not even Home Guards, members of Auxiliary Units were not covered by the Geneva Convention. Absolute secrecy was their only safeguard against capture and summary execution, coupled with unrestricted reprisals against the local community.

On recruitment, every member signed or gave an oath of secrecy

> BERKSHIRE TERRITORIAL ARMY ASSOCIATION.
>
> To: 2/Lt. C. R. Bent.
>
> Yeomanry House,
> Castle Hill,
> Reading.
>
> 1 July 1945.
>
> According to instructions received from Headquarters Southern Command I have to inform you that you have been granted the Honorary Rank of 2/LIEUT (H.G.)
>
> J. J. Bygott
> Brigadier,
> Secretary,
> BERKSHIRE TERRITORIAL ARMY ASSOCIATION.

*A few members of Auxiliary Units were given officer rank, but their promotion was never published. This less than formal document came long after the war ended, as the only official confirmation of a commission. (Bill Bent)*

under the Official Secrets Act. To ensure that they could betray nothing if captured, men knew only their immediate comrades. Few knew the members or location of any other patrol. Not even their families knew their special role, although wives sometimes suspected something when the house was used as an arsenal. Training in the maintenance of secrecy was precise:

> Above all, be modest. Never attempt to cut a dash. Pretend your job is dull and uninteresting.
>   Never be mysterious, it only makes people curious. Be matter of fact, and when questioned think out a plausible and simple answer.
>   When asked what you are doing, never say "Something secret, I'm afraid I can't tell you". Make some matter of fact reply. For instance say you are a fighting patrol or a scout section with observation duties or a runner or give some other simple explanation why you are not forming one of the road blocks.
>   Never try and justify yourself. If a senior officer or a contemporary implies that you are not pulling your weight, do

*At Charterhouse, 50 years after the war ended, Somerset's Lord Lieutenant, Sir John Wills, presented the Defence Medal to veterans of Auxiliary Units: Arthur Parsons (Cheddar), Arthur Walton (Wells), Sir John Wills, Nora Trego (widow of Sgt Cecil Fred Trego, Weston), Bryan Green (Gurney Slade) and John Sealy (Westbury-sub-Mendip). (Author)*

not be tempted to explain just how important you are.

They learned their lesson well. During the war itself, they certainly never talked. Driving back to Bristol late at night from duty with the Pensford unit, Jim Hooper was stopped by the police checking insurance and petrol entitlement.

> I wasn't in uniform. I was using my vehicle on a G licence to come out to the Unit. We had instructions that if the police ever questioned us, we had to answer: "I must refer you to the Chief Constable".
> 
> I was arrested and taken to Court. The captain in charge of the area came with me. When the magistrates questioned me, we still couldn't say why, wherefore or anything. But he confirmed that I was not breaking the law.

Wandering the Chewton Mendip woods at night, Reg Rendall of Bathway inadvertently witnessed the arrival of a lorry load of military stores. The soldiers handed him over to the nearest civil authority, Special Constable Edgar Salvidge, Waldegrave estate carpenter. Edgar escorted the unfortunate Reg to Wells where both received a strong warning that they were now subject to the Official Secrets Act. Reg had at least escaped a poaching charge, but Special Constable Salvidge got back home at 7 am from a duty meant to end at midnight, unable to explain to his wife where he'd been.

At a Mendip Auxiliary Units reunion 50 years later, two cousins found that they had served in patrols in neighbouring villages. Two others, members since the war of the same club, discovered that they had served in the same Unit, one coming in as a replacement when the other left. What's more, the men kept their secrets through the Cold War, in case they were needed again. Even now, over half a century later, some are unwilling to talk about their service.

This absolute secrecy and the consequent absence of records explains why their work was never officially acknowledged and most never received the Defence Medal, awarded for all other voluntary uniformed work. A list of Somerset's auxiliers, compiled from the memories of men who served, is given in Appendix B.

'It's only since it came up in the paper this last year that I've talked about it,' said Tony Loxton. 'Medals don't mean anything to me. We were just doing what we thought would be right.'

During talk about the Units, Arthur Parsons' wife heard the name Reg Barber mentioned as a volunteer: 'That was my father. I never knew he was doing anything like that.'

Sergeant Trego's younger brother suspected something, but his widow says,

> Even when the war finished, up to when he died in April 1991, he never talked about it. I'm glad it's all made public now so that people will know what they really did.

# 13
# WARTIME LIFE

While the Auxiliary Units trained to kill and commit sabotage, Mendip settled down to a long war.

Everyone carried Identity Cards. Regularly in morning assembly, schoolchildren held up their cards and practised putting on their gas masks. The Women's Voluntary Service gave lessons on constructing field kitchens from bricks and a stovepipe. Old soldiers remembered how to cook in 'hay boxes', using insulation to eke out fuel.

On 5th July 1940, housewives heard Lord Beaverbrook, Minister of Aircraft Production, enlist them in the battle: 'Women of Britain, give us your aluminium. We will turn your pots and pans into Spitfires and Hurricanes, Blenheims and Wellingtons.' They responded by collecting waste materials as salvage for re-cycling. Churchill villagers stacked scrap metal behind the Churchill Inn.

Suddenly, everything was in short supply. Newspapers shrank in size to a single sheet, folded into four pages. RAF man Jim Morris encountered an unexpected wartime problem: the girls couldn't get hair curlers. He won popularity by handing out off-cuts of Air Ministry electrical cable as a substitute.

Cigarettes and matches were desperately scarce. When Sam Gilling first went to Shipham,

> I thought I'd go down and have a drink on Sunday night. I was walking down Cuck Hill and Jack Lock was walking up. He had a Woodbine in his mouth and he couldn't find any matches.
> "Excuse me, young sir," he said. "Have you got a light?"
> I said, "Yes."
> He offered me a Woodbine but I didn't take it. I handed him my matchbox and he said, "Well, you won't want these no more then if you don't smoke," and put them in his pocket and went on up the hill.
> I only refused his Woody because I liked Capstan Full Strength.

CONFIDENTIAL AND
NOT FOR PUBLICATION.

Circular E.422.

## SOMERSET COUNTY COUNCIL.

### THE COUNTY EDUCATION COMMITTEE.

*Enclosure.*

COUNTY HALL,
TAUNTON.
10th February, 1942.

DEAR SIR OR MADAM,

### THE POSITION OF SCHOOLS IN THE EVENT OF INVASION.

1. In an Administrative Memorandum received from the Board of Education in March of last year reference was made to the general question of the position of schools in the event of invasion. The Board have now made further suggestions dealing with this possibility and the action to be taken in such an event. It is stated in the Board's latest communication that in the event of invasion day schools in the area of operations and as may be necessary in areas immediately adjacent will be closed, instructions for closure being issued by the Regional Commissioner with whom the educational services should co-operate in the fullest degree, and that plans should be laid now for placing at the disposal of the Commissioner any facilities of which he might wish to avail himself, while at the same time maintaining as full a measure of education as is possible in the circumstances of each area.

With the object of carrying out the instructions of the Board in this matter the Committee feel that it is desirable to communicate fully with the managers, governors and staffs of elementary and secondary schools and to submit to them certain preliminary advice and suggestions for dealing with the situation which may arise however likely or unlikely that may be. In doing so the Committee realise that in the interests of the children in the schools and also of the residents in the locality generally they will have the whole-hearted co-operation, help and support of all connected with the school in carrying out these and any further instructions which it may ultimately be necessary to issue.

2. Regional Commissioners on taking control will have as their advisers Regional Officers of certain Government Departments and as far as education is concerned the Board of Education's Divisional Inspectors have been instructed to place themselves at the disposal of the Regional Commissioners in case of emergency and will act as Regional Education Officers. Education Authorities are required to be prepared to put into effect at once any instructions received from the Regional Commissioner whether directly or through the Regional Education Officer (Miss F. M. Tann, H.M.I., 12 Oldfield Road, Bath).

3. In order that such instructions may be carried out promptly it is necessary for the Committee to consider now how they could most quickly get into contact with the schools if in session and with the teachers and the pupils if the schools are not in session. Every possible step must be taken to ensure such contact, it being borne in mind that telephones and certain roads might not be available. Use will be made of the normal services of communication for so long as they are available and possibly of personal messengers, but the possibility of failure of direct contact with this office makes it imperative that all schools should be able to maintain contact with their managers or governors who in turn should be in close contact with the Local Defence Committee, and in cases where managers or governors are not available instructions should be taken direct from the Local Defence Committee. Methods, other than those mentioned, by which the Local Education Authority may establish contact with schools may on investigation of the matter be found to be possible and in this event further information will be issued at a later date.

**It is important that persons receiving directions in an emergency such as that to which this circular relates should as far as possible unless they are entirely satisfied as to the source of such directions, take all possible steps to verify them before taking action thereon.**

4. Since a proportion of the teachers might in the emergency be employed upon urgent duties in connection with the Home Guard, Civil Defence, etc., it is necessary for the Committee to ascertain which teachers will remain available for service with the children. As regards members of the Home Guard on the staffs of schools, it should be noted that on consideration of a communication from the Board of Education in the early part of last year the Committee decided "that while in the event of invasion the Home Guard may be called upon to give whole-time service it is fully recognised that certain members of the force might not be available for such service, as their ordinary duties must come first." Since this decision of the Committee the responsibilities and duties of the Home Guard have been somewhat altered and the Committee propose to consider if it is necessary to vary the instruction quoted above, and a further communication on this point may be issued to schools. Lists of all teachers and their private addresses must now be prepared by Local Education Authorities and kept up to date, and arrangements should therefore be made for the enclosed card (Form E.98 or E.99) to be completed and returned to me as quickly as possible. The form should contain particulars in respect of each member of the staff including war-time temporary teachers, but **not short-time emergency teachers, and any changes of teachers and/or their addresses that may subsequently occur, should be notified at once to this office.**

Any methods of contacting the school which can be suggested by teachers, other than those referred to in paragraph 3 above can be stated on the reverse side of the form. Teachers' telephone numbers (or those of a neighbour at which a call could be received) should be given in Column 4, though in this connection it must be repeated that in the event of actual invasion the use of the telephone may be denied to the education service. In the case of evacuated public elementary schools Form E.99 should be used in respect of the staff at each separate set of premises occupied

*A confidential circular sent to Somerset schools in 1942, it included the directive that in the event of invasion: 'Care should be taken by teachers to preserve the school attendance registers so that the children in the locality can be more easily accounted for in the event of heavy bombing or ground operations.' (Author's collection)*

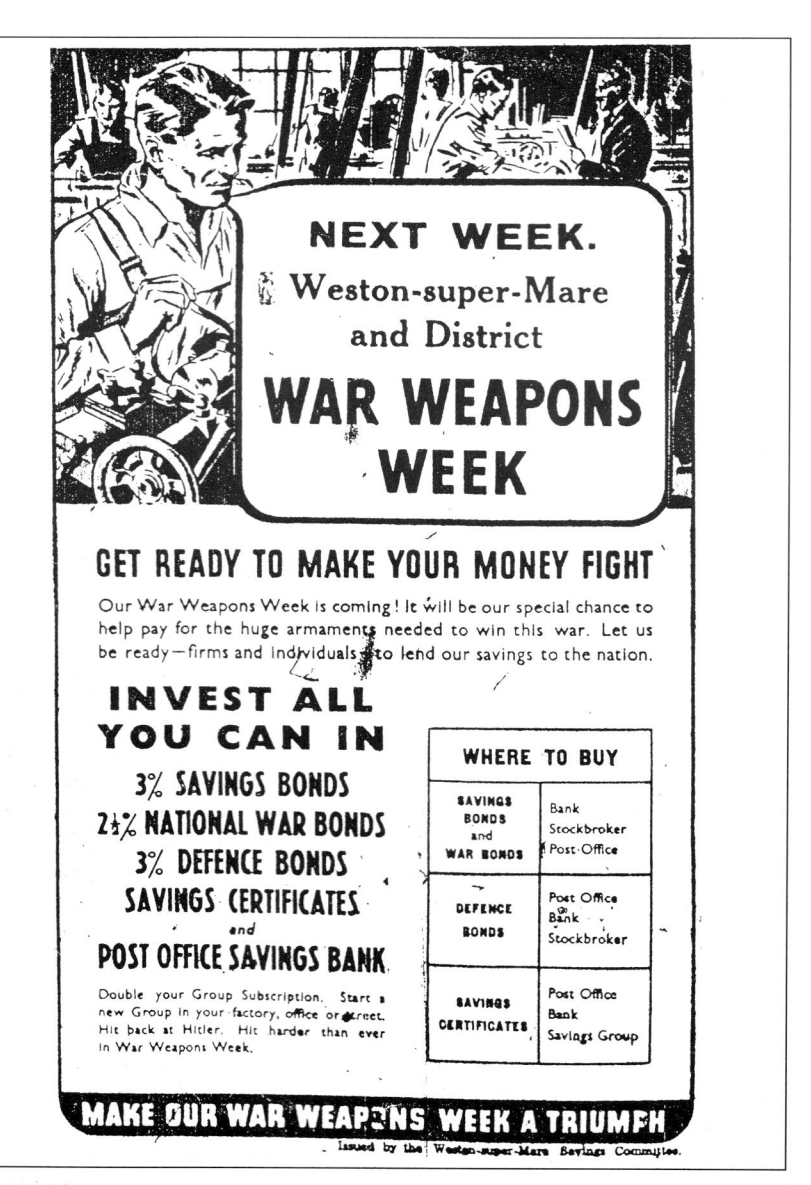

*Already heavily taxed at 8s 6d in the pound, communities collected huge sums in national appeals to buy 'Wings for Victory' or 'War Weapons'. Axbridge area raised a quarter of a million pounds for Warship Week. (Weston Mercury)*

With no petrol available for private use, most people stored their cars 'for the duration'. Drained of oil, fuel and water, the treasured vehicles stood on blocks, with the wheels off.

On her 17th birthday, Helen Boileau passed the last driving test to be held in Weston until after the war. The family Vauxhall did 20 miles to the gallon. As country dwellers they were allowed six gallons of petrol a month, to be used only on journeys to Axbridge, Winscombe or Weston railway stations. Helen got extra petrol for specific WVS jobs, like delivering evacuees. Once a year, she drove Food Control Office staff round the village halls to issue new Ration Books, clothing coupons, vouchers for National Dried Milk, orange juice, cod liver oil, vitamin tablets.

The cost of the war hit people in the pocket. Income tax went up by a shilling to 8s 6d (42p) in the pound, and a new Purchase Tax levied 24% on luxuries and 12% on most other goods. Yet the public responded generously to fund-raising appeals. In Wings for Victory Week, Axbridge Rural Districts aimed to raise £35,000 for the cost of seven fighter aircraft, 'in order to help in the ultimate hanging of Hitler and his fiendish friends.'

The same people then raised £225,000 for Warship Week in 1942. They adopted the destroyer HMS *Goathland*, sending 'comforts' – books, cigarettes and clothing – for its crew on convoy duty and during the Normandy invasion.

All the villages raised money for Services welfare funds. Children sold hedgerow fruit. Gardeners raffled rare onions. Whilst drives, dances and film shows raised money and provided entertainment as well. Shipham ran a dance to buy a parachute for the RAF. The Services reciprocated. Terry Heal and Joyce Hooper went to school in wartime Cheddar and recall, 'We could go to the Army's ENSA concerts. The RAF men had a band which played at village dances.'

Villages filled with evacuees. The Wainwrights moved out of their home at Barleycombe in Christon to release it for city families. Other children, who arrived without parents, were billeted in Webbington House, owned by the Tiarks family. In Churchill, evacuees from Bristol and London went into The Beeches and Mendip Lodge as well as the Methodist church hall. Shipham billeted its evacuee mothers and babies in Penscot House, then a centre for adult education. The school expanded into the Wesleyan Sunday school but, as in most villages, still had to teach classes in shifts.

*Trainloads of evacuees arrived in the villages without their parents. They were billeted in any house with a spare room, large or small. Mrs Slim from Lower Weare acted as Matron for 25 London children, aged 5 to 15, in Webbington House, home of Mr Herman Tiarks. Both Webbington pictures were taken by an American journalist in 1940, over here to report on the realities of war. (Mrs Margaret Jordan)*

A complete London school arrived by train in Cheddar on 1st September 1939. Bernard Parsons remembers their arrival:

> They were from East Ham in London, some 300 of them. They were billeted around Cheddar and if there was room in your home you were expected to take them in. They brought their own teachers and schooling was organised using the Church House Hall and the Methodist Hall as well as the British School and the National School.
>
> As the war progressed we were gradually integrated. I remember being taught by Mrs Young in the Church House Hall. She wore riding breeches because she lived up at Charterhouse and came down to school on horse-back.

Mrs Kathleen Young was one of the teachers who had accompanied the evacuees. She married a local farmer, Bill Young of Lower Farm, Charterhouse, and stayed on after the war.

Other evacuees were less eager. Barton Camp had been built to provide simple countryside holidays for deprived Bristol children. The first bombed-out evacuees from London were billeted there until local accommodation could be found. WVS driver Helen Boileau transported two of the women there, with their children. They looked at it, and, says Helen, 'offered me ten bob to go to Weston station instead.'

There were some strange stories. In Banwell, John Chapman recalls:

> One woman arrived in a house lit by gas downstairs and candles upstairs.
>
> She was given the front bedroom which was seldom if ever used. Putting her candle down, she sat on the edge of the ancient mattress, took off a shoe and pushed it just under the bed. She sat up, took off the other shoe and leant down to put it beside its partner.
>
> The first shoe had gone.
>
> She straightened up in horror – and the second shoe was whisked out of her hand.
>
> Seizing the candlestick, she ran downstairs. Up came the housewife with another candle. They bent down at a safe distance and looked under the bed. Nothing. Not a shoe in sight.
>
> With all her fears confirmed about rural life, and rural after-life,

*Iris Edmonds and Moyna Gilbertson came on an evacuee train from London's Isle of Dogs to Wells. They stayed with Col McDonnell, playing with his daughter Peggy's dolls. Moyna now has the OBE for charity work for the disabled. (Mrs M Lees)*

*In 1940 Gladys Bailey, barmaid at the Crown Hotel, Wells, married Stanley Derrick, a nurse at Mendip Hospital, then in the RAMC. Stanley spent the rest of the war in India where he met Cyril Price, his bride's nephew. (John Sealy)*

the evacuee spent the rest of the night downstairs with the gas light on. She left next morning for the safety of the city.

Never having heard of a ghost in all her years there, the Banwell housewife called in the vicar. In broad daylight, they went back upstairs and dragged the clothes off the bed.

Beneath the mattress spiralled a network of broken coil springs. Enmeshed in them were the missing shoes. As the evacuee sat on the edge of the bed, the mattress went down and the springs reached the floor. As she sat up, a broken spring hooked a shoe up with it, out of sight.

With the papers and pubs full of spy stories, the police checked on anyone who arrived unexpectedly. A foreign accent invited particular suspicion. Mr R.J. Keel recounts a story from 1940 of Otto, a refugee who arrived in Chew Stoke from Germany. In the desperate atmosphere of the time, he was suddenly interned, as were most other fugitives from the Nazis. Almost immediately, the unfortunate Otto took on spy status. Rumour soon equipped him with a radio transmitter, tracked down by GPO detectors. A stick of bombs on the local RAF unit served for some as final proof of his hostile activities.

Support for popular belief in a spy-ring came from German broadcasts in English. Irreverent listeners nick-named the reader 'Lord Haw-Haw' and treated his threats generally as a joke. But the broadcasts sometimes forecast air-raids and then described damage in detail that could only be obtained on the spot. Sam Gilling relates a suspicious encounter:

> On the farms, we were getting people from all sorts of walks of life. I had this lad with me, about 19, 20 something like that, teaching him to drive the tractor. He'd been to college and he didn't speak like I do, thee's know. I was cutting corn so it must have been late August. I had him on the tractor for quite a while. He kept going round and wasting a lot of corn.
>
> When we were sitting down and having our sandwiches, he told me he was a relation to Lord Haw-Haw.
>
> A few days later he got picked up at Puriton signalling with a torch. At that time when Haw-Haw was speaking on the radio he was threatening to bomb the factory at Puriton.

Shepton Mallet shared the spy stories. Charles Wainwright was warned by his parents to be careful what he said in the hearing of one suspect:

> One of our family married and lived in Europe. Then they were overrun by the Germans. Out of the blue, her husband arrived at Shepton, having left his family behind. He was suspected right from the start as nobody could have got out unless helped by the Germans.
>
> He went to live with distant relatives in Evercreech. My mother and father thought he might try to pump us boys for information as he was a sort of relation. They said we had to refuse to answer any questions and then tell the police.
>
> He never spoke to us, but father said he had a radio and sent Morse messages from his room. The police used to listen and take it all down. A lot of it was very far from the truth because the police planted ideas for him to use.
>
> He was restricted in movement to a two-mile radius and had to report three times a day to Shepton police station. The village constable checked that he was in his quarters every night at Evercreech. When the war came to an end, his wife came home.

*Threatened by air-raids, London and Bristol stored civic and art treasures in Cheddar, Charterhouse and Shepton Mallet. One local legend even placed the Crown Jewels in this water-works tunnel at Rowberrow. (Author)*

He stayed here and they ran some shops until he died. He daren't go back to his own country.

Some bombs fell around Shepton Mallet but missed the prison. By now a 'glasshouse' - a military jail – it also guarded priceless and irreplaceable national documents, stored there alongside its involuntary occupants. Domesday Book was inside, with royal and parliamentary records dating back over a thousand years. Charles Wainwright writes:

> Quite a number of us youngsters were shown the Domesday Book when it was being prepared for transit back to London. Records from Somerset House were in the Ladies' Wing.

Bristol City regalia found safety in disused lead-smelting flues behind Charterhouse; other treasures were hidden in Cheddar Caves. A legend persists that the Crown Jewels spent the war in the Bristol

Waterworks tunnel at Rowberrow. A special Home Guard unit, the story goes, was recruited secretly in Bristol to stand guard. But Albert Frost, then chairman of the Parish Council, dismisses the notion:

> Our Home Guard officer did come from Bristol, but only because he was bombed out there. The Churchill Home Guard did put sentries on the tunnel, but only because all tunnels had to be guarded.

Bristol Water deny any knowledge of the whole business.

# 14
# DIG FOR VICTORY

After *blitzkrieg*, the next enemy was slow starvation. Hitler proclaimed a 'total blockade of the waters of Britain' with an order to 'concentrate every means of waging war by sea and air on enemy supplies.' The German navy launched such devastating submarine attacks on our food convoys that Churchill later admitted, 'I would have exchanged a full attempt at invasion for this peril.'

Food reserves were stockpiled. John Nurse of Wick Farm, Coxley, remembers sacks of flour stacked up in the piggeries. 'More was stored in three or four big brick buildings with corrugated asbestos roofs, just beyond Farrington Gurney.' In Shepton Mallet, says Ralph Vowles, 'Bacon and butter were stocked in the Co-op cold store', and Sam Gilling knew of 'warehouses in Midsomer Norton, full of corned beef.'

Intensive farming and strict rationing saved the day. Within a year, bread was the only food not 'on coupons'. And, cultivating a vastly increased acreage of land, the country's farmers doggedly worked their way towards self-sufficiency in food.

Around Compton Bishop, cultivation spread ever higher on the hillsides. Children collected wild berries, orchard fruit and village mulberries. The Women's Institute boiled these up at their Jam Centre, on the site of the old Pound, filling thousands of jars with home-made jam.

Observing the slogan 'Dig For Victory', gardeners grew vegetables instead of flowers. Fred Villis remembers that Cheddar's strawberry growers turned over to vegetable crops, and Bernard Parsons tells how, 'School children over ten years old were given 20 half-days each summer to assist with gathering the harvest.'

Albert Frost remembers seeing town youngsters on a farm camp at Charterhouse, laid out after drinking cider. Helen Boileau was made of sterner stuff. Still in her teens, she worked on a farm at Cross with three men:

> Worle Senior School, Weston-super-Mare.
>
> January 15th. 1941.
>
> **Hot Dinners for Schoolchildren.**
>
> Dear Sir or Madam,
>
> If support is sufficient, it is proposed to provide hot dinners for children attending this School. Two courses would be served and the cost would not be more than 4$^d$ per day per child. At a later date, it may be possible to reduce the cost for a second child of the same family. The menus would vary from day to day and every effort made to make the meals attractive and appetising.
>
> The value of a hot meal in the middle of the day is apparent to everyone and it is hoped that as many parents as possible will take advantage of the service. If you wish your child to take School Dinners please sign and return the attached slip.
>
> Yours faithfully,
>
> L.W.Cosgrove
>
> ---
>
> I wish my child to take School Dinners.
>
> Signed:—

*Wartime pressures brought social advances. As well as providing a rich source for jokes, school dinners were free and 'off the ration'. For many children they provided the first regular square meals they had ever seen. (Author's collection)*

E.L.3

Licence No. E.L.389(C)
S.W.177

# Ministry of Food

### The Defence (General) Regulations, 1939, as amended
### The Food (Licensing of Establishments) Order, 1943

Pursuant to the above Order and subject to the conditions set out overleaf, the Minister of Food hereby licenses

L. W. Bisgrove, _____ (Name of Licensee(s))

* Strike out whichever is inapplicable

to carry on a catering establishment* at ~~an institution~~*

Worle Senior School Canteen,
Worle Senior School,
Weston-super-Mare.

(Address of Premises)

and to obtain for the purposes of that establishment the following specified foods :—

Bacon and ham, uncooked
Bacon and ham, cooked
Biscuits, rusks and crispbreads
Blancmange powder, cornflour and custard powder
Bread
Butter
Cakes
Canned beans
~~Cereal breakfast foods~~
Cheese (including processed cheese)
Cocoa
Coffee
Coffee essence (including coffee and chicory essence)
Edible and cooking fats
Edible egg products
~~Eggs~~
Fish, wet
Fish, cured or dried
Fish, in cans, glasses or other airtight containers
Fish pastes
Flour

Fruit, bottled or canned
Fruit, crystallised
Fruit, curds
Fruit, dried or evaporated
Fruit, fresh
~~Game~~
Honey
Jam and marmalade
Lard and compound lard
Macaroni, spaghetti and vermicelli
Margarine
Meat, chilled, fresh or frozen
Meat, canned or preserved, other than canned corned beef, canned corned mutton and canned corned pork
Meat, cooked
Meat pastes
Meat pastries (including sausage rolls) and meat pies
Meat products, manufactured or canned meat not in airtight containers
Meat roll or galantines, canned

Milk, fresh
Milk, canned
Milk, dried
Mincemeat
~~Nuts~~
Oatmeal and oatflakes
Pickles and sauces
Potatoes
~~Poultry (including turkeys)~~
Rabbits
Rice and edible rice products
Sago and tapioca
Sausages
Semolina
Soups, canned or desiccated
Soya flour
Sugar
Syrup and treacle
~~Table jellies~~
~~Tea~~
Vegetables, fresh, other than potatoes
Vegetables, bottled or canned other than canned beans
Vegetables, dried

FOOD OFFICE STAMP

WESTON-SUPER-MARE
BOROUGH
S.W.177
FOOD OFFICE

Code No. _____

For and on behalf of the Minister of Food

_____ D/Food Executive Officer.

Dated the 23rd day of Nov. 1944

P.T.O.

*Every school had to be licensed to obtain essential foodstuffs. (Author's collection)*

Tom came from Compton Bishop and another Tom came from Weare. They were both 50. Old Jack was 60. He had corns. The boss was always busy on Axbridge Council and the men wouldn't work unless told what to do. They just stood around. So I told them what to do and they did it.

Sam Gilling recalls,

> As farm workers, we were entitled to coupons for extra food rations at hay-making and harvest and other busy times. The farmer's wife bought it and issued it. We got fats, sugar, tea and tinned meat. You never saw a farmer go hungry. Quite a few made their own cheeses and butter.
> They'd play skittles for leg-of-mutton suppers. To get a leg of mutton, they'd push a sheep in the rhyne and declare it as an accident. Then they could eat it themselves.
> I never witnessed one, but some places had badger suppers. They said it was very much like pork.

Most farmers relinquished their paltry bacon ration in exchange for permission to slaughter two pigs a year which they duly cured and hung in the cellar. Sam can still savour the delicious pork faggots he used to enjoy at Hewish when they slaughtered a pig.

Bernard Parsons' family made the most of what they could find:

> Dad caught rabbits in Cheddar Wood and Art shot the odd Mallard duck on Cheddar Moor. I haven't seen a sheep's head boiled up since the war but mother often did one then. Hares, geese and pigeons were on the menu, as were the larger birds' eggs if you could find them. Being market gardeners we had plenty of fruit and vegetables so we did quite well. Most families out in the country kept chicken and a pig but all animals slaughtered for food had to be reported to the Ministry of Food. Hubert Pimm of Cheddar, a cattle dealer, was involved in that procedure.

Farms were generally small, with mixed livestock, chickens scratching round an unpaved yard, an orchard and a few acres of crops worked with horse-drawn equipment. In spite of government insistence on increased output, agricultural workers were called up

*Gardeners cultivated every scrap of land to produce food. Town Hall certificates recognised the best allotments – and encouraged growers' competitive instincts. (Author's collection)*

for the Forces at ever younger ages. Call-up could be deferred only for 'key workers' with carefully defined experience and skills. Others like nurserymen, pigmen and poultrymen were classed as being in 'subsidiary occupations' and were conscripted. Bryan Green was an agricultural key worker:

> In those days they used to reckon one man to ten cows. We had a 200 acre farm being worked by one man of 55 and an Old Age Pensioner. I was the oldest brother. Another was in the RAF and one at school. My father had been ill and I got deferment as the key worker. They took 19-22 year olds for the army, but a key worker of 25 or 26 would be deferred.

The War Agricultural Committee, the War Ag, directed which crops were to be grown and where. During 1941, farmers' efforts increased the area of cultivated land by almost 50%, helping Britain become self-sufficient in vegetables, cutting food imports by a third and beating Hitler's blockade.

Twice sent home from the Army because he was serving in an Auxiliary Unit, Sam Gilling found employment with the War Ag:

> We had a little office in Passey & Porter's yard in Winscombe, where Jack Chew worked. Clifford Cook was on the War Ag at Rolstone, Hewish. First time I went in he said, 'Hello young man, you want a drink of cider?' He gave me a bottle out of his barrel. I had a few sips and took it home to my Dad.
>
> The farmers were instructed what they had to grow. We'd have a list of the farms under orders to plough so many acres. They all had to plough one eighth of the land for potatoes or some form of food. Then we'd have to go and see the farmers and arrange to do the ploughing.
>
> We started off at Winscombe, the main depot, with seven or eight blokes. If you rolled a field for a farmer and it was twenty acres, that would cost him £2, two bob an acre. Ploughing was anything from 17/6 to thirty bob. Everything was on a contract and the farmer paid the War Ag. We were responsible for gathering the money up.
>
> We did contract work for farms down on the levels. You wouldn't find anybody home for the first five farms, then you'd find them all in the cider cellar in the next farm. That's all they

used to do before the war. They'd pick up the eggs, milk the cows, go in and have their dinner and then go down in the cellar drinking cider all day until milking time at night.

The cider was in 120-gallon barrels. The farmer would have a quart or a three-pint pot, double-handled, and he'd fill it up, drink, and pass it round and when it came back it was empty and you'd fill'n up, drink, and pass it round. That cup never got washed from one year's end to another

There's stories about what went into the cider. I've heard of putting beetroot in to colour sweet cider. And beef. I'm not sure about dead rats. Of course cider would eat it all up. And that's what it does to your stomach.

Most farms were dairy or general. A lot of the farmers had never seen a plough when the war started. The only tractor I remember was in Langford House, a farm which the War Ag took over from Sir Sidney Hill. We turned it into a bull breeding station. It wasn't a tractor, it was a crawler, like a caterpillar, with a trailer mower. I could plough a field quicker with a pair of horses. To cut eight acres, they'd take a day and a half, two days.

Bernard Parsons observes,

The most significant change on Mendip was that a lot of wheat was grown on land that for decades had been rough ground or pasture land. Most of the ploughing was done with standard Fordson tractors which had changed very little since the first world war when Mendip had had similar treatment. There was still a lot of ploughing being done by horses at this time. The Fordsons were fuelled by Tractor Vaporising Oil or TVO, which laymen call paraffin. Later in the war other tractors were brought in from the USA, like John Deere and Allis-Chalmers.

Charles Wainwright's father chaired the War Agricultural Committee at Wells:

Every farm had to give a weekly return of all the eggs they collected, the number of hens they had, the cows, the yield, corn acreage and production, everything. Inspectors assessed how much ought to be produced on each farm, which didn't always agree with the farmers' figures. The Food Minister once came to

Wells. He said he couldn't understand how farmers needed extra feed for extra hens, although their returns claimed egg production had gone down.

Father was a dowser. He could cut a stick from the hedge and find water. When they needed more water for the extra wartime cultivation on Mendip, he selected a place for a well just past the Castle of Comfort. Clements sank it but they dug it too deep. They should have gone to 150 feet, but went to 154 feet, so the water didn't rise. An old chap in the office said drop a sack of beans in. They did that and the water came and it's still producing.

Mary Small spent her wartime childhood on her father's farm at Tynings:

In 1941, the War Agricultural Committee came with a mandate to produce food. The fields had all those stone cairns there to stop the gliders. They were not going to plough and sow round them, so men with lorries, tractors and trailers removed them all. The stone was put to good use, rebuilding walls that had fallen into disrepair during the depression of the thirties, filling in old insanitary ponds and putting firm foundations into farmyards.

It was said that the field, named Green Ground, would never grow anything, but when the site was cleared, it was ploughed, with a high expenditure of patience and ploughshares, and grew a good crop of oats with the exception of a few yellow patches. The land produced good pasture until 1957.

With hindsight, clearing and cultivating these slopes was a hair-raising job, although we seldom regarded it as such. We were always told to 'keep the wheels straight'. Oats and potatoes were grown on the gentler slope, but the steepest part was re-sown directly with grass and rape, to be grazed by sheep – a great day when animals returned to the farm.

Sam Gilling reclaimed land that was more than marginal:

In the wintertime when we couldn't do much else, we'd plough up between the rocks at the top of Cheddar Gorge. Patches of an acre, acre and a half, two acres. That was made into good land.

Between Green Ore and Mendip Inn was all forest. It was felled

*Without our farmers, the war would have been lost. Tractors revolutionised their pre-war horse-drawn methods. (Author)*

and all the stumps were left there, just over a hundred acres. We cleared that and turned it into a farm before the end of the war.

Francis Stott of Westbury looks back to his first attempt at ploughing:

Father bought a standard Fordson tractor and a 3-furrow Cockshutt plough and I set off. First time I went, I had no idea. He showed me how to mark out and I didn't do it straight enough to please him. He come up the other end of the ground and he looked back and he said, "If I couldn't drive straighter than that, I'd bloody give up."

I ploughed up most of the top of Mendip. When I started, that ground up there was so tough, if the furrow did break going along, he'd run back right the way down and fall back in to where he'd come out. That was so tough, so fibrous, it took three years to break down. It was a late season, always late up there.

Over at Chewton Mendip, Bryan Green was improvising:

We were using old cars, £5 cars. You could buy a Morris, and do your chain harrowing on the back of it. You could use the old mowers that had the pole on for two horses. You took the pole off and lifted it over the back of the car. Then my father bought a tractor. My own came in 1941 with Lease-Lend from America. I've still got it at the back of the shed.

Bryan remembers the old Mendip landscape as

Yellow. That was the colour of the grasses. You still get them on the very poor bits that's left now, the springy wiry grass that makes a lovely lawn.

There was only about five or ten acres to a village that were ploughland until the War Ag came along and you had to do all the extra. A lot of them didn't want to plough. Some were unable to do it with their horse-drawn single plough. The War Ag got a new tractor and new plough, but their man was used to a Ransome plough and couldn't use the new one. Tommy Thomson, a young ploughman from the Scottish Borders, was at Cannington. The War Ag sent him and he taught the old chaps how to do it.

Fred Villis tells how the new technology reached Cheddar:

When all the fields were ploughed up for corn, the problem was how to thresh it all. They went for advice to Henry Tiarks. He was said to be a bit of an eccentric. He ran the Mendip Hunt and kept the hounds up at Priddy Hill Farm. He used to fly his own biplane from there. He listened to them, sat down and wrote a cheque and said "Don't bother me again." They bought their own threshing machine.

Tony Loxton was keen to study new methods:

One of the most advanced farmers then was Tom Nurse at Coxley. We'd go down there with the Young Farmers and see the silage making. We learned a lot.

Other new practices spread from the Long Ashton Research Station and Langford. Sam Gilling worked on them:

> They were always coming up with different kinds of seeds and fertilisers for different kinds of land. We had combine drills that used to drill corn and fertiliser together. Rollers were a thing of the past but then they come out with gang rollers, the big one behind the tractor, then two wing ones which covered more land. In about 1943, I was in charge of one of the first combine harvesters in Somerset. They took a lot of getting used to, but eventually they saved an awful lot of work.
>
> If you had a combine and fine weather, you could cut somewhere the size of Felton Common in a week. But if you had to cut it with a binder, you've got to stook it, you've got to rick it, you've got to thrash it. Eventually all that died out.
>
> With War Ag work all day and Auxiliary Unit duties all night, I put in well over a hundred hours a week. I had to pick the grain up from the combine and take it into Avonmouth so it could be dried in the drier. I remember going up the hill with ten ton on a seven-ten lorry, elbow on the side and this hand hanging on the steering wheel so if I fell asleep I'd turn in to the pavement.

No wonder Mendip farmers were glad to see the Land Girls.

# 15
# BACK TO THE LAND

From her poster, the smiling girl looked across neat fields of wheat towards rolling hills. 'For a healthy, happy job,' she urged, 'join the Women's Land Army.' Dorothy Chalker remembers joining:

> In June 1942, I cycled from Street to Cannington Open Day and Mrs Young took my name for the Land Army. I had to have a medical certificate from my own doctor. He looked at my tongue and said, "You'll do."
>
> It was a very hot day! I cycled to Wells, found the road for Wookey Hole, trudged up over Ebbor and thankfully free-wheeled down to Priddy and found the hostel.
>
> Hostel accommodation was quite basic. It catered for sixteen girls with two-tiered bunks and flock mattresses. There was officially plenty of hot and cold water but the boiler and pump were out of action so we used rainwater.

The girl in the poster looked smart, glamorous even, in her Land Army uniform of green sweater, khaki shirt and corduroy breeches. But it wasn't quite like that for Dorothy at Priddy:

> My uniform consisted of two pairs of dungarees, three shirts and a pair of heavy leather boots with blakeys in the sole. No breeches, stockings, coat, jumper, hat or shoes.

At Priddy, training was directly practical:

> The first day we were called at 6 am and told to be ready to leave by 7.30 am. Breakfast was porridge, cooked overnight, and toast.

*Steanbow Farm became a training centre and hostel for Land Army recruits, smart in their uniforms. (John Sealy)*

Packed lunch was doorstep sandwiches with cheese or meat paste.

A van took us to Steanbow Farm where I got my first experience of stooking. After a couple of hours, we walked to another farm where we planted cabbages by sitting on a machine and dropping the cabbages down metal funnels as the tractor pulled us along. We were back at the hostel by 9.30 pm.

A week later we were sent with a tractor and water trailer from Cheddar Head to Priddy. Alice, the driver, had never driven on the road before and had no licence. Going up Cheddar Gorge, she showed me how to stop and start and let me drive a couple of miles. That was all the training I received about handling a tractor. The rest came by practice.

Help was wanted at Tynings Farm, seven miles away. Daisy Palmer and I went because we were the only ones willing and able to cycle that distance and back every day. After six weeks, we went to live at Tynings with Gilbert Small, his wife Hilda and daughter Mary. We were accepted as part of the team and our

*Stanley Duddon photographed young John Sealy perched on the wing of his father's Standard Fordson tractor, driven by Brian Catell with William Moyle on the binder at the top of Stoke Hill. The tractor, which worked on the farm throughout the war, came second-hand from Locking airfield where its standard steel-cleated rear wheels had been replaced with pneumatic tyres. (John Sealy)*

mates were very helpful. Two of them, Cliff and Douglas, were conscientious objectors, living in a caravan in the yard. Old Harry had a cottage down the track. Alf Hodges, the mechanic, came in daily from Cheddar, Ted Targett the ploughman from Compton Martin, and Arthur Day from Blagdon. That was our work force for eight hundred acres, a thousand sheep, about fifty steers, a horse or two and a few pigs.

Life for the Land Girls ran to a rural calendar:

It seems amazing that girls straight from factories or shops were adaptable enough to work on the land using tractors and implements within a few days. Being harvest time, we started by cutting with the binder, hauling to the rick and manoeuvring in rick yards. As the fields were cleared, we learned to plough. Ploughing went on from September to February, in between baling and threshing. In Spring, we needed discing, harrowing and drilling skills to prepare the soil for the crops, oats, wheat, silage (oats, peas and beans) and tons of potatoes. Then came haymaking, cutting and turning, and hauling to the ricks which we learned to build. In July, we began lifting potatoes before harvesting began again in earnest.

There was more:

In between tractor work, we helped catch sheep to look for maggots, to administer pills, dip them and drive them where we wanted them to go. When they had been sheared, we learned to roll their fleeces. In wet weather, we white-washed sheds and barns with long house brooms, cleaned and greased machinery, chopped swedes for sheep and sorted straw for thatching ricks.

We also tried our hand at fire-fighting when a straw pile caught fire on a very exposed part of Mendip and again when an oil stove blazed up in the hostel early one morning.

Leisure was welcome, but not much easier:

I could get from my home in Street to Priddy in an hour and a half by bike, so after a week-end off I'd cycle back on Monday morning before work. We walked or cycled three miles each way to Cheddar twice a month for the Pictures or to see friends. Sometimes we rode seven miles each way to see the girls at the Hostel. We had a wireless that should have worked on batteries but rarely did, so we relied on our work-mates for news of the outside world.

Priddy Hostel closed in July 1943, as the city girls unsurprisingly found it too isolated. But Dorothy Chalker insists, 'I thoroughly enjoyed my Land Army days.'

Marion Davis came from North Wootton. After working on Horace Godfrey's farm she joined the Land Army:

I trained at Steanbow Farm with 30 to 40 other Land Girls. It was a big farm and we learned on the job. One of the instructors, Miss Tyler, used to come up from Taunton. Another was Miss Madiver. They taught us milking, cleaning out, poultry, horses. Some girls just learned arable farming. We didn't do tractors or machinery.

*The pretty side of Land Girl work: Dyl, Dorrie, Margaret Sealy and Cholie Bryce fed lambs at Croft Farm, Westbury-sub-Mendip. The rick base behind them was supported on staddle stones to keep rats out. (John Sealy)*

Some girls stayed at Steanbow hostel and some went out to farms to live in. Ted Croker asked for me: "I'll have Miss Davis." They always called me Miss Davis.

At Ted Croker's they took the manure out with a heavy horse and a putt. It was all deep in mud and we had to jump up on the seat: "Jump on that, Miss Davis, and keep the horse going," they'd say, to see if I could do it or if I'd fall in.

Kitty Mullins confirms that the Land Girls were not mollycoddled: 'We milked by hand and did all the chain harrowing with horses and

*Dressed for real farm work, Land Girls and labourers by a rick. (John Sealy)*

raked and pitched by hand onto the ricks.' Bryan Green agrees,

> Women made better milkers than men but the Land Girls were a mixed bunch. Our first was absolutely hopeless. The next was Elsie Ritson from Jarrow. She had previously only worked in hotels. Her uncle had walked with the Jarrow marchers down to London and she told us all about the life of the industrial unemployed. I can't really believe how I'd grown up and didn't know how the rest of the world lived.
>
> Even with the Land Girls and Italian prisoners of war, we were still short of labour and they brought Irishmen over to help.

John Small also remembers 'gangs of Irish labourers here until 1947. They kept fighting the Italian prisoners.'

A Land Girl from the hostel at Dunball worked in Sam Gilling's area:

> Daphne was a London hairdresser, she married my mate. She had a hell of a tractor and could never start it. There wasn't anti-freeze about in those days. If it was frosty you just let the water out

*Elsie Ritson in her Land Army uniform. (Bryan Green)*

overnight and you had to refill it in the morning.

This particular morning Daphne was working in Puxton Moor and I went down to start the tractor. About two fields away from the farm-house I saw this Italian prisoner of war dripping water. A real frosty morning it was.

Daphne was raving mad: "Did you see that bloody Eyetie?"

I said, "Yes. What did he do? Did he fall in the rhyne?"

She said, "No, I put the bugger in there. I was down getting a can of water out of the rhyne for the tractor and he come and caught hold of me."

She was a big girl, Daphne, tall girl, well built. She knew how to deal with him.

# 16
# THE THREAT FROM THE AIR

Farm-workers watched the sky as well as the land:

> The day the Germans bombed Filton, we saw them coming over. Old Teddy Locking who was a First World War veteran and myself, we were stood on top of our tractors watching. But Wally Watts, he was underneath his. Wally had just been invalided out of the Grenadier Guards. "Ah," he said, "when you've seen what I saw in France, you'll get underneath as well."

What Wally had seen in France was the German air force smashing any ability to resist out of the French people. As soon as France capitulated, Hitler set 12th August 1940 as the date to open a similar onslaught on Britain. He code-named it *Adlertag*, Day of the Eagle. On the evidence of the war so far, German fliers expected to dominate the skies within a few days and to destroy the RAF in a few weeks. From their tractors, Wally, Teddy and Sam Gilling were watching *Adlertag* in action.

Wherever the raids created a social need, the Women's Voluntary Service prepared to meet it with canteens, accommodation, clothing depots and Rest Centres. The Red Cross and St John Ambulance staffed First Aid Centres and taught skills that saved many lives when the raids came. Cadet units trained teenagers preparing to join the services. Norman Salvidge of Ston Easton heard about the Special Constabulary from his father:

> Every Special Constable in Chewton was an old soldier from World War 1. My father, Edgar, was in it with Leslie Chapel, Stanley Jones, Maurice Payne, Walter St John and Charlie Church.

Bryan Green knew them all:

> Stanley Jones was in charge. Charlie Church worked in the quarry at Bathway, Walter St John was the village baker and Maurice Payne had a garage. Maurice was a fine shot. He had his own Remington .22 and could fire it from the hip, one-handed, like a pistol. The muzzle never wavered. We had competitions between the volunteer defence organisations and Maurice won them all.

In one of his regular Sunday night broadcasts, playwright J.B. Priestley recognised this surge of patriotism, describing it as 'a citizen's war'. At the eastern end of Mendip between Axbridge and Weston, 2,000 of Priestley's 'organized militant citizens' joined the ARP – Air Raid Precautions – as unpaid volunteers. The Somerset ARP Handbook defined their job as to 'minimise the effects of air raids when the enemy penetrates the active defences.'

Like the Home Guard, ARP Wardens came home from work, put on their blue battledress and went out again on all-night duty. When the raiders came, they cleared people from the streets and were first on the scene after an attack.

In Cheddar, volunteers like Terry Heal set the system in motion. Terry worked in Cheddar telephone exchange at what is now Magnolia House. At night she joined an ARP shift in the Fire Station from 5 pm to 8 am and remembers the routine:

> Air Raid Warnings came by phone from Weston. The Yellow warning said the raiders were coming. When the Red warning came, I pushed the ON button. That sounded the siren on the roof. It was a warbling note. After another Yellow, the Green All Clear message came and we sounded the siren again. That was one continuous note.

Cheddar had the only real Fire Station in the area, although Blagdon pump unit enjoyed the use of the Wills estate private station at Coombe Lodge. In 1938, Axbridge RDC depended on two old fire-engines with solid wheels and one even older manual pump. In Shepton Mallet, however, Charles Wainwright remembers two open-style Rolls-Royce fire-engines – until one toppled into the river on an exercise, to be replaced by a humbler Leyland.

*Navigators of German bombers worked from British Ordnance Survey maps overprinted in*

**Nur für den Dienstgebrauch!**

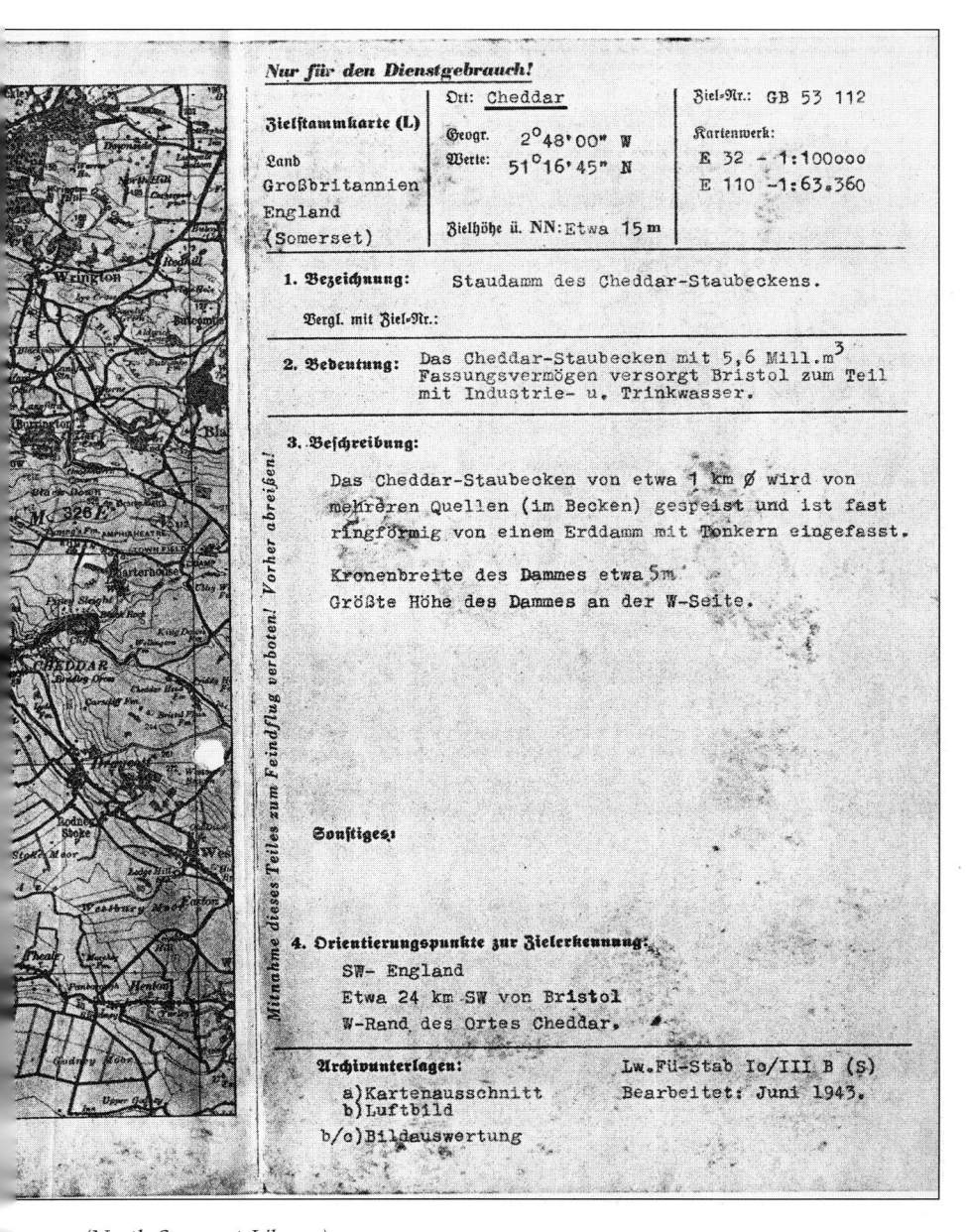

| | Ort: **Cheddar** | Ziel-Nr.: GB 53 112 |
|---|---|---|
| **Zielstammkarte (L)** | Geogr. 2°48'00" W | Kartenwerk: |
| Land Großbritannien | Werte: 51°16'45" N | E 32 – 1:100000 |
| England (Somerset) | Zielhöhe ü. NN: Etwa 15 m | E 110 – 1:63.360 |

1. **Bezeichnung:** Staudamm des Cheddar-Staubeckens.

   Vergl. mit Ziel-Nr.:

2. **Bedeutung:** Das Cheddar-Staubecken mit 5,6 Mill.m$^3$ Fassungsvermögen versorgt Bristol zum Teil mit Industrie- u. Trinkwasser.

3. **Beschreibung:**

   Das Cheddar-Staubecken von etwa 1 km ⌀ wird von mehreren Quellen (im Becken) gespeist und ist fast ringförmig von einem Erddamm mit Tonkern eingefasst.

   Kronenbreite des Dammes etwa 5m.
   Größte Höhe des Dammes an der W-Seite.

   *Mitnahme dieses Teiles zum Feindflug verboten! Vorher abreißen!*

   **Sonstiges:**

4. **Orientierungspunkte zur Zielerkennung:**
   SW- England
   Etwa 24 km SW von Bristol
   W-Rand des Ortes Cheddar.

| **Archivunterlagen:** | Lw.Fü-Stab Ic/III B (S) |
|---|---|
| a) Kartenausschnitt | Bearbeitet: Juni 1943. |
| b) Luftbild | |
| b/c) Bildauswertung | |

*rman. (North Somerset Library)*

*In the Air Raid Warden Post on Weston's sea-front, a camp-bed offered rest between raids. Duty rosters covered the notice-board by the telephone and a stirrup-pump hung on the wall. On the floor, hurricane lamps and a car battery were ready for when the electricity failed. (Geoff Holburd)*

W.J. Egan was the wartime Fire Chief at Axbridge. From a Report Centre in the Council Offices basement, he controlled brigades at Axbridge, Banwell and Cheddar. With a training centre at Sidcot School, his volunteers eventually peaked at 275 firemen, on duty from dusk to dawn in brigades, pump stations and village fire-parties. A further 2,000 volunteers, organised by Mr Godwin of Blagdon, stood ready as Fire Guards with stirrup pumps.

Cheddar Fire Station also housed the First Aid Post, staffed by Red Cross volunteers who trained in a barn behind the bakery. Confident perhaps in the cave system, Cheddar had no public air-raid shelters. Head Warden was Mr J.J. Tyson, head of the Junior Council School, once known as the 'British School', taking children up to 14. The Warden's Post was in the school's back classroom: tel 146.

After the war, Mr Tyson's son Hugh came across a Luftwaffe aerial photograph of Cheddar reservoir. Drawing on his own active service in RAF Bomber Command, Hugh analyses the picture as:

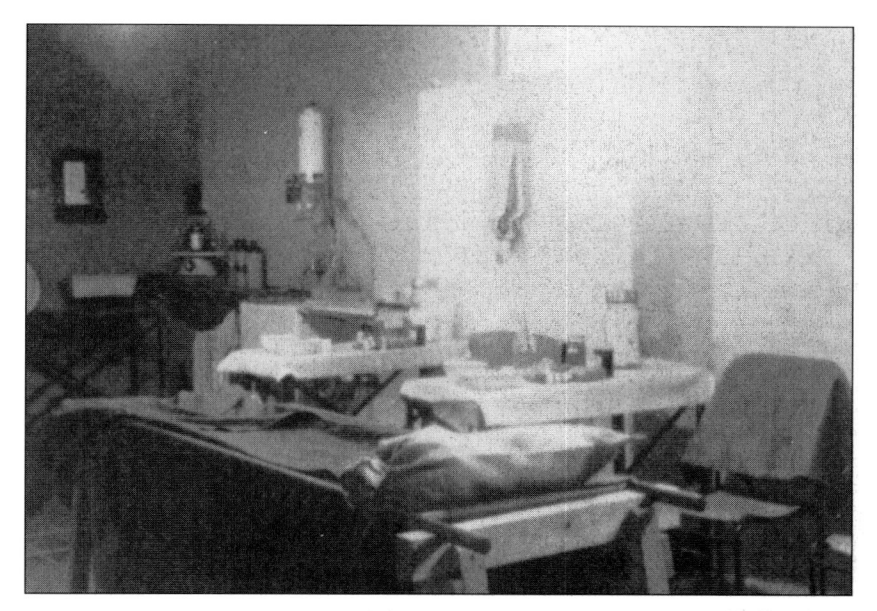

*Simple equipment in this First Aid Post stood on tables against brick blast walls built against the windows. Rubber hot-water bottles hung on the wall and stone hot-water bottles stood by the gas-heater and kettle. Trestles supported a blanket-covered stretcher. (Geoff Holburd)*

... taken around noon, probably in autumn 1940 as the tree shadows near Hythe Bow are long and pointing north. Recently cut hayfields show up as a lighter colour and there are stacks in some of the fields. The triangular field opposite the pumping station shows huts and a path leading to the searchlight there. It is marked *Scheinwerfer* – German for "searchlight" – in red.

The reservoir and pumping station would have been hard to hit using 1940 bombing techniques. Statements by German bomber crews after the war show that the reservoir was useful to them as a navigational marker.

In 1942, Bristol Waterworks Company painted the rim of the reservoir grey to make it harder for enemy bombers to spot.

Near the reservoir, the Cheddar searchlight crew had their own anti-

*A stick of bombs fell across the little village of Banwell, in September 1940, killing five. Leslie King of Pool Farm photographed the destruction in West Street. (Roy Rice Collection)*

aircraft Lewis machine-gun. At Star, three searchlights operated from a field behind Laneside Cottage. The soldiers lived in huts in a corner of the field and power came from a noisy generator at the bottom of Cheddarcombe Lane. Another searchlight was based on Mendip at Higher Pitts Farm and one was sited on the corner at Littleton. Francis Stott remembers a searchlight and Lewis gun at the bottom of Westbury where the soldiers lived in huts on the site, with a Tillings Stevenson generator for power.

Searchlights dotted the area, particularly round Weston's aircraft factories. Most were operated by TA units of No 448 Battery, controlled from Headquarters at Churchill Gate House. In November 1940 the HQ moved to Banwell Abbey. With searchlights placed at two-mile intervals, their task was to illuminate enemy raiders, ideally in a cone of beams, to help anti-aircraft gunners lay their sights on them. Another function aimed to blind the German airmen with a sheet of light known as 'Dazzle Defence'. Single searchlight beams served to point our fighters towards the enemy, or to guide lost learner-pilots back to base.

*Special Police headed the funeral procession in Banwell of air-raid victim Ron Clark, killed on his 49th birthday when on duty as a Special Constable. A World War I veteran, Ron ran the village's electrical shop. (Roy Rice Collection)*

*German land mines were dropped by parachute, exploding on impact, causing immense blast damage at ground level. An airman from Locking stands inside this land mine crater on Summer Lane, Banwell. (Roy Rice Collection)*

By 10th October 1940, half the allocated 24 lights were in service and by Spring 1941 some were linked with a new Searchlight Control Radar which locked on to the target and then illuminated it. At the end of 1941, the searchlights were moved from north Somerset to a newly defined 'Killer Belt' in the south of the county.

The first German bomb fell on 30th June 1940 in a field at Weare, just south of the Mendips. The Red Cross turned out, not to treat casualties, but to rattle collection cans at sightseers.

Casualties came in September when a stick of bombs killed five and injured 50 in Banwell. Two telephone operators were trapped in the burning post office, three houses were demolished and a hundred damaged. As the roads were blocked, bodies had to be carried out over hedges and through fields. James Hunt was seven years old:

> Poor old Sam Lewis's house and tailor's shop was just a mass of rubble, broken wood and furniture. I noticed one of Trixie Lewis's shoes in the tangled mass and wondered what had become of her.
>
> Onlookers were still tight-lipped and shocked and I realised people had been killed.
>
> I saw an open lorry. Sticking out of the back was an unexploded bomb. It looked huge to me, about ten feet or more in length and almost two and a half feet wide. It was a 1,500 lb bomb complete. I wished they would take it away quick, but the men who had done it were celebrating in The Bell!

After the attack, No 955 (Mobile Balloon) Squadron established their HQ in Banwell Castle. By 3rd May 1941, 24 barrage balloons ringed Weston and its aircraft factories. The following year, crews from the Women's Auxiliary Air Force (WAAF) took the balloons over.

Their triple-finned LZ (Low Zone) Kite Balloons flew at 5,000 feet, tethered to winches with steel cable, preventing enemy aircraft from making low-level attacks. Unfortunately, they also stopped trainer aircraft taking off from Locking airfield. The solution was to ground them until an enemy approach was signalled as imminent.

One balloon flew from Devil's Bridge, at the seaward end of Bleadon Hill. Within a month, on 28th June 1941, it broke away, fouling electricity cables as it trailed its cable across the countryside. A month later, lightning struck several other balloons. Some broke loose, this time damaging a local pub, the Borough Arms.

German bomber fleets crossed Mendip to attack Bristol, Bath and

Weston in 1940's daytime blitz, the night raids of 1941 and the 'Baedeker' raids of 1942. Bombs and parachute mines fell on Bleadon, Wells and Winscombe, Compton Martin and Cheddar, Mells and Radstock. In the last 'Steinbock' raids in 1944, bombs dropped at Milton near Wells, and incendiaries fell on Wookey Hole and Leigh-on-Mendip.

Francis Stott lived in Westbury and recalls that:

> We had 21 bombs here one night. One down there below the village, he spewed the ground up but he never went off. He's still down there somewhere.

A bomb in September 1940 reduced Compton Bishop School and School House to a crater full of rubble. The school mistress, Mrs Howell, and her family survived but their dog was killed. Although some evacuees went home, lessons continued for the remaining 50 pupils in Mr Amos's garage until June 1941 when they moved to Cross Memorial Hall.

In 1941, Rosemary Hodges won a scholarship to the County School for Girls at Weston-super-Mare. She found girls from two other schools sharing the building, evacuees from Barking Abbey and Mitcham. One Monday in June 1942, Rosemary got off the bus from Blagdon to find her classrooms burned out by incendiary bombs. 'I don't think I'll ever forget the acrid smell of burnt books, gym-shoes and exploded chemicals which greeted us,' she recalled. 'Within a few days the London schools had gone.'

John Small lived in Manor Farm Cottage when a land mine fell on Blackdown a mile away, bringing the ceiling down. 'You could see all the laths. My father patched it up with cardboard and it stayed like that until long after the war.'

Down in Congresbury, Lt Reynolds won the George Medal for defusing a 500 lb unexploded bomb near the White Hart. Terry Heal recalls other unexploded bombs:

> The only bombs on Cheddar were dropped on the night the Americans arrived from Southampton. But none of the bombs exploded. They landed on the strawberry fields. We were told the bombs were made in Poland and the factory workers had fitted fuses that wouldn't go off.

*Clive Morris stood gleefully on a German unexploded bomb with his father Jim's Vauxhall in the background. Jim said the thousand-pounder fell above Battscombe, Cheddar, in 1943 and was excavated after the war. (Jim Morris)*

Sometimes all was not as it seemed. Hugh Tyson of Cheddar remembers one unexploded bomb:

> Bombs fell in a small wood just south of Battscombe quarry. One failed to explode but the casing split open. Bill Hill, who was in charge of the Fire Brigade, loaded it on to the back step of the Buick fire tender and took it to the Fire Station. They put it on display for Red Cross funds. When the Bomb Disposal men arrived, they found it was still alive and fused. They removed it with great rapidity.

Blagdon's first ARP fire-watchers, reports Joan Lyons, then Joan Stokes,

> used the summerhouse in the garden of "Fairways" above the Mendip Hotel. The summerhouse was on a turn-table and so gave a good view round the valley. Transport was provided by a lady from Batcombe whose car was converted to using fuel from a large gas bag on the roof. Later they were given a pick-up truck and a 1914–18 army ambulance.

On the night of 27th March 1944, their ARP Rescue section sped away in their truck to help in an air-raid on Weston. They were all men: Bill Drake, Reg Hollier, George Light, Arthur Lyons, Arthur Maybee, Colin Redwood and Ike Smart. Two women, Joan Stokes and Frances Riley, hurried to the George Inn where their ambulance was parked. Joan had not driven this particular vehicle before and only now found that it had no self-starter, just a starting handle:

> Luckily, there were American soldiers stationed in the village and I asked one to turn the handle and get us going. I remember dreading changing gear in case I stalled the engine. Metal hoods over the headlamps gave a very dim view of the road but we reached Hutton safely and then waited for the Rescue team to dig out any survivors.

Joan and Frances took an old man to Weston Hospital and returned for more, but he was the only survivor. Four civilians and a Home Guard died there.

Thousands of incendiary bombs showered down in air raids. About a foot long, their magnesium content burned with an intense heat. Some held an explosive charge. Frederick Reed grew up in the Bristol blitz. His daily job before going to school was to climb a ladder to see if any unexploded incendiaries had lodged on their roof. He spotted this one and kept it as a souvenir. Its casing is dated 1936, the time of the Spanish Civil War. (Author)

*Volunteers staffed First Aid Posts. These young Red Cross nurses served in Wells: Thelma Yarrow, Queenie Gillard, Audrey Price and Gwyneth Weekes. Audrey married John Sealy and Gwyneth married Tommy Webster of the Auxiliary Units. (John Sealy)*

We were there all night. Next morning, the men started our ambulance and then went on ahead, back to Blagdon. We followed but at Sandford we got a puncture. We couldn't change the wheel, or start the engine if we did, so we had to sit there, waiting for the men to realise we were missing and come back to find us. They were not pleased.

People sought refuge on Mendip from the city raids. Sam Gilling watched:

I don't know where they got their petrol from, but thousands came out into the country away from the raids. In Burrington Combe there were vans, cars, all sorts, and lots of caravans at Rock of Ages. Just up there in the corner there's a big cave. That was all full. A family from Bristol lived in our boiler house at Rickford all through the blitzes. When we wanted a bath we had to turn them out.

Communications were uncertain says Helen Boileau, recalling that Mr Ashby of Cross was the Axbridge Head Warden. 'A message from Mr Watkins at Brent Knoll took five hours to arrive because the ARP Messengers were all hay-making.'

Most damage was naturally suffered by the towns. Nearly 300 High Explosive bombs and 2,000 incendiaries fell on Wells where 40 buildings were damaged. Over 8,000 Weston buildings were damaged by 200 bombs and 31,000 incendiaries.

The Post Office did well during the blitz on Bristol, rescuing letters from the flames. Bryan Green still has one, proudly delivered to him in its scorched envelope. It contained a bill for £153 0s 7d.

Sadly, the danger from the air did not come solely from enemy action. Fifty three Allied servicemen died in crashed aircraft on and around the Mendip Hills. Half involved pilots under training, many from Number 10 Elementary Flying Training School at Locking. Working the Mendip land, Francis Stott saw some come down:

> Several planes crashed while we were up there. The first one, it was the first time he'd ever been on his own. He went straight across the ground and he saw a wall and he put the brakes on and he tipped upside-down. He hung up inside there and I had to chop him out of it.
>
> Another, he went into the field we were ploughing. It was foggy, and he went straight down in. I picked up his thumb and one finger in his glove, and a leg in one boot.
>
> Two Harvards, American trainers, were flying in and out the clouds, and they collided and that was the end of them. One baled out and he came down about three fields away from where we were. The other one caught on fire when he hit the ground.

Wreckage was removed rapidly. As usual, schoolboys knew what was going on. In Shepton Mallet, Ralph Vowles says, 'The Air Ministry took over the Anglo-Bavarian Brewery on the Wells Road as a store. They recruited local men as guards.'

Charles Wainwright saw inside: 'They had crashed aircraft in there, and stocks of bombs.'

Schoolboy Hugh Tyson was a meticulous aerospotter. Unlike most, he recorded his sightings in a diary. On 27th April 1942, he noted,

> I saw a Spitfire crash at Axbridge just above the village. After

hearing cannon fire above the cloud layer, I watched it dive out of the clouds inverted. It turned topside up but still flew in and was totally destroyed. I went over on my bike. Both cannons were driven into the limestone as far as the breech mechanisms and the Merlin had gone in as far as the supercharger casing at the back. The remains of the pilot were being collected in sandbags.

In May 1943, a New Zealander pilot at RNAS Yeovilton wrote home describing his training in low-altitude flying. Shortly afterwards, he followed his instructor down into a swoop over Downside Abbey School. Schoolboys watched with their customary wartime interest which turned into horror as his Hurricane clipped the tree-tops and crashed into a cricket match, killing nine boys. The pilot is buried in the school cemetery beside the boys.

Schoolboy survivor Philip Jebb, later to become headmaster of Downside, recalls the stoicism needed in those times:

After the crash, the boys were sent out on a walk in the hills.

*A Hurricane on a training flight from Yeovilton crashed into a 1st XI cricket match on the playing-fields of Downside Abbey School. Jeremy Grantham-Hill, who was among the younger boys watching the game, took this picture. Nine boys and the pilot died. (Jeremy Grantham-Hill)*

*Sgt Michael Durrant of 582 Squadron Bomber Command was shot down in a raid on Kiel in September 1944. His mother, Catherine, served in the London blitz as a nurse. Her father, Charles Wainwright, placed this window in Christon Church to commemorate both. (Author)*

Fortified by their faith and supported by the prayers of the monks, they resumed normal school the next day.

Every year, ex-airborne padre Bob Browning of Uphill takes a British Legion remembrance service for 23 British servicemen who died on active service in Double Hills field near Farrington Gurney.

On 17th September 1944, they climbed into their Horsa troop-carrying glider RJ113. Their mission was to seize the Rhine bridges at Arnhem in Operation Market Garden. A Stirling bomber towed them to 1st Airborne Division's Assembly Area over Bath, where they joined a vast aerial fleet that filled the Somerset sky as it wheeled south. But Horsa RJ113 broke up in mid-air and crashed into Double Hills field, killing both glider pilots and all 21 soldiers of 9th Airborne RE Field Company.

# 17
# STARFISH WARS

Coming home from Burrington village school one afternoon, young John Fear found a new gate across Link Lane. During the day, a squad of RAF men had arrived at Tynings Farm to take over Blackdown's bleak plateau.

Sworn to secrecy, these airmen were part of a national aerial defence system, designed to lure German bombers from their scheduled targets. Their task on Blackdown was nothing less than to create a replica of Bristol at night. Jim Morris was one of the squad:

> After basic training, eight of us went to Harwell in Berkshire. They told us we'd be attached to the Air Ministry in London and they had a job for us in Somerset.
>
> It was the end of 1940. I was billeted first at the Jefferies in Manor Farm. Mike Beddoes and Eddie Edwards went to Mrs Villis at Brook Cottage between Tynings and Charterhouse. They fed us and did all the washing. They got about £5 to £6 a week so they were pleased to have us. We flew from Harwell in a Wellington bomber and took aerial photographs of the marshalling yards at Bristol. People from Shepperton Film Studios superimposed them on the Mendips.

Piles of stone – 'tumps' – marked out streets and railway lines of the decoy city. Viewed today from the air, they show up as a double dotted line of lighter vegetation running east-west across the dark surface of Blackdown. Similar straight lines radiate north and south. North-west of the east bunker, scaffold and canvas simulated Temple Meads station, marshalling yard and goods depots.

On each tump sat a 'glow-box', a glass-topped wooden box containing a light bulb. Three switches like theatrical dimmers faded the lights up and down or turned them off. Jim Morris explains:

*In 1940, a replica of Bristol appeared at night on Blackdown, complete with streets, railway station and lights. Long demolished, the ghost town's plan is still visible from the air. (Author)*

*Blackdown's Starfish city, fires and guns were controlled from three bunkers equipped with generators and switches. The bunkers protected the airmen from the bombs they hoped to attract. (Author)*

We expected to be bombed because the idea was to attract the bombers. We would get a signal to light up the electric simulations and would gradually bring the lights on with the big slide switches. One had a red lamp inside. Every few minutes, a red glow would come out and then close up, like a chap stoking his railway engine. As the aircraft passed over Bristol or came near us, we got another signal and dimmed the lights down to look like turning them off.

I flew over the site once in a Lysander. On the way out from Lulsgate, it was daylight and we couldn't see much on the ground at all. But when we came back it was dark and it looked just like Bristol. I couldn't believe my eyes even though I'd helped build it.

The project had primitive beginnings:

A wooden hut, 8 by 6, and a lorryload of cable. That was the beginning of it all. Then we built two bunkers. The roof was made of concrete poured on, about nine inches thick. But the props on

*Chew Magna Starfish did its job, attracting incendiaries and HE bombs onto the decoy target. Robert King stood guard alongside a defused bomb case outside the guard-room. (Robert King)*

one bunker gave way and the wet concrete fell in. We had to shovel it out by hand quickly and do it again. The walls were brick with earth piled on.

Three generators in each bunker provided electricity for the site. It was all well thought out and neatly done. They were very smart the electrical people. The cables mostly ran along the surface, but went under the paths.

Driver Howard Edwards, known as 'Eddie', had problems with his vehicle on Blackdown's soft surface, but found a local solution:

The machinery at Blagdon Waterworks was coal-fired in those days. Mr Williams, the engineer, let us have his boiler ash to put on the tracks over Beacon Batch to stop our vehicles bogging down.

Just after Bristol's first raid, Robert King was suddenly posted away from Bomber Command:

We didn't know where we were going. We got to Filton first and then this place Chew Magna. We'd never heard of it. We started in a bell tent and a sandbagged shelter. We built our own guardroom and then got a Nissen hut. A lot of bombs fell on the site, some round the tent.

As a corporal I had a Triumph motor-bike to get around. We had sites at Whitchurch, Downside just behind Lulsgate, Kingston Seymour, Coxley and Uphill, all small ones.

Our local HQ was at Lulsgate, just inside the main gate. I had to phone every evening and give a cloud report which helped assess the likelihood of enemy air attack.

Some days I had to go up to Brockworth in Gloucestershire. We worked on an aircraft plotting table that showed the German aircraft coming in and then signalled the information to the RAF and army ack-ack.

These German bombers flew in from France following radio beams known as *Knickebein* which intersected over the target. As soon as this invisible menace was identified in June 1940, top priority went to Britain's Radio Counter-Measures programme. Run by RAF 80 Wing at Radlett in Hertfordshire, RCM stations soon ringed the country from

*Decoy fires were part of the Starfish system. From raised tanks, a mixture of creosote and water flowed into troughs of flammable material. When ignited, these flared up like fires from incendiary bombs. (Robert King)*

Aberdeen to Devon. Churchill called it the 'Wizard War'; Hugh Tyson tells how the wizards arrived in Shipham:

> An officer selected a site on Cuck Hill and commandeered the land on the direct authority, people said, of Churchill. Within days, a squad of men moved into local billets and started construction.
>
> From December 1st 1940, they were operating a radio listening-post that remained in action until 1st September 1944. Their job was to bend the German beams, leading the bombers away from their target. Having done that, they signalled the code-word "Blackie". That lit decoys below the enemy, persuading them to drop their bombs over open country.

Power came from the public grid, backed by a Lister diesel generator. Working a three-watch 24-hour day, the national RCM network reported all German directional signals to Radlett, hoping to work out

*One of the surviving Z-rocket bases on Blackdown. (Author)*

points of intersection and thus the next target.

By now, 80 Wing HQ was code-named 'Headache Control' while the stations were termed 'Aspirin' or 'Bromide', according to their radio frequency. A worse headache came when the Germans introduced *X-Verfahren* directional beams from France. These were countered by Masking Beacons – abbreviated to 'Meacons' – which received the enemy signal at one station and re-transmitted the same signal from another several miles away, throwing German navigators well off their expected track. One Meacon station was based near Doulting and another at Highbridge, re-transmitting from Lympsham. Eddie Edwards takes up the story:

> Because the Germans were short of skilled navigators, pathfinders led the way, following the radio beams. They dropped incendiaries on the target to light fires as markers. The main force followed up and bombed the fires.
>
> Our plan was to put the fires out fast in Bristol and then light our own fires on the decoy.

This system of dummy fires developed after the Coventry raid in

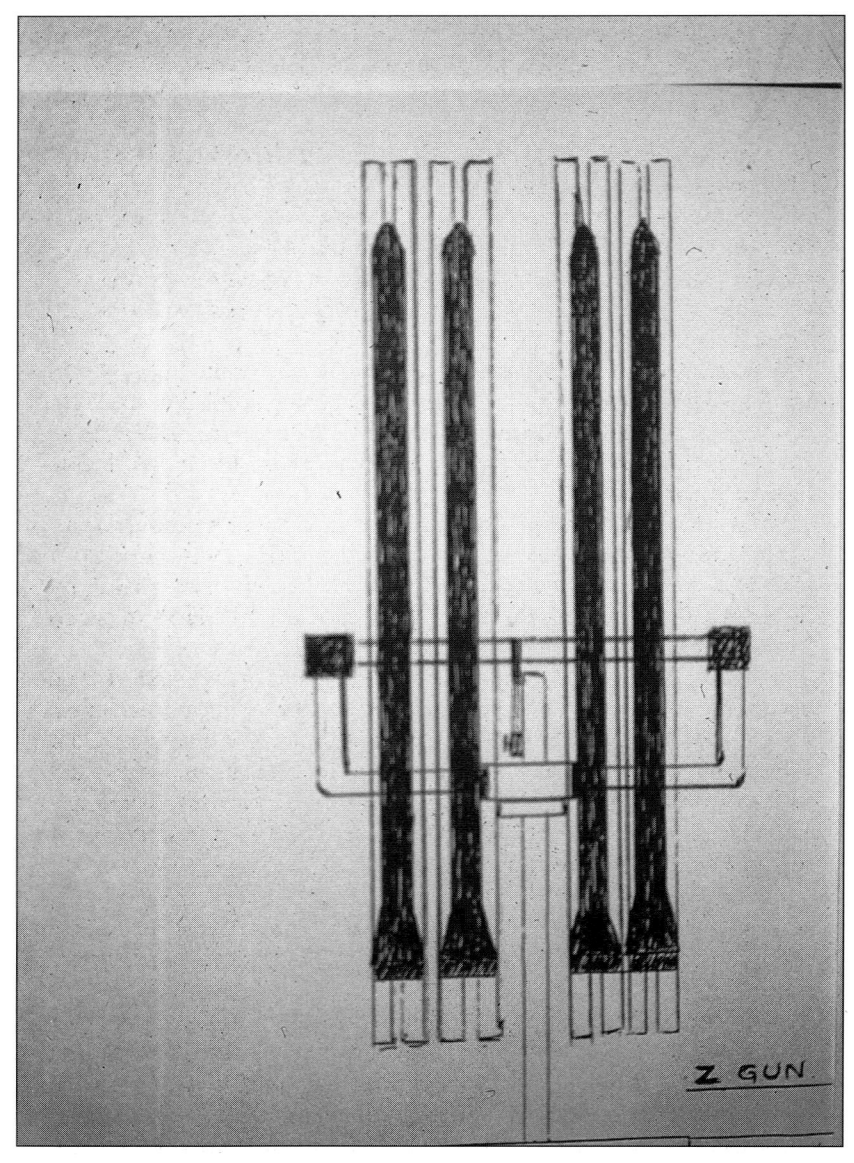

*Some Starfish sites were armed with secret Z-batteries of rocket-guns. Jim Morris sketched from memory details of the battery he helped build and operate on Blackdown. (Jim Morris)*

November 1940. The code SF – Special Fire – soon evolved into the name 'Starfish' as a general term for all the decoys. Jim Morris continues:

> Down at Tynings Gate, we had rows of iron troughs full of bales of straw, soaked with creosote ready to catch fire quickly.
>
> Well away from them we built elevated tanks with valves like the ballcock on a WC cistern. We could let an intermittent flow of more creosote or water from the tanks down pipes to the fire-troughs. The creosote kept the fire going but when the water flowed, it flared up.
>
> It was unbelievable. It wasn't red fire, it was white and yellow, brilliant, like magnesium. Once it got going you couldn't get anywhere near it. And you couldn't turn it off or stop the flow of fuel. Ignition was with an electric switch in the bunker five hundred yards away.
>
> Once I was down in Cheddar and a terrible storm started. Lightning was flashing everywhere and a terrific wind got up. I saw this glow over the site and I said, "We've been struck by lightning. I've got to go up there." I jumped on my bike and when I got there the site was on fire.
>
> It was 50 years before I found out what happened. I met another airman from up there and we got talking about old times. He said, "I started that fire. I was burning some rubbish and the wind blew up and sparks started the fire in the baskets. I expected to be put away for life but Flying Officer Richardson was very good about it. He said I could just pay for the damage. But it meant I had to go without any beer."

Mendip's air defences went beyond bent beams, decoy cities and decoy fires. Defence turned into attack. Jim Morris tells the story:

> The Z-guns were the biggest secret of all. We didn't even go on a training course because they were so secret. There was a gate across the road to the gun site with an armed guard 24 hours a day. No one, not even an officer, could get in.
>
> I was the corporal and I was told, "The rockets are on the way. They've been developed for the Z-guns and you've just got to follow the instructions."
>
> But we hadn't got any instructions. Along came another

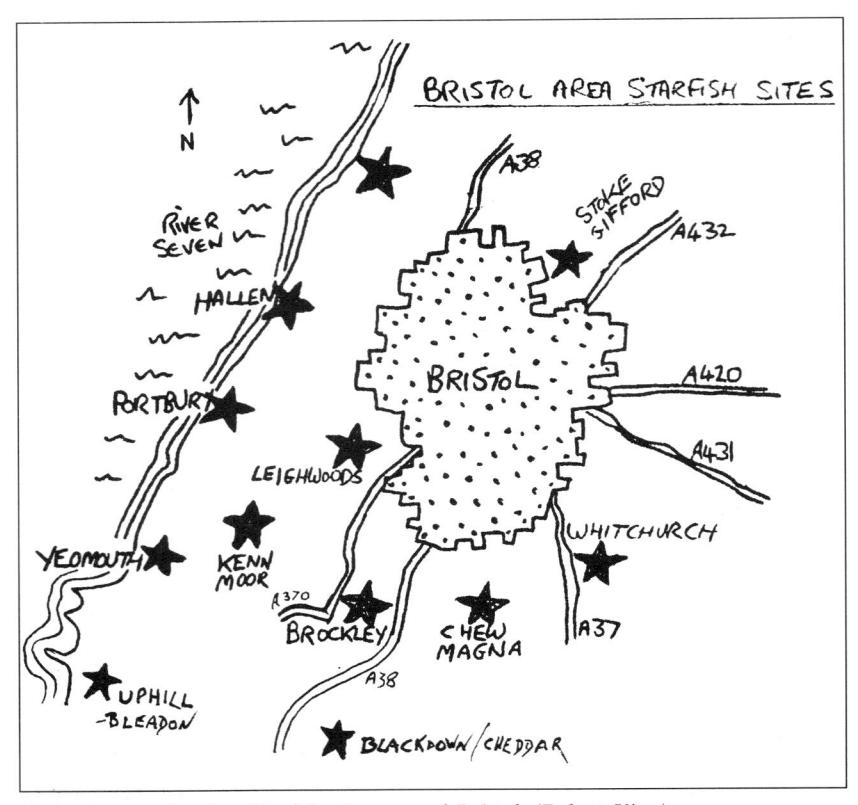

*A sketch map showing Starfish sites around Bristol. (Robert King)*

corporal, Jock Kidd, a dispatch rider, with a paper.

It said: "Place the rocket nose upward, a foot away from the contacts. Lower it down onto the contacts. When the order comes to fire, press the button."

We built twelve concrete blocks about three feet across, mounted with metal scales marked in degrees like a protractor. This controlled the aim.

A man came up and made launchers out of two pieces of scaffold pipe about two inches in diameter. He welded them five or six inches apart with a strip across the back and we fitted them on to the protractor bases.

The rockets were about three or four inches in diameter. They lay between the two pipes and slid back onto an electrical contact. Four rockets on each block made forty-eight in all. Firing was done by operators in the bunker, by electrical circuit.

Corporal Robert King passed on the orders:

We set the elevation and direction as instructed, and the altitude at which they were to explode. All the rocket sites fired simultaneously and between us we hit a box of five cubic miles. Some warheads were explosive and some released miles of wire.

Jim Morris continues:

Ignition of glow-boxes or fires or rockets was ordered from RAF HQ – telephone number 126 – via a GPO phone at Lower Farm. The Flight Sergeant received the call and passed it on through our field telephones which rang in all three bunkers. This was called a 126 call.

One night, Percy Smith got the 126 call from the sergeant with an order to fire the rockets. I was in the top bunker by the lights and I went out to watch the rockets go off.

At that moment a German land-mine dropped by the side of the shelter. It made a crater the size of a room. We felt the whole shelter lift off the ground.

Then one minute later the rockets fired. I was stone deaf for a long while and got perforated ear-drums. That was from the mine first and then the rockets going off. We were told later that we had hit a bomber with that salvo but it wasn't credited to us because we were secret.

Mary Small lived literally in the middle of it all at Tynings Farm:

Our home at Tynings was between the two sites. The airmen used to come in to fill their flasks and buy fried egg sandwiches to eat while on duty.

The family was ordered out when the decoy was lit at night. But as the farm was twenty yards outside the official danger zone, we didn't qualify for an air-raid shelter.

Chew Magna was the first decoy target to go operational, on 25th

*Within a month of going operational in November 1940, Chew Magna Starfish decoy attracted many HE and incendiary bombs, triumphantly displayed here by the crew. (Robert King)*

November 1940. It attracted half-a-dozen bombs on the night of 2nd December 1940. A month later, on 3rd January 1941, over a thousand incendiaries showered the site.

The next night, bombs fell on another Starfish decoy, in the fields south-west of Uphill. This was a QF site, designed to simulate a burning airfield. During the night of 4th January 1941, Weston's first big raid, the order came to ignite the target in an attempt to draw the bombers away from the town. Soaked by heavy rain, the switches failed.

One of the Starfish airmen, AC2 CFM Bright, filled a bottle with petrol and went out to light the target manually. For nearly two hours, he crawled along wet ditches to ignite the dummy hangars as bombs fell all round him. Next day, 42 big craters and 1,500 incendiary fins were counted there. AC2 Bright won the Military Medal but the citation remained secret.

Mr B.S. Counsell of Uphill tells another side of the Uphill Starfish story:

Arthur Jefferies of Flat Roof Farm was going down the lane in his pony cart to do his milking when he met Farmer Amesbury of Bleadon. He was crying, "For God's sake come and help me!"

They found a dreadful scene at the end of the lane. The bombs had fallen just where Mr Amesbury's dairy herd was lying down for the night. There were dead cows, cows stumping about with legs blown off, others with their entrails dragging on the grass. Farmer Jefferies had to shoot several with his shotgun.

# 18
# MENDIP SKY WATCH

Every minute of every wartime day and night, men and women of the Observer Corps watched the skies over Mendip.

When war came, Somerset already had 29 Observer posts, mostly sandbagged shelters. Located at five mile intervals, they maintained continuous contact as planes passed over. In the Mendip area, making up 23 Group, there were posts at Frome, Glastonbury, Radstock, Shepton Mallet, Westbury-sub-Mendip, West Harptree, Weston-super-Mare and Winscombe (see Appendix E).

From each post, a team of two Observers monitored every aircraft that flew overhead, Allied as well as German. They passed these visual sightings on to Observer Headquarters in Bristol to be plotted on to a large map-table. Their findings were phoned through to RAF Fighter Command Operations Room. There they were collated with radar trackings and weather reports to present the clearest possible picture of what was happening in the air. If invasion had come, the Observer Corps role would have extended to reporting enemy airborne landings.

West Harptree was one of five ROC posts in the area to be rebuilt underground after the war to cope with nuclear attack. Leading Observer Mike Parfitt and the post-war team have renovated the bunker as a museum and tribute to Corps members.

Beneath a heavy steel trapdoor, a ladder leads down a narrow shaft through a roof seven feet thick. The bunker is a concrete box inside bedrock that was blasted out to a standard size. Down below, the air strikes cold and the floor is insulated with strips of old machine belting from Somerset collieries: Observers worked with their greatcoats on. Bunks and an Elsan provided basic creature comforts. A petrol generator ran on the surface, charging batteries that could run lights for 110 hours. A telephone line linked the post directly with HQ at

Lansdown and with the local master-post at Clutton where there was a radio.

In April 1941 the Corps was designated 'Royal' and members, all civilian volunteers, were given RAF-type uniforms. Their crest features a Spanish Armada coastal beacon-lighter.

At Westbury-sub-Mendip, the ruins of a concrete bunker lie at the top of the escarpment. It was still a sandbagged post when the first local part-time Observer, Henry Moore, pushed his bike up the hill from the village after a day's work on the farm, free-wheeling back down at the end of his duty. In his spare time Henry served in the Rodney Stoke Home Guard.

Shepton Mallet's Observers had good views from their post on the Ridge above the town. There were 15 of them, including Derby Miller, the High Street hairdresser, and Bertie Jacobs, senior clerk in Mr Wainwright's farm estate office. Another, Mr Angwin, worked as deputy head of the secondary school where the boys knew they could distract him from anything by asking about aeroplanes. Two valuable members reputedly made the best tea in the county, not only warming the pot, but pre-heating their fine china cups. Trading as Bowden Bros, Grocers, their reputation was at stake.

In 1940, after a scattering of bombs through July, the war came home to Mendip on the afternoon of 14th August. Directed by the Observer Corps, Spitfires of Blue Section, 92 Squadron, intercepted three Heinkel He 111 raiders over Glastonbury.

In a 15 minute action, they shot down all three. One crash-landed at Charterhouse, being hit on the way by Lewis gun fire from the Cheddar searchlight unit. Another came down at Puriton where all five crew were captured. The third crashed into Bridgwater Bay. Only one body was recovered, that of Uffz Hans Dolata. He is buried in the war grave section of Weston cemetery. Hugh Tyson watched the action:

> I was an ARP messenger in Cheddar, on duty outside the Fire Station. We first saw the Heinkel 111 at about 2,000 feet, flying slowly between Cheddar and Nyland. The undercarriage was down and it was obviously in trouble. It disappeared over the Mendips and around the same time we saw another Heinkel 111 to our south-west, diving vertically. This latter machine crashed at Toogood's Farm in Puriton. We heard that the first Heinkel was down at Charterhouse and we cycled up to see it. By next day we had heard about the Puriton crash and cycled there as well.

# SOMERSET v HITLER

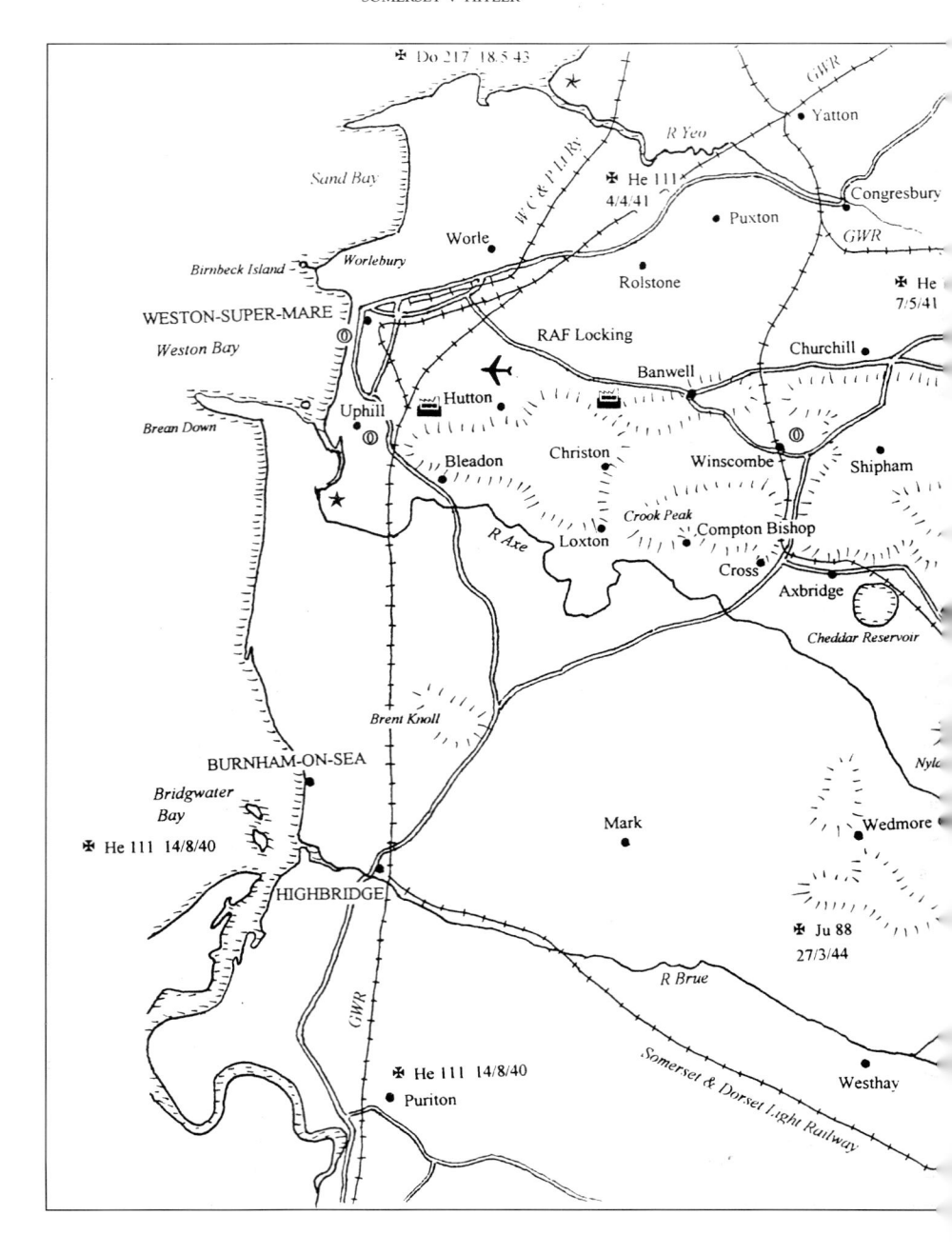

✠ Do 217 18.5.43

R Yeo

• Yatton

*Sand Bay*

✠ He 111
4/4/41

• Puxton

• Congresbury

GWR

• Worle

*Birnbeck Island*

*Worlebury*

• Rolstone

✠ He
7/5/41

WESTON-SUPER-MARE

RAF Locking

• Churchill

*Weston Bay*

• Banwell

Uphill

Hutton

*Brean Down*

Bleadon

Christon

Winscombe

• Shipham

Crook Peak

R Axe

Loxton

Compton Bishop

Cross

Axbridge

*Cheddar Reservoir*

*Brent Knoll*

BURNHAM-ON-SEA

*Nyla*

*Bridgwater Bay*

• Mark

• Wedmore

✠ He 111 14/8/40

HIGHBRIDGE

✠ Ju 88
27/3/44

R Brue

*Somerset & Dorset Light Railway*

✠ He 111 14/8/40
• Puriton

• Westhay

# MENDIP SKY WATCH

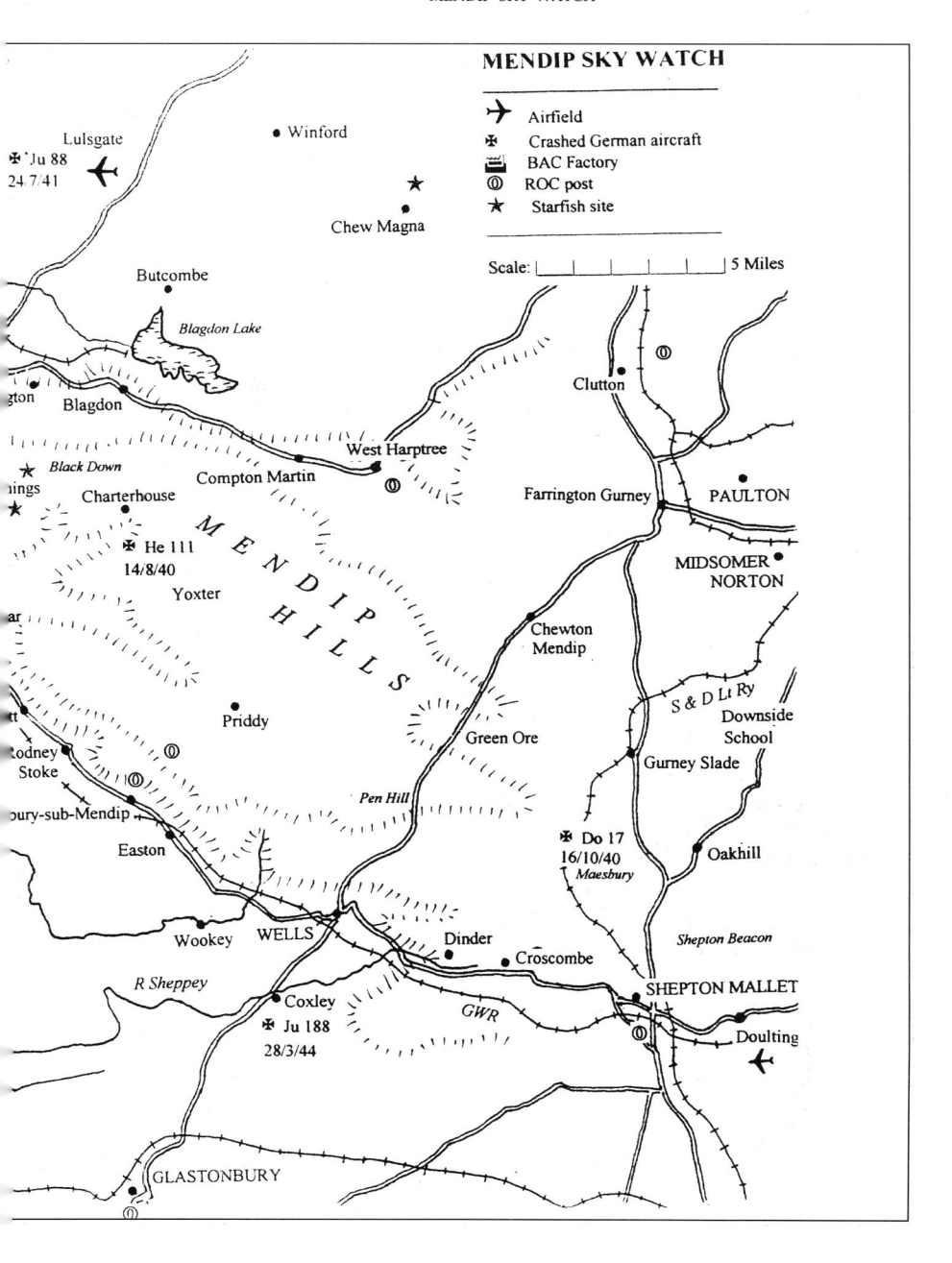

- ✈ Airfield
- ✠ Crashed German aircraft
- 🏭 BAC Factory
- Ⓞ ROC post
- ★ Starfish site

Scale: |＿|＿|＿|＿|＿| 5 Miles

Lulsgate
✠ Ju 88
24/7/41 ✈

• Winford

• Chew Magna

• Butcombe

Blagdon Lake

• Blagdon

★ Black Down
Charterhouse
★

• Compton Martin
West Harptree Ⓞ

• Clutton Ⓞ

Farrington Gurney

PAULTON

MIDSOMER • NORTON

✠ He 111
14/8/40
Yoxter

M E N D I P   H I L L S

• Priddy

• Chewton Mendip

S & D Lt Ry

Downside School

odney Stoke Ⓞ

• Green Ore

Gurney Slade

bury-sub-Mendip
• Easton

Pen Hill

✠ Do 17
16/10/40
Maesbury

• Oakhill

Shepton Beacon

• Wookey  WELLS
• Dinder  • Croscombe

SHEPTON MALLET Ⓞ

R Sheppey

• Coxley
✠ Ju 188
28/3/44

GWR

• Doulting ✈

GLASTONBURY Ⓞ

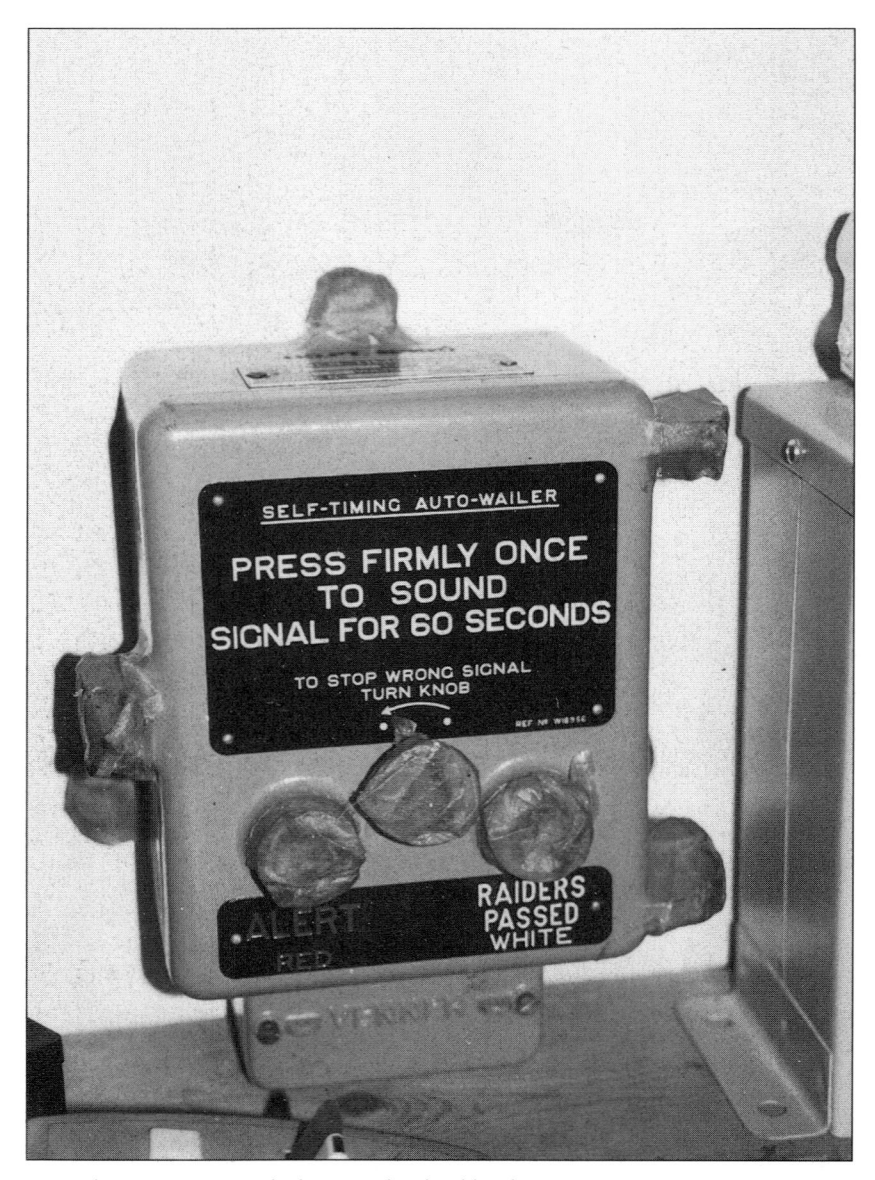

*A wailing siren warned that people should take cover as enemy bombers were approaching. A single-note siren sounded when the raiders had passed. Switches like this activated the Alert and All-Clear signals. (Author)*

*In a Battle of Britain fight over north Somerset, a flight of Spitfires commanded by air ace Stanford-Tuck shot down three Heinkel bombers. One crashed near Steep Holm, one at Puriton and this one on Mendip near Charterhouse where Home Guard captured the crew. (Imperial War Museum)*

At the time, Fred Villis was working in Springfields 'fat factory' at Charterhouse:

> Percy Walters, the school-teacher's husband, saw the aircraft come down. He rang the factory manager, Cecil Upton. Cecil was the Home Guard sergeant and he jumped into his Singer 10, picked up Percy and drove to the crashed plane. He captured the crew but wouldn't hand them over to the soldiers until he got a receipt for them.

The soldiers were from the Gloucestershire Regiment, stationed at Yoxter. George Tricks of Litton fills in some detail:

> My father Dennis Tricks was second-in-command of the Blagdon Home Guard. He and my brother Norman were the first people at the crash. Dr Peacock was called out in case anybody was injured. When they arrived at the plane, the pilot was trying to burn his papers and father stopped him.

More spectators arrived. Joyce Hooper went up on her bicycle from Cheddar:

> It was near Mrs Small's farm. The pilot was only about 17. All the farmers went for him with their pitchforks. They were going to march him off but the farmer's wife said, "He's not going anywhere till he's had a cup of tea." She had the kettle on this big black range with a whole tree burning in it.

When the news was phoned to Blagdon Police Station, PC Bailey went over to the Live and Let Live Inn. Joan Stokes lived there:

> My father, A.J. Stokes, was the landlord. He had a car for his work at Lulsgate and PC Bailey commandeered it to drive him to the crashed plane. I went as well. People were clambering all over it, when someone said the Germans had left a time-bomb in it. They couldn't get out fast enough. To make sure, they brought two of the Germans back to sit in the plane. I thought how young and frightened they were. Later, Oliver Lyons of Blagdon Lioness Coaches, ran trips for the villagers to see the plane.

Local people still produce souvenirs from the wreck. One has a flying helmet and pencil-case with the name Uffz A. Blumenthal.

That must have been the most intensively witnessed wartime episode on Mendip. By contrast, nobody saw another German bomber hit Maesbury Ring at midnight two months later, leaving the crew of four dead. Ted Parsons of Doulting discovered the crash. He writes:

> I left school at 14 during the summer of 1940. My first job was digging anti-invasion trenches. The foreman told me to go over the Ring to the ditch on the other side. Walking up by the wood

on the south side, I noticed the top of an ash tree was knocked off, and there was a great scar up the bank where a large patch of gorse had been ripped out.

Looking down into the saucer of the Ring, I saw an amazing sight. There was this jet black plane with the starboard wing torn off and the tail snapped off. I can vividly remember the tyre was made by Dunlop. Walking to the fuselage, I was stopped in my tracks for all round me I saw a number of bombs lying on the grass.

Talking about it later, a schoolmaster in the Observer Corps at Shepton Mallet told me this plane was hit by gunfire over Portland. It put its navigational lights on and flew northwards over Dorset and Somerset. The Observer Corps at Yeovil handed it on to the Shepton unit who contacted Radstock. The plane never reached them. An RAF guard told me that maps in the plane showed the target was Liverpool.

The RAF crash report says the bombs were fused and fitted with whistles so that they would shriek as they fell. It identifies the aircraft as a Dornier Do 17z, painted with a crest: 'Grey and black eagle attacking a map of England with claws and beak. England marked in red with white cliffs, sapphire sea, pale blue sky, all within a black and white shield.'

Henry Esain was among the first on the scene:

They were all dead. One was over by the Ring, he must have crawled there. Two were thrown out and one was still inside. They were not marked, although one had his leg broken. There was ammunition scattered all over the place. When I went to leave, somebody had already pinched the boots off the one by the Ring. Then the Welsh Guards arrived from Midsomer Norton to guard it.

Because the Germans were short of aircrew, the observer was a naval flier, so he became the only German naval officer killed in action in Somerset.

Roy Philips joined the stream of boys who turned out at every incident of the war. He cycled up to Maesbury from Wells Blue School to find the plane loaded on a trailer. Later he saw the dead airmen carried past his school on an RAF Queen Mary transporter, draped

*All four crew members died when their Dornier Do 17 bomber crashed into Maesbury hill-fort near Wells in October 1940. After a funeral with full military honours and Last Post, they were buried in Wells. Ever since, flowers have been laid on Heinrich Faupel's grave, even after re-interment in the central German war cemetery. (Henry Esain)*

with the German flag. The *Wells Journal* reported the burial, with full military honours. 'An Army chaplain officiated. All four coffins bore a brass plate with the name of the victim. After three volleys had been fired over the grave a bugler sounded the Last Post.' Henry Esain remembers:

> All four were buried in one grave and there were always flowers on it. After the war, they were re-buried in the German War Cemetery at Cannock Chase and in 1985 there were still fresh flowers under the name Heinrich Faupel. We heard that he had relations in Birmingham and they were responsible.

Nobody died and no schoolboys watched as a Junkers 88 made a perfect landing on Lulsgate airfield at 6 am on 24th July 1941. But Jim Morris of the Blackdown Starfish was there:

> I was working at Lulsgate when this German plane landed. The pilot got out and asked a workman something in German but no one understood him. Then a truck came roaring up with a squad of soldiers from the guard-room. The Germans pulled out their pistols but then dropped them and surrendered.

When questioned, they said they had mistaken the Bristol Channel for the English Channel and thought they were landing in France. What they did not know was that their *X-Verfahren* navigational radio beam had been 'bent' by the Meacon radio counter-measures station at Lympsham. The RAF gladly took over their aircraft, a new model of the Junkers 88, and attached it to a special unit of captured enemy aircraft, RAF 1426 (Enemy Aircraft) Flight, at Farnborough.

There was little left to collect from the German Junkers 88 bomber that crashed just before midnight on 27th March 1944 near Wedmore. Ken Banwell farmed there:

> For years there was a sock hanging over the beam in our cider cellar. This German plane had been hit and the crew had baled out but this chap's parachute didn't open. Bits of his clothes came off. They found his first boot where we do the cider, the second boot just up past Westlake's and one sock in our orchard. They found his body in a turf pit out on Tadham Moor and the plane in another turf pit.

Fleeing from night fighters, the crew had jettisoned their bombs on Weston and Highbridge, only to be brought down by anti-aircraft fire. The dead Luftwaffe flier, Uffz Heinrich Schink, is buried in Weston cemetery. The official record credits the hit to gunners at Weston. But some think this could have been the bomber brought down by Blackdown's secret Starfish Z-gunners.

Built in Bristol Aircraft's shadow factory at Banwell, the Beaufighter entered service as a night fighter in January 1941. It was immediately successful. Equipped with Airborne Interception radar and linked with Ground Controlled Interception radar, Beaufighters shot down two Heinkel He 111 bombers near Weston.

The first, on its way to bomb Avonmouth, crashed behind the Woolpack Inn at Hewish. Three crew were captured; two are buried in Weston Cemetery. The other, bound for Liverpool, came down between Langford and Wrington. Five crew parachuted down to be captured by Congresbury Home Guard, four near the Bell Inn, Congresbury and the fifth near the Star Inn on Rhodyate Hill.

Of all the local Home Guard engagements with enemy airmen, Charterhouse remains the only one to take place well away from a pub.

# 19
# YOXTER

Everyone from Somerset who has served in the Home Guard, Territorial Army or Cadets knows the name Yoxter. It's the army camp on top of Mendip where skylarks sing between snowstorms.

The oldest active military base on Mendip, Yoxter Camp straddles a ridge between Charterhouse and Priddy. Volunteers, Regulars and Territorials had already trained there, living under canvas in the

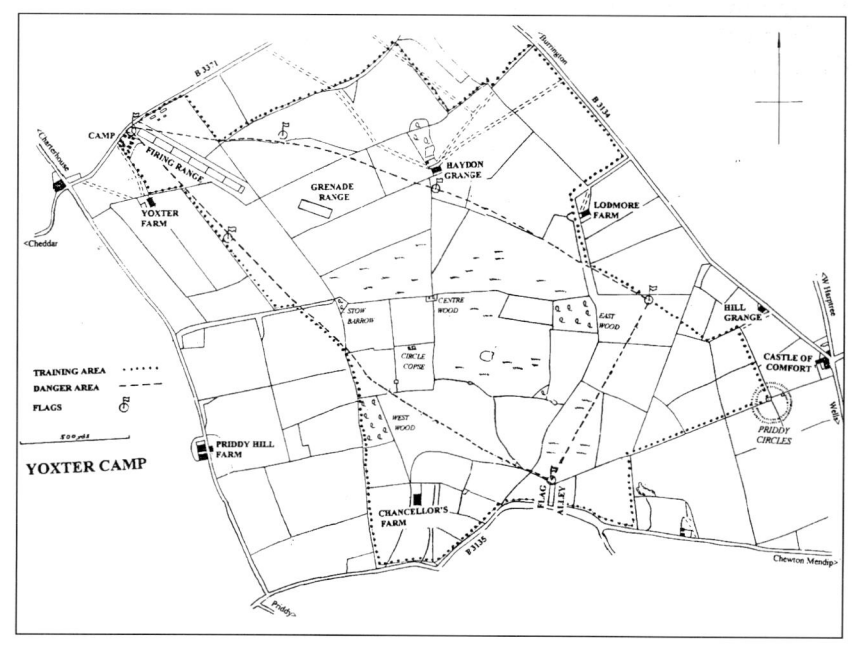

*Before D-Day, Yoxter training area was doubled by extending south-eastward onto Chewton Rabbit Warren. To the north-west, the range was sometimes extended to 1,000 yards, by closing the B3371 and firing across it.*

*In 1933 the army built a 600 yard firing range on the Mendips, with a training area of rough moorland, dotted with mine-workings and prickly with gorse. Ten years later, this tiny, ramshackle camp at Yoxter became the centre of a massive D-Day arsenal. (Author)*

villages, marching or riding up for manoeuvres. The name Camp Fields on the edge of Wells recalls one of their tented sites.

In 1933, the army came to stay, buying land for a permanent camp, a training area and a 600 yard rifle range, with 'shootover rights' across neighbouring fields. Local labourers built the rifle butts in 1934, cutting stone from a quarry 100 yards from their south side. They transported the stone and soil in tubs on a light rail-track. By 1938 Yoxter Camp still comprised just two huts, one for cooking, the other for officers. Everybody else lived in bell tents and washed in troughs under standpipes outside the cookhouse. Water came from a well at Stow Barrow. It was stored in large metal tanks on the edge of the wood and piped downhill to the camp.

The Second World War saw Yoxter expand to accommodate a series of units including REME, RAOC, RASC, the Green Howards, Glosters and other infantry regiments, as well as the Home Guard. The Guards Armoured Division school at Weston trained their tank crews there. They camped near the road just north of the range and drove on their

*Armed with his Lee-Enfield rifle, Fred Sawyer of Knowle, Bristol, guarded Yoxter Camp in September 1939. He shared a sandbagged Lewis gun emplacement with a Gloucestershire Regiment TA comrade who had brought his own dog to share guard duties. (Fred Sawyer)*

own track to a driver training area behind the butts.

After the war, Yoxter reverted to the Territorial Army. The North Somerset Yeomanry returned first, reputedly driving their tanks by road from Keynsham up Burrington Combe. The Somerset Light Infantry came back – and former Home Guards turned up again, this time as civilians in their own Rifle Club.

Years of intensive war-time use had added buildings, but left the camp badly run down. In 1964, the Royal Anglian Regiment sent working parties from Donniford to help with renovation. They promptly burnt nearly 200 mattresses. The old rusty black iron folding bedsteads went to Shepton Mallet military prison for repair. Sleeping quarters were fitted out with metal double-tier bunks and modern

*Boasting just two wooden huts when war broke out, Yoxter Camp accommodated thousands of soldiers from all arms over the six war years. (Author)*

mattresses. New dining furniture replaced traditional six-foot wooden folding tables and forms. Into the kitchen went bigger cooking ranges and a full scale of utensils. Within an amazing six weeks, Yoxter was back in use with new entrance gates, freshly painted buildings and neatly mown grass.

As mains services had still not reached that part of Mendip, coke and coal provided heating and cooking until about 1975, when Calor gas was installed. Water was pumped up from the mains Pump House at Velvet Bottom to a twin water tank tower near Top Range Gate. When direct mains water was finally laid on, the tower was removed as a week-end training exercise by Captain Blackford and his TA troop of Royal Engineers.

After an accident in 1957, a wartime grenade range behind the rifle butts was also removed. To cater for more .22 shooting, particularly by the Cadet Force, a Wessex tube range was constructed. This is a concrete drain-pipe with the firing-point at one end and illuminated targets at the other.

The training area continues in almost constant use by the Regular Army, Royal Marines, Territorials and Cadets for tactical and survival

*Gloucestershire Regiment Territorials from Bristol share one rifle and one dead rabbit. Fred Sawyer (centre) started his war at Yoxter Camp in 1939 and ended it in Bremen in 1945, rounding up war criminals. (Fred Sawyer)*

exercises. It is also used for rough-driving training, with old lead mine workings providing extra hazards. Thanks to its military isolation, a rich plant life survives in the area.

A long line of veteran soldiers has served Yoxter as Range Wardens, most in Somerset Light Infantry uniform. The first, in 1938, was ex-RSM 'Skinny' Rogers DCM. In 1946 ex-WOII Hector Holder moved in, assisted by another former CSM, Bob Stickles. In 1964, the longest serving Warden arrived, Captain E.R. 'Mick' Emery, who retired as major in 1985 with a BEM. Captain Jim Cooke followed and Sergeant-Major Ron Dawson took over in 1987.

# 20
# TURNING THE TABLES: D-DAY

Military camps massed on Mendip as the country prepared for the invasion of Europe. Bryan Green watched the first troops arrive in 1943:

> The Priory at Chewton Mendip was taken over by Military Police of the Guards Division. We had Irish, Scottish and Grenadiers, a complete mixture.
>
> The Vicar of Binegar, the Rev Warren, had nine children. The third boy went to Australia, farming. When the war came, he joined the Australian Army and was posted to England. His unit was being moved on the Somerset and Dorset railway line, the old Slow and Dirty. The train kept slowing down and starting again until it just stopped. He peered out of the window – to find himself looking down on Binegar Rectory where he grew up.

Eion Fraser saw more troops in Blagdon:

> Blagdon Court had 77 Brigade HQ and an RA Field Gun unit. 1st Division were in Coombe Lodge. After I went in the Army, the Americans came here ready for D-Day.

Terry Heal recalls the regiments stationed in Cheddar:

> The Pioneers were here, the Suffolks, the Green Howards and the King's Own. They were billeted in all the church halls, the Cliff Hotel and rooms down the Valley. One Officers' Mess was in Hill View, Cliff Street.

*Somerset became home to the American 9th Army as it prepared for D-Day. While billeted in the Crown Hotel, Wells, these smartly-uniformed GIs took the chance to visit the Cathedral. (John Sealy)*

Fred Villis adds that Hobswell House was another Officers' Mess:

> They left and the American MASH unit moved into the same billets. They put on a demonstration of their tented hospital. The Americans had a wonderful band that sounded just like Glenn Miller – they played for the village dances.

Ronald Denman, Vicar of Cheddar for nearly 30 years, reports:

> The Americans commandeered a five-room flat in the Vicarage as their HQ and immediately demanded seven telephone lines. The very next morning, a truck load of black GIs turned up to dig a trench in the road and the lines went in that afternoon.
> In 1982, a BT engineer arrived at last to remove the extra lines. As a GPO telephone apprentice 40 years earlier, he had heard the American colonel's original demand for the lines.

The Americans were part of the US 9th Army, massing in Somerset for the invasion. Cheddar's unit was the 24th Evacuation Hospital which parked its ambulances in a field over the road from Yoxter. An American Casualty Reception Centre was also based at Edgarley Hall in Glastonbury.

Frome housed a battalion of the 3rd Armored Division while various artillery units sampled the joys of Blagdon and Chewton. A special railway siding augmented Somerset side-roads to bring war material into a huge American depot near Maesbury Ring. Down in Weston, American guns and vehicles covered the golf course and Beach Lawns, while US airmen moved into RAF Locking. Amphibious vehicles plunged into the sea from Weston beach to test their waterproofing.

Like our own troops, the Americans worked up to battle readiness on improvised training areas. Wally King was one of the local boys who watched them firing their machine-carbines on Sandford Hill, Dolebury Warren, Rowberrow and Blackdown. Sadly, a memorial tablet in Churchill church records the death of two youngsters, Johnny Bartlett, an evacuee, and Dennis Brooks, killed by a live rifle grenade picked up with spent cartridge cases.

The top of Mendip became a vast arsenal. Blister huts, stacked with munitions and explosives, filled the fields. From the beginning of 1943, the whole area was declared a military exclusion zone. To get in, everyone, residents, schoolchildren and visitors had to have a permit.

## SUPREME HEADQUARTERS
## ALLIED EXPEDITIONARY FORCE

Soldiers, Sailors and Airmen of the Allied Expeditionary Force!

You are about to embark upon the Great Crusade, toward which we have striven these many months. The eyes of the world are upon you. The hopes and prayers of liberty-loving people everywhere march with you. In company with our brave Allies and brothers-in-arms on other Fronts, you will bring about the destruction of the German war machine, the elimination of Nazi tyranny over the oppressed peoples of Europe, and security for ourselves in a free world.

Your task will not be an easy one. Your enemy is well trained, well equipped and battle-hardened. He will fight savagely.

But this is the year 1944! Much has happened since the Nazi triumphs of 1940-41. The United Nations have inflicted upon the Germans great defeats, in open battle, man-to-man. Our air offensive has seriously reduced their strength in the air and their capacity to wage war on the ground. Our Home Fronts have given us an overwhelming superiority in weapons and munitions of war, and placed at our disposal great reserves of trained fighting men. The tide has turned! The free men of the world are marching together to Victory!

I have full confidence in your courage, devotion to duty and skill in battle. We will accept nothing less than full Victory!

Good Luck! And let us all beseech the blessing of Almighty God upon this great and noble undertaking.

*Dwight D. Eisenhower*

General Eisenhower issued this call-to-arms to the Allied troops embarking for Normandy on June 6th 1944 and to supporting forces. Hugh Tyson received his copy when serving with Bomber Command. (Hugh Tyson)

Those coming up Burrington passed a military petrol supply point. From there, vehicles were parked as far as the Miners' Arms, tight in, at right angles to the road, leaving a single central lane open. Camouflage netting concealed lines of tanks. Even the netting was local, made by Somerset women of the WVS who cut lengths of scrim and knotted it into the net.

Yoxter Camp became Headquarters of 21st Army Group's Vehicle Reserve Depot (21 VRD). Home Guard Jim Loxton was still serving in the Westbury-Easton platoon:

> On Sunday mornings the Home Guard were taken by Army lorries to Yoxter Camp, where we were formed into squads with a regular soldier in charge. Those who could drive had to move new vehicles which had been delivered and left in the fields. We parked them on the wide road verges in perfectly straight rows.
>
> Other men went to huge tents placed at the cross-roads. They had to prepare kits for the vehicles which were going to the various battlefields.

Army Cadets helped. Ralph Vowles was one who learned about lubricating vehicles while in week-end camp at Green Ore.

From mid-May 1944, Mendip began to empty as the invasion force moved into embarkation camps at Avonmouth and Portishead and on the English Channel. American military police, nick-named 'Snowdrops' from their white helmets, patrolled the roads on Harley Davidson and Indian motor-cycles or in jeeps. Bernard Parsons recalls, 'The tanks came down off Mendip and were loaded onto rail transporters at Cheddar Station.'

At 2359 hours on 5th June 1944, the Somerset skies filled with aircraft of the 101st US Airborne Division. By a nice twist of fate, they assembled above the line of advance that might once have brought German invaders north from Lyme Bay to Mendip. But these gliders and paratroops were flying south, to Normandy.

One glider lost its tow but came down safely on the moors. Its C47 tow-plane landed at Lulsgate and unloaded a jeep from the cargo bay. Ground-crew drove the jeep out to the glider, attached a looped cable to its tow-point and hoisted the cable over two poles. RAF fliers from Lulsgate watched the C47 take off, hook up the cable – and pull the glider off. The jeep returned to the airfield as another C47 landed to pick it up.

*Having trained Somerset's secret Auxiliary Units, Major Ian Fenwick was killed in a fierce SAS action behind the German lines at Chambon-la-Fôret. French villagers erected this memorial to him and two Frenchmen killed with him. (David Ingrams)*

*Many Auxiliary Units' instructors moved on into special service units for the invasion. From Cranmore, Sgts Ron Garnham and Freddy Chapman (first and third from left) went to Normandy as Glider Pilots. Lt Keith Salter, between them, landed on D-day with the top-secret Phantom intelligence unit. Sgt Tommy Webster, later Mayor of Wells, joined the Parachute Regiment. (Freddy Chapman)*

Among the first British troops into action were men of the original Scout teams who had trained the Auxiliary Units. They now turned their nefarious skills from defence to attack. Some had followed Gubbins from Coleshill into the Special Operations Executive (SOE), taking AU techniques to resistance movements throughout occupied Europe.

Others found a natural niche in the Special Air Service (SAS), expanding fast and training for a major role in the invasion. Ian Fenwick was one: he left Somerset to command D Squadron of 1st SAS, parachuting into the Forest of Orleans, far behind German lines. For two months his squadron operated there on the pattern he had taught his AU patrols, lying low by day and attacking by night. They cut communications, blew railway lines, attacked convoys and sent back daily reports on enemy movements. They also met the fate that the Germans had promised the Auxiliary Units: capture and death.

The SAS magazine *Mars and Minerva* quotes a tribute to Major Fenwick: 'The loss to his family, his friends, those who served with him and those many thousands who knew him through his art and inimitable humour, is irreparable.'

From the Cranmore Scout team, Sergeants Freddy Chapman and Ron Garnham went into the Glider Pilot Regiment, Sergeant Tommy Webster into the Parachute Regiment and Captain Keith Salter into Phantom. This aptly-named if little-known unit operated ahead of the battle in Normandy, reporting directly in cipher to Field Marshal Montgomery.

By the end of July 1944, Somerset was empty of soldiers, leaving the Home Guard with full responsibility for local defence.

D-Day also ended the German air threat to Somerset. In June 1944, all balloon barrages were moved to the south coast to counter Hitler's secret weapon, mass attacks with V1s, the first pilotless missiles. By the end of the year, Somerset's radio counter-measures stations and deception sites were closed, the AA gun batteries were made non-operational and Civil Defence was relaxed. Only the Royal Observer Corps remained to watch the Mendip skies.

As nobody doubted the German capacity for launching daring commando raids, the Auxiliary Unit role was redefined. Instead of silent sabotage, their mission now was to attack and destroy any raiding force. Sam Gilling was whisked away from the Sandford patrol:

> I was working on the War Ag and I just had to tell them I was called up. Nothing was said about where we were going or what we were doing. Of course we thought we were off to France.
>
> We got picked up and taken to Bishops Lydeard and fitted out overnight. We left next morning, about half past seven, and it wasn't till we got to Southampton that we knew where we were off to. We got on this boat and were taken over to the Isle of Wight, into Parkhurst Prison. There were ack-ack sites on the Isle of Wight and we were stationed on one of them.
>
> They thought the Germans might send paratroops over. The invasion communications went through the Isle of Wight. And PLUTO, the big oil-line. That's what we were guarding.
>
> We were all AUs, no Home Guards. We were on duty all night and used to go back in the camp and have breakfast, a good clean

up and a couple of hours sleep. We had to recce likely German landing points. Then we selected the best defensive positions to stop them. That went on until a fortnight after D-Day. Then we went home again. It was all very secret.

Sergeant Cecil Trego went with Sam. His wife remembers:

He never said what he was doing and I didn't know where he was going or where he had been until it gradually came out later. I thought he was going overseas.

Arthur Walton and Tom Bush of Midsomer Norton were there as well. Arthur says,

The day before D-Day, I went with three lorry loads of Bath area Auxiliary Units. We passed through the American army camps and got on a boat. We sailed to the Isle of Wight past their invasion ships.

Their contribution did not go unnoticed. On 4 July 1944, a letter, classified SECRET, from 38 (Welsh) Divisional Commander noted: 'I would like to express my appreciation of the work of the Auxiliaries (from 201, 202 and 203 Bns Home Guard) who have been sent to assist in the defence of the ISLE OF WIGHT during the past few weeks.'

At last, in November 1944, the country lowered its guard. At their final meetings, the Invasion Committees ordered the removal of road blocks and the restoration of sign-posts and place names.

Verdon Besley could volunteer for the army now, after serving in the Sandford Auxiliary Unit:

I joined at 18, in 1944. Just after D-Day I was transferred into the Queen's Royal Regiment in 7th Armoured because they'd had heavy losses. I went with them all the way to Berlin.

We captured a farm house but were counter-attacked by about 80 Germans and cut off. They got into the house and that's where my training with Molotov cocktails in the AU was useful. I threw a phosphorous grenade at them and that got them out.

Then we heard this voice outside, shouting in German. I fired at it through the window with my last bullet.

A man burst in, wearing British battledress. He spoke German

*Bryan Green remembers Lt Robert de Latour taking part in local events when stationed at Chewton Mendip. In 1944, Princess Elizabeth inspected 6th Airborne Division, speaking to Lt de Latour. A few days later, he was killed in Normandy. (Bryan Green)*

and was shouting at the Germans to surrender. I found later he was Captain Robert Maxwell. He got the Military Cross for rescuing us. It was the day after I was 19.

# 21
# FOR YOU, THE WAR IS OVER

Some enemy soldiers did reach the Mendips. They came under escort as prisoners-of-war.

A hut and the water-tower survive from Penleigh (No 107) Prisoner of War Camp on Wookey Road, Wells. Housing has replaced Stoberry Park (No 666) POW Camp in College Road, Wells, but the access road passes between stone pillars of the old camp gateway. A flat patch remains on one pillar from the original wartime sign. More prisoners were held at Maesbury.

*In College Road, Wells, a pair of stone pillars flank a side road. They were built as the gateway to Stoberry Park Prisoner of War Camp. (Author)*

*An Italian prisoner, stone-mason Gaetano Celestra, built this statue to Romulus and Remus in thanks for his kind treatment in captivity. The statue stands outside Wells beside the A39 road. (Author)*

Just outside Banwell, the Knightcott Industrial Estate once housed prisoners, with their guards billeted at Summer Lane camp-site. There were other big camps in Bridgwater, Backwell and Brockley.

The Italians arrived first, captured in African desert campaigns. On his way up to the Blackdown Decoy, AC2 Howard 'Eddie' Edwards used to pass them working round Burrington. Jim Morris, also stationed on the Decoy, remembers them on Tynings Farm. He says there was nothing to stop them running away, but they preferred farming to fighting. He recalls them carving little crucifixes from scrap material. Dennis Dyke says: "We had no Land Girls or POWs living in with us. we just went to the camp and asked for POWs when we needed them.'

Having de-commissioned all the Decoy sites, Robert King spent his last year of service, 1946, living in Cheddar but working at Lulsgate:

I had charge of the Italian prisoners. They looked after themselves in a Nissen hut at the extreme left hand side of the airfield in a little hollow. We used them for labour, like carrying coal. And they worked at the boneyard where the butchers' bones were rendered down to make glue. That was a mucky job.

A permanent reminder of the Italian presence stands beside the A39 road as it rises from Wells to Pen Hill. While repairing the old wall, an Italian stone mason, Gaetano Celestra, built a statue of Romulus and Remus as a tribute to the kindness he received while a prisoner.

That wasn't the only bit of local Italian stone-work. Tony Loxton tells what happened in Ebbor:

> The two stones that mark Deer Leap were in our ground. After father sold the farm, they had Eyeties up there that took away a lot of the walls. They smashed up one of these stones and Cyril Hodges told them, "You mustn't do that. That's history."
>
> So they went and found another great rock and put it there instead. They put the stones the same distance apart but they shifted them a bit over so they're not in the original place.

After the war, some Italians chose to settle here, Gaetano Celestra in Chewton Mendip, others in Wells and Weston.

German prisoners arrived after D-Day, captured in Normandy. Once checked politically, they were allowed to volunteer for farm work. Some were employed in Shipham Quarry. In Uphill, Germans rebuilt the stone revetting of the Great Rhyne when it collapsed after a storm. It's still in good condition. In 1946, German prisoners landed on Steep Holm to dismantle the military jetties.

It wasn't just Italians who stayed on. German prisoner Alec Eisentrager settled in Backwell and went on to play for years for Bristol City. Sam Gilling watched him play: 'He was a winger, quite small.'

Former leader of Dinder Auxiliary Unit, Horace Godfrey, says:

> I had a German POW on the farm. He was a sergeant and he had trained German troops in France to invade England in flat-bottomed boats. If they had come, I could have met him in action.

Arnold Arnold worked on various Mendip farms and in Mendip Hospital. Rather than be repatriated to East Germany, he stayed on in

*After British victories in Libya, thousands of Italian prisoners of war came to Somerset, where they worked voluntarily on farms. This hut and the water tower remain from Penleigh Camp, Wookey Road, Wells. (Author)*

Wells. His last job before retirement was as a security guard in a factory built on the site of his old POW camp at Penleigh.

Long after the war, Heinz Dietrich came to Mendip on holiday. He first came on 7th May 1941 as a Luftwaffe sergeant, captured by the Home Guard when his Heinkel bomber was shot down near Langford. This time, he brought his wife with him to show her where his war had ended.

# 22
# PEACE RETURNS TO MENDIP

In April 1945, the War Office publicly admitted that a British Resistance Organisation had existed since 1940. On 14th April General Sir Harold Franklyn wrote a letter about the Units to *The Times*. A week later, *The Times* ran a leader on the subject.

But excitement over the imminent end of the war naturally overshadowed a newpaper item about unknown civilian volunteers whose services had not been required. Jack Chew remembers:

> When it finished, we went down to Exeter. We marched up and saluted and the captain or whoever he was shook hands and thanked us and gave us this little badge. We never had a Defence Medal.
> If the Germans had come, we'd have done a bit of good.

And Dennis Dyke's wife comments, 'I'm glad this is all coming out, because people never knew what those men did.'

Meanwhile, Mendip marked victory with more bonfires than had signalled the Spanish Armada. Francis Stott celebrated in Westbury:

> They burnt an effigy of Hitler in the square. Everyone was dancing at night, all impromptu. People decorated tractors and farm trolleys and we went round Wells with them. They had a carnival.

While flames rose from the Sidcot School bonfire on their playing-field, some senior boy boarders slipped down to the Star Inn to buy cider. Next morning, at least two were sent home to cool their enthusiasm and face the ire of their parents.

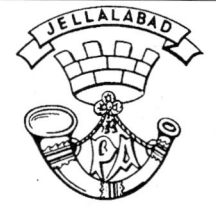

## 9TH SOMERSET HOME GUARD

# FAREWELL PARADE
*at*
# WELLS

### SUNDAY, DECEMBER 3, 1944

---

**MARCH PAST.**

**MESSAGE FROM THE COLONEL-IN-CHIEF, HIS MAJESTY THE KING.**

**HYMN.**

OFT in danger, oft in woe,
    Onward, Christians, onward go,
      Fight the fight, maintain the strife,
Strengthened with the Bread of Life.

Onward, Christians, onward go,
Join the war and face the foe;
Faint not! Much doth yet remain,
Dreary is the long campaign.

Shrink not, Christians! Will ye yield?
Will ye quit the painful field?
Will ye flee in danger's hour?
Know ye not your Captain's power?

Let your drooping hearts be glad;
March, in heavenly armour clad;
Fight, nor think the battle long;
Victory soon shall tune your song.

Let not sorrow dim your eye;
Soon shall every tear be dry;
Let not woe your course impede,
Great your strength, if great your need.

Onward then to battle move;
More than conquerors ye shall prove;
Though opposed by many a foe,
Christian soldiers, onward go. Amen.

**PRAYERS.**

**For the King and his peoples:**

O MOST MIGHTY and merciful Father, the sure stronghold of them that trust in Thee, We beseech Thee to arm with sound counsel and stern resolve our Sovereign Lord, King George, his Ministers, his Forces and his peoples, contending as one for the liberties of all; that, in strong assurance of Thy heavenly help, they may wrest victory out of danger, and restore to all nations the kindly blessings of peace; for Thy dear Son's sake, Jesus Christ our Lord. Amen.

*After four years on duty, the Home Guard stood down in December 1944 as the Allied armies rolled into Germany. In Wells, as all over the country, a final church parade and march-past marked the end of this citizen's army. (Mrs M Lees)*

Lt Peter Wise of Bristol welcomed British soldiers returning from captivity in German POW camps:

> Shortly after VE Day, thousands of our POWs were coming back to the UK. They housed some of them in a camp on the Mendips prior to being demobbed. As the Home Guard catering officer, I recruited a civilian chef from Horts Restaurant to feed them.
>
> The camp was staffed with Italian POWs and British "conchies", who were an awful nuisance. Most days one would come to the office and say he was refusing to take any further orders, and he was then taken away by the Military Police. We used to let the Italians go out to pick wild mushrooms.
>
> The repats were all officers, most of whom were taken at Arnhem. I well remember three captains, Jock Hannigan, a Scots Guard WO who was commissioned in the field – he later became a prison officer at Dartmoor – and John Murray, and Woods who became a vet in Sussex.
>
> One night they climbed on top of the 15 cwt truck and drove round the camp dropping plastic grenades down the stove pipes. It only lasted a few weeks, but was great fun.

*Banwell ran its own village fire brigade, drawn up here at the end of the war in front of their Coventry Climax pump towed by a Vauxhall tender. (Roy Rice Collection)*

# WINSCOMBE
## *Victory*
# CARNIVAL

IN AID OF THE SOMERSET COUNTY
BRITISH LEGION WAR MEMORIAL HOME

### JUNE 1st to 9th, 1946

THE BRITISH LEGION WAR MEMORIAL HOME
AT WESTON-SUPER-MARE

**SOUVENIR PROGRAMME**

*Winscombe's Victory Carnival was typical of many throughout Somerset. (Mrs Pam May)*

*The Services, Home Guard and local volunteer organisations joined together in Victory Parades when the war in Europe ended in May 1945. Here, Red Cross nurses in Wells marched past blocks of brick air-raid shelters. (John Sealy)*

Five years after his appointment as the Admiralty's oldest coastguard, Steep Holm warden Harry Cox, put on his uniform to light a VJ-Day bonfire on Brean Down, part of a fiery pattern along both coasts of the Bristol Channel.

An American contingent returned to St Cuthbert's church, Wells, to present and dedicate a Colour in memory of their forces who had been stationed in the area. And as local men and women came home from wartime service, their town or village welcomed them with more carnivals and gifts. Chew Magna presented each one with a certificate. The names of those who did not return were added to the war memorials that already listed the dead of the First World War.

There are, sadly, many of these. The oldest Mendip memorial, in Burrington church, dates back to the Napoleonic Wars. Below the 1918 memorial window inside the church, First World War names are inscribed on a brass plate.

*After the victory parades came the parties. Draycott laid out an unrationed feast in the village hall. (John Sealy)*

Inside Compton Bishop's St Andrew's church, a framed Roll of Honour 1914–1918 lists the men who served, naming seven as Fallen in Battle. Those seven names, and three from the second war, are carved on an oak board, flanked by the flags of St Andrew and St George.

Cheddar's dead of 1914–1918 are listed on a wooden memorial inside St Andrew's church and again on a stone pillar in the churchyard. Two War Graves Commission headstones stand separately in the cemetery. Away from the church, names from both wars appear on a tall stone cross.

A simple memorial on Shipham Square and a plaque in St Leonard's church remember five Second World War dead from the village.

A roadside plaque at Sandford gives no names, simply stating '1914–1918, 1939–1945'. Sandford is part of Winscombe Parish, where names of the dead from both wars are carved on a stone cross looking north from the top of Winscombe's sloping churchyard. In the church porch, a wooden board lists 22 names on a 1914–1918 Roll of Honour. A Roll of Service acknowledges all who served in that war, including Brev Lt Col Yatman DSO whose name reappeared in the second war in command of Axbridge Home Guard.

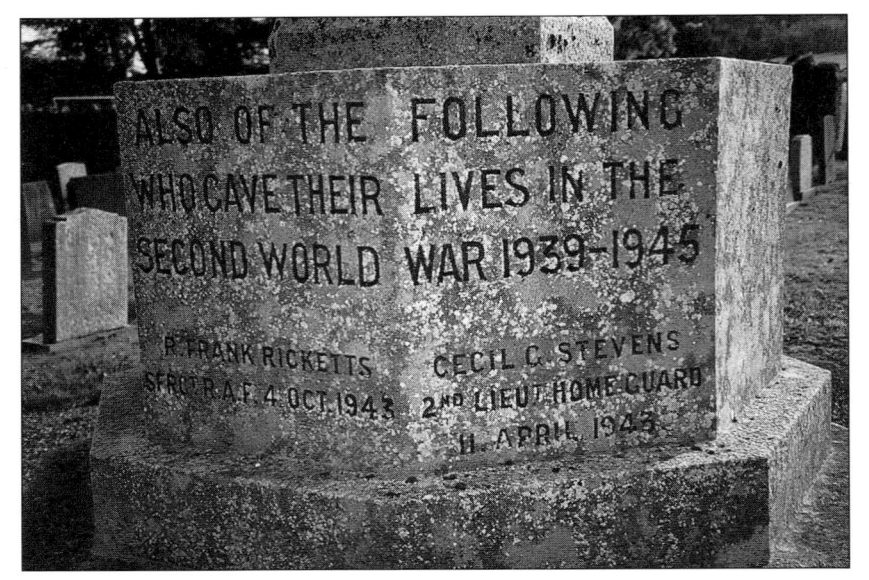

*Chewton Mendip's war memorial. (Author)*

Easton seems to have been one of about 30 villages in the country with no war memorial as all their men returned safely from the wars. In the Somerset volume of King's England, Arthur Mee terms them 'Thankful Villages'.

It was 40 years before a memorial was built to mark the crash of the Arnhem glider at Farrington Gurney. The dead are buried in the War Graves section of Weston cemetery alongside fallen German fliers.

Where the Mendips reach the sea at Uphill, the old church of St Nicholas stands above a sheer quarry face. On 11th March 1920, a 13-year-old choirboy, Charlie Howe, walked out of the church carrying the processional cross at the dedication of Uphill's new war memorial. Music was a problem, there being only a small harmonium in the old church. But among the names on the memorial was Sgt Stanley Smith whose brother-in-law, Charlie Baker, was the leading cornet player with Mogg's Band, well known around Weston.

Telling the story 70 years later, Charles Howe was still moved by his memory of the soaring notes of Charlie Baker's cornet as the villagers sang the words, 'Hark the sound of holy voices, chanting in the crystal sea.' Far below the church, the sun shone on Weston Bay and the River Axe, where boats were coming in on the tide.

After the second war, twelve names were added. Among them, unusually, were six Home Guards killed by enemy action in air-raids while serving in the village platoon. As Weston's senior Ambulance officer, Charles Howe received them all into the mortuary. Two were brothers, aged 16 and 14, not much older than choirboy Charlie Howe had been when the memorial was consecrated.

# Appendix A
# A Home Guard War Book

*Home Guard jokes conceal a professional seriousness of military purpose. Former Home Guard lieutenant Bryan Green found these faded and flimsy typed sheets among forgotten papers. They cover the defence of one Mendip cross-roads. Similar plans covered the entire country.*

WAR BOOK – MENDIP COMPANY

INFORMATION
1. (a) Neighbouring Units:-
    NE        Farrington Gurney Platoon
    N & NW  Litton Platoon at Litton
                     at E Harptree
    W         Cheddar Platoon
    SW       Cheddar Valley Coy
    S         Wells Coy Strength 303 (total)
               DL Sadler St Strength 188 MR 988668
               Tor Street Strength 130 MR 992670
               Coy Battle HQ Sadler Street
               Communication 4 Chamberlain St. Tel. Wells 12
    E         Ashwick Coy Strength 412
               DL Lynch House & Nettlebridge
               MR 072698 & 092698

Posts in ring round CHQ at Emborough, Chilcompton, Stratton & Holcombe.

  (b) Strength of Fighting Base at Green Ore Farm – Map Ref Sheet 111 017710.
       7 Officers
       132 Men
       57 Rifles
       17 E.Y.
       45 Sten
       1 Medium B.M.G.
       3 B.A. Rifles
       3 D.P. Lewis

4 Northovers
3 Spigots

INTENTION

To deny the enemy use of road, Wells-Bristol, and Burnt Wood to Miners' Arms, in vicinity of Cross Roads 017710.

*Method* (a) General

Two Battle Platoons, comprising 3 Sections, with Parapatrol, Recce Patrols, will engage Paratroops or such enemy elements in the vicinity – to harass and destroy.

C.H.Q. will be at Green Ore Farm. Phone Contact C. Mendip 86.

Chewton Hill Platoon in reserve, for reinforcement and defence.

*Phase 1*

On Action Stations:

Chewton Hill Platoon assemble at Chewton Reading Room

Priddy Platoon assemble at Priddy Green

Horrington Platoon assemble at Old Chapel Horrington

All immediately proceed to CHQ Green Ore where Green Ore Platoon will muster.

O.P. at Nedge Hill, to be manned by Chewton Hill Platoon.

*Phase 2*

Enemy reported in vicinity – Parapatrols and Recce Patrol to make contact.

*Phase 3*

On contacting the enemy, if in force, DR attached to Parapatrol will report and the fighting Patrol will move, by lorry, in support.

If far superior force, Reserves to be called out, and, if necessary, to fight a harassing and delaying action.

*Phase 4*

In event of enemy evading action, and deploying to road, Reserve at Base will contact and engage.

BATTLE AREA

Priddy, Horrington, Chewton Mendip Area.

(a) The Company will be at Green Ore Farm, with Battle Qtrs ready for action.

(b) The Platoon in reserve will be responsible for the defence of the Base and will be reinforced by Battle Qtrs until called out.

*Task.* To cover approaches to Base and deny use of roads.

*Method*
Location. Corner of bull house, facing Wells.
> Squad Cmdr. BMG. 3 men. 2 riflemen.
> Task: Cover road and approaches from South.

Location. Lambing shed, facing NW.
> Squad Cmdr. 2 men. LMG. 6 rifles, lambing pen.
> Task: Cover approaches from E.

Static. Cottage facing NE.
> 1 L/c. LMG. 2 men.
> Task: Covering main Bristol Road and Crossroad.

Wood NW of Base.
> Squad Cmdr. 5 Sten. Patrol of 8 Riflemen.
> Task: Deny enemy cover of wood.

Static. 2 Spigots. Paddock and Buildings.
> Squad Cmdr. 3 Spigots. 11 men. (1 Spigot and 5 men mobile).
> Task: To destroy AFVs using road in support of all round defence.

DEFENCE WORK
Dig gun pit for BMG and slit and communication trenches, and remove wall on East for field of fire. Loophole in Lambing Shed and wall of pen.
Cottage to be loopholed – window reinforced – glass removed – window wired.
Perimeter of base to be wired if available.

CIVIL DEFENCE
The Chewton Mendip Civil Defence will provide.
EA James, Chairman. Phone Chewton Mendip 84.
Men, tools, shovels, picks, axes.
Task. As per Defence work.

FOOD
Each man will bring food for 48 hrs.
Food control arrangement with C. Mendip Co-op Society after 24 hrs.
Meat – Payne, The Ford, C. Mendip.
Bread – St John, Bathway, C. Mendip.

## WATER
A miniumum of 10,000 galls of water available on premises – alternative supply at garage (30 yds).
Lighting: Hurricane Lamps.
Fire Precautions: Stirrup Pump in Base – water from pond.

## AMMUNITION
300 per man.
Battle Pn   60 per man. 500 DP Lewis, Sten 100, Grenades 36
Reserve     60 per man. 500 DP Lewis, Sten 100, Grenades 36
Mobile Spigot 20.
Lorries conveying fighting patrol – 1200 (reserve).
Reserves 300          300 MG        Sten      Grenades

## MEDICAL
First Aid Post at CHQ under Mr Oatley, St John Ambulance.

## EVACUATION
Occupants of premises remain until Action is imminent.

## TRANSPORT
Each Battle Pln will have a lorry detailed, with one in reserve.
DRs 1 each to accompany Parapatrols.
      2 at CHQ.

## PETROL
50 galls each to be held in reserve until Filling Station (30 yds) is exhausted.

## E.L.
To be used on Action Stations.

## ANTI-GAS
Rooms at rear of premises will be used.
Respirators carried after Action Stations.
Warning signal – Rattles.
Report to Base first use of Gas.
Base will report BHQ immediately.

INTERCOMMUNICATION
By phone, if working, to neighbouring Units – otherwise DRs and bicycles.

PATROLS
Observation by Defence Units by day – 3 Squads comprising 1 NCO, 7 men to patrol by night, to patrol perimeter of Base, making contact at specified points.

# Appendix B
# Mendip Auxiliary Units

*There being few public records, the following lists have been compiled largely from the memories of men who served in the Auxiliary Units.*

COMMAND STRUCTURE

1. Auxiliary Unit activities and training were controlled nationally from Coleshill House, c/o GPO Highworth, nr Swindon, Wilts. Commanders: Col Colin Gubbins 1940; Col C.R. 'Bill' Major 1940; Col Lord Glanusk 1942; Col Frank W.R. Douglas RA 30 Nov 1944. Staff included Col G.H. Beyts, Capt Lord Delamere, Capt Neale, Maj N.V. Oxenden MC, Royal Northumberland Fusiliers. Instructors came from Guards regiments and the Lovat Scouts.

2. In 1944 Maj W.W. Harston, Dorsets, commanded Auxiliary Units, SW Region, from 21 East Street, Ashburton, Devon (tel. Ashburton 371).

3. Somerset Auxiliary Units comprised an Operational Section under an Intelligence Officer (IO) who was an Army captain with his HQ at 68 Monmouth Street, Bridgwater. This HQ later moved to The Lodge, Bishop's Lydeard, near Taunton (tel. Bishop's Lydeard 200). Stores were held at Bishop's Lydeard.
The first IO, Capt Ian Fenwick KRRC, set up the Somerset network. He was followed by Capt L. Strangman RAOC, Capt John Holberton, Capt C.M.P. Coxwell-Rogers MC, Glosters, and Capt J.M. Martin.
Somerset was run as two areas, each under a Scout Officer with a Scout Section of 14 men to instruct the Auxiliary Units and help build their Operational Bases.

4. Lt V.A. Gough, Somerset LI, was Scout Officer for South and West Somerset, based at Goathurst near Bridgwater.

5. The Scout Section for North and East Somerset was based in the stables of Southill House, Cranmore, Shepton Mallet.
Lt John A. McCue, Wiltshire Regt, was its first Scout Officer, with a

team from the Welch Regiment, including Sgts Freddy Chapman, Ron Garnham, Tommy Webster, Ptes Gracey, Griffiths, Kitts, Rootes and RASC Driver Townley. Lt Keith W. Salter, Somerset LI, took over in 1941 and 1942.

On invasion, this Scout Section was to join the Bruton patrol at Creech Hill OB.

6. Each Auxiliary Unit was led by a Patrol Leader, usually a sergeant.

7. Individual Units later came under Group Commanders, usually captains. Some of these had Assistant Group Commanders, usually lieutenants. They distributed ammunition and stores to their Units.

## MENDIP GROUP COMMANDERS

Axbridge: Capt H. Radford, Wine Merchant, Town Square, Axbridge; Lt Pike, Willets, millers of Sandford.
Midsomer Norton: Capt Malcolm T. Shackell, Swainswick farmer.
Pensford: Lt Charles William Trussler, later captain, Hunstrete gamekeeper.
Wells: Lt EA Harrison, master at Wells Blue School

Other Somerset Group commanders: Bath: Capt L.A. Aves, Capt J.G. Spearman, Lt W.R. Hornett; Bruton: Capt Richard Hunt, farmer; Blue Anchor: Sgt F.M. Hepper; Bridgwater: Capt T.A. Baird; Taunton: Lt J.S. Bent; Washford: Capt B.I. Chambers; Watchet: 2/Lt T.H. Down; Yeovil: Lt E.E.G. Loder.

## MENDIP AUXILIARY UNITS

*In Somerset, 300 men served in 44 Units, using 50 bases. The following Units came under the command of Cranmore. Most were based on or around Mendip.*

BALTONSBOROUGH
Sgt Edwin Gould, World War 1 soldier, village newsagent.

Bill Dunkerton, farmer's son.
Hugh Champion, farmer, (also World War 1) replaced Bill Dunkerton.

## BATH
Capt L.A. Aves, followed by Capt J.G. Spearman, commanded five Admiralty Patrols with Bases at Bathampton, Landridge, Kelston House, Lansdown, Milson Street, Prior Park, Southstoke.
Capt Malcolm T. Shackell and Lt W.R. Hornett commanded three Town Patrols.

## BLAGDON
Base: Foxes Hole, Burrington Combe.
Sgt Bob Brock, Blagdon, worked for Electricity Board.
Eion Fraser, Blagdon, BAC worker, joined army.
Wilfie Light, son of Blagdon post office manager.
Ron Saint, ran local dance band.
Sammy Sampson left the Specials to join AU, village newsagent and barber.
Sid Shepston, Blagdon smallholder.
Bill Wilson, lived near Bob Brock.

## BRUTON
Bases: Bramble Ditch and Creech Hill.
Capt Richard Hunt, Drop In Lane Farm.
Archie John Roberts, farm worker.
All others from Bruton, including a farmer, a teacher and a farmer's merchant.

## BUTLEIGH
Base: on Granville estate.
Sgt Leonard B. Haimes
Frederick Ball.
Robert C. Burrough.
W. Harding (former member).
Stanley J. Higgins.
Henry G. Marsh.
H. Whitehead (former member).

CHEDDAR
Base: Great Oones Hole, Cheddar Gorge.
Sgt Arthur H. Pavey, general builder/decorator in Cliff Street, Cheddar.
Jack Chew, employed at Passey & Porter's garage, Winscombe. After the war, he and John Tunstall ran a garage off North Street, Cheddar.
Kenneth P.V. Channon, Axbridge.
John Hewlett, farmer.
Philip L. Leigh, youngest of three brothers, all market gardeners with parents. Phil later drove Cheddar hearse. After war, auxiliary fireman.
Bryan A. Painter.
Arthur G. Parsons of Cheddar, War Agricultural Board tractor driver, served May 1940 to 31 December 1944.
John Tunstall of Cheddar.
Another man, not local, lodging in Cheddar.

CHEW MAGNA
No firm information.

COMPTON BISHOP
Base: Denny's Hole.
Arthur Brinson, lived near Denny's Hole.
Lewis Croker, First World War soldier, postman, lived between Compton Bishop and Cross.
Christopher Ellis, Cross.
Henry Charles Lattimer, Cross.
Frank Lee, Bourton Farm, born Compton Bishop.
Sidney J. Martin, Axbridge.
William T. Vowells, Compton Bishop. Ran Willetts Corn Store in Winscombe after the war.

DINDER
Bases: Dulcote Hill and Lyatt Wood.
Sgt Fred J. Shatwell of St Andrews St, Wells (evacuee schoolmaster from London in Blue School).
Horace P. Godfrey i/c patrol, poultry farmer, North Wootton.
Charlie H. Clark of Keward; worked at Dinder.
Sidney F. Down, farmer in Dinder.

Dennis R. Dyke, farmer in Dinder. Joined later.
Percy H. Hull, son of postmistress in Dinder; worked on Somerville Estate.
Clifford R. Taylor of Poulsam, Coxley Wick (youngest at 21).

EBBOR
Bases: Ebbor Gorge and Cook's Hill Hole.
2/Lt P. Jack Lunnon i/c patrol, worked at F.G. Clements water company (dowsing and drilling), Easton.
Charles A. 'Bertie' Barnes, landlord Burcott Inn, footballer, printer at Clares.
'Biddy' Irving H. Farley – dental mechanic.
Jack Farley, brother of Irving.
Jonathan Harrison, son of Lt Harrison.
Harold E. Lane, Wells, printer at Pettigrews.
C.W. Tony Loxton. Farmed at Easton.
Wilf L. Paul, journalist on *Wells Journal*.
G. Tyley, Westbury-sub-Mendip.

LONGLEAT HOUSE
Base: The Knoll.
Sgt Bill Buckett, gamekeeper.
Francis and brother Bert Crossman.
Kenneth W.C. Fricker.
3 others.
Unit inspected by Col Lord Glanusk and Col Beyts from Coleshill.

MIDSOMER NORTON
Base: Old Mills.
Sgt Ken Hartry from Street.
Cpl Charlie Lanning from Pickett Mead.
Len Bailey, worked for Shepherds sawmill in Chilcompton.
Tom Bush.
Dennis A. Chard, Temple Inn, Temple Cloud.
Arthur Parsons.
Mervyn Powney, colliery blacksmith.
Arthur Walton, miner, explosives handler.
Two from Standard Check Co.

PENSFORD
Base: Lords Wood.
Lt, later Capt, Charles William Trussler, estate gamekeeper for Mr Hugh Langbourne Popham.
Henry C.G. Bailey, lorry driver from Compton Dando.
Lewis G. Crow, Chelwood.
Harding, miner from Pensford.
Jim Hooper, builder, Bristol.
Vic Hooper, Jim's brother, two years younger.
Arthur J. Lovell, Temple Cloud.
Edwin C. Thomas, builder, Keynsham.
A farmer from Ston Easton.
A builder from Keynsham.

SANDFORD
Base: Sandford Levvy.
Lt Cliff H.G. Coombs, Weston, owned shoe businesses in Taunton and Regent Street, Weston, making footwear for RAF: therefore reserved occupation.
Cpl Ken V. Watts, Shipham, labourer at Winterhead Hill Farm.
Cliff Banner, had market garden with brother on the A38.
Verdon Besley, Hill Farm, Winscombe, aged 16, joined later before going into army.
Roy Clark, hairdresser, Upper Bristol Road, Weston.
Sam Gilling, Burrington, worked on land for War Agricultural Committee.
Fred Hayter, insurance man.
Arthur Lovell, quarry worker from Shipham.
Edward Pearce, from near Exeter, directed to work in Banwell or Oldmixon BAC.
Cecil (Fred) Trego of Worle – later sergeant. Call-up deferred because of AU membership – later in RAOC.
Ken Weymouth, Holland Street, Weston. Worked at David Greig. Army call-up cancelled as he was in AU.
A former army officer who lived near Sidcot School.

SHEPTON MALLET
Base: Shepton Beacon.
No firm information.

## STOKE LANE
No firm information.

## WEDMORE
Bases: Oldwood and Churchill.
Explosives store in derelict cottage near Old Wood. Look-out post, watching the Axe.
Sgt Arthur Duckett, carpenter, Billings Hill.
Cpl Francis S. Banwell, Old Wood Farm, Sand, Wedmore.
Ernest Bethell.
Charles Binning, local baker.
Stan Clarke, farmed at Theale.
Austin Higgs, farmed at Theale.
John Morgan, Electricity Board engineer.
Albert G. Tucker.
Three of these Wedmore Unit surnames were already engraved on the World War I memorial at Theale: W. Higgs SLI, A.S. Higgs RWR, C. Bethell WSY, E. Tucker MGC.

## WELLS
Bases: Chewton Mendip and Green Ore.
Sgt Percy W.J. Reid, Ash Lane, Wells. Textile manager in Clare's brush factory, Wells.
Reg Barber, Westbury – joined later.
Hughie Bisgrove – joined later.
F. John Sealy, farmer, Westbury-sub-Mendip.
Francis Stott, farmer, Westbury-sub-Mendip.
*Left before stand-down*:
A. Battle.
John E.G. Bazley, Wells (replaced Bryan Green), railwayman.
Eric H. Brown, Wells, school-teacher evacuated from London.
Charlie Ford, Waldegrave estate worker.
H.E. Bryan Green, farmer, Chewton Mendip. Rejoined Home Guard.
Denis S.S. Nicholson, veterinary surgeon, Wells.
'Coffee' Parfitt, farm-worker, Shepton Mallet.
Reginald C. Rose, milk roundsman. Joined army.
Henry Joseph (Harry) Western, Sheldon's engineering.

WRINGTON
Base: Kings Wood.
Sgt W.H. (Bill) Porter, estate forestry worker in Cleeve Woods.
Mr Attwell, Congresbury.
Frank E. Bennett, Redhill.
Steve Fairhurst.
William A.C. Price, the local undertaker.

WELLS GROUP
These members of the Wells Group met at the Bekynton Cafe, Wells on Friday 15th December 1945 for a reunion meal. The names are as listed for the reunion.
Lt E.A. Harrison OC
2/Lt P.J. Lunnon*, W.L. Paul*, C.A. Barnes, I.H. Farley*, H.E. Lane*, J. Harrison, C.W. Loxton; former members M.G. Scott, G. Tyley
Sgt P.W.J. Reid*, E.J. Sealy, F. Stott, H. Bisgrove, Reg Barber; former members G.W.F. Hawes, A. Battle, D.S.S. Nicholson, H.E.B. Green, C. Ford, R.C. Rose, E. Brown, H. Western, J.E.G. Bazley, F.E. Bennett
Sgt F.J. Shatwell* (Blue School master), P.H. Hull*, S. Down*, C.R. Taylor, C.H. Clark*, H.P. Godfrey*, D.R. Dyke; Sgt L.B. Haines†, R. Burrough†, F. Ball†, G. Marsh, S.J. Higgins; former members, H. Whitehead, W. Harding.

---

\* served in AU since formation
† served in patrols (cells) since formation

# Appendix C
# Auxiliary Unit Operational Patrols

*Coleshill wasted no words in its definition of what was expected of an AU patrol:*

Patrols will never go out aimlessly but always as a result of something that has been observed. Generally speaking, the patrol will be undertaken in darkness or fog (but always on known ground) as a result of daylight observation.

No night can be missed. There MUST be a target every night.

Your task is either to destroy by incendiarism, demolition or ambush, enemy stores, aeroplanes and vehicles, or to overpower isolated sentries, stragglers, HQ DRs. The weapons you are given are for self protection, for destruction of stores etc by burning and demolition, and for overpowering of *individual* men. You must therefore lie low if encountered by an enemy patrol, and never accept battle unless the odds are overwhelmingly in your favour. Whilst en route to your task, do not return the enemy's fire. He thus will remain in doubt, and will either come nearer to investigate or go on his way.

On arrival at the last R.V. or springboard, close observation of the enemy will always be necessary before 'going in' to the target. The Patrol Leader and possibly one or two others will then go ahead – the rest remaining hidden – to look out for obstacles and watch the movements and reliefs of sentries.

Plenty of time must be taken over this as the execution of the final plan, the success or failure of the patrol and the lives of all concerned are dependent on accurate observation and deduction of enemy sentries' dispositions.

From here the patrol will split up and go to its appointed tasks. Remember that we want to be back in bed before the explosion occurs – the time pencil is therefore our chief ally. In all your movements proceed deliberately, as haste merely leads to excitement and confusion.

A simple plan is therefore the keynote to success. Each member of the patrol must clearly know the task in hand and his own particular role *before he leaves the Operational Base*.

Never leave a wounded comrade, who should be taken to a friend's house, and never to the Operational Base.

*****

The duration of an invasion of this country must be limited to about three weeks at the outside. We therefore have only from 10 to 20 nights in which we can operate; and to make ourselves felt, we must waste no time. A target must be attacked every night, and in order to do this it may be necessary for every man in the patrol to be an observer or scout by day.

A patrol cannot operate without a definite target. The finding of a reasonable one is, therefore, its primary task.

The area officially allocated to each patrol is a circle of $2\frac{1}{2}$ miles radius, but many are confident of being able to cover four times this area, which would mean operating sometimes five miles from their base.

A patrol would only be aware of a target so far away if the observer had been there to find it.

This is the order of priority of the targets that we hope to find:
1. Important military HQs.
2. Landing Grounds.
3. Dumps.
4. Vehicles.

By 'attacking an HQ' we do not intend that five men should make a commando raid upon it and attempt to wipe out personnel who may number 150, but rather that it should be rendered inoperative as an HQ. This can be done by destroying wireless transmitting sets, sabotaging telephone wires and ambushing DRs.

Opportunity may occur to ambush a flagged staff car, but it must be remembered that armoured cars will probably be used.

If the fighting is fluid, such targets may be gone within a day or two, and in any case must be considered the exception rather than the rule.

Broadly speaking therefore, our patrols will be divided into two categories:
(i) those which have been formed near landing grounds (LG) with

the express purpose of raiding them; and

(ii) those whose primary role will be the destruction of dumps.

It is no longer considered likely that Hitler will be content to count upon his aircraft for one single journey and crash-land them in fields, if he can capture an LG.

He will probably attempt to organize ferry services to evacuate his wounded and bring in more and more men and stores. Every plane wrecked, therefore, means 35 wounded not evacuated and 35 fully equipped men unable to arrive.

Those patrols who have their bases near airfields have the greatest opportunities of all. Their observers have an easy task, since it is only necessary to locate the dispersal areas. The patrol can penetrate the perimeter and find their targets with comparative ease, and can achieve the maximum of results with the minimum of explosive.

The defence will probably be in the form of fixed posts at intervals and patrols with dogs. Wind direction should therefore be studied, and training should include experiments with 'Renardine', turpentine or T.C.P. on the hands, knees and feet.

It may be considered necessary, if charges are being placed on the tails of dispersed aircraft, to arrange for them to go off within as short a space of time as possible, by breaking all the pencils together, say, at the springboard or when the first charge is laid. Safety pins are, of course, withdrawn only at the last moment. If two or three planes blow up at intervals, the others will probably be examined by the crews in time to save them.

Dumps are likely to be small and numerous, to localise destruction by shellfire or bombing. Below a certain size they would not justify the attention of the R.A.F but would provide very useful work for us.

They cannot be located at random but must be (a) on a firm track or road, first to avoid the bogging of laden vehicles, and secondly to avoid making new tracks that can be seen from the air, and (b) under trees, so that they are screened from air reconnaissance. A firm track through a wood is ideal, but the difficulty of finding a known target in a dark wood is familiar to all auxiliers from many exercises; and to find dumps, guns or vehicles that are only known to be somewhere in that wood is incomparably harder, especially if the wood is a large one. It is, therefore, essential that the observer should not only know the exact spot where they will be found, but should be able to describe it accurately to the rest of the patrol.

As the number of possible dump-sites in a given piece of country is

limited, a patrol should get a 1/25000 map of its area and, from the combined local knowledge of its members, should mark on it in colours:
  (i) all stretches of road that can be used as dumps, and
  (ii) the points from which they can be seen.

Next, a circuit or series of circuits should be planned, by which a scout can visit a chain of these points and report to his P.L. which, if any, of the roads covered by his beat are in use as dumps. From the reports the P.L. can choose his 'Target for Tonight'.

(i) In districts where the war is intense and enemy troops thick on the ground, it will not be necessary to go far to find a target.

(ii) In modern and highly fluid warfare there will be nothing unusual in the sight of the odd man, or even a small body of men, moving about; and should the observer show himself for an instant, he may attract very little notice from troops whose whole attention is on their own tasks and progress.

All stretches of road that can be used as dumps or vehicle parks should be regarded as traps for the enemy. The observer's duty will be to visit his traps daily and report to his patrol leader whether the enemy has walked into them, i.e. whether they are in use as dumps, or whether they have been – and therefore may be again – used as A.F.V. laagers.

Should all traps be empty, however, the answer is to stage an ambush. Time must not be wasted!

*The AU approach to ambush was meticulously planned.*

If a patrol can ambush a vehicle on a difficult piece of road, they will achieve results far greater than mere destruction of stores – the holding up of the whole supply column while the road is cleared. The operation will be comparatively safe as there will not be any appreciable defence and certainly no personnel to follow up the attackers when they make their withdrawal.

An ambush cannot be organized vaguely but must be laid out for a definite type of target.

The stage setting is most important – high hedges, narrow road, a bad corner and uphill gradient are ideal. There must always be a covered 'getaway'.

To intercept motor-cycle D.R.s, a wire stretched across the road at body height will probably decapitate the rider. The black trip wire (not the thin 'trap wire') should be used. The wire is raised and fixed when the observer signals; the debris is then removed, the wire lowered and the attackers return to hiding until the next target is signalled.

*Ploys to stop a selected vehicle included simply shooting the driver, felling a tree, mining the road, disturbing the surface to make it look mined, and, simplest of all, hanging a screen of sacking across the road.*

To destroy vehicles and stores, rifles and Stens will be needed to deal with the personnel, then incendiary and demolition charges, previously prepared, to carry out the destruction. Such an ambush must be close up so that the drivers are killed and have no chance of taking cover and firing on the men who emerge from cover to lay the charges. These should be used to make the vehicle as difficult as possible to move off the road, which is most easily done by blowing off two wheels or capsizing it. The petrol tank should always be holed and fired.

To attack lorried infantry, the patrol should remain at a greater distance and rely on heavy automatic weapon fire as long as confusion reigns. Once any organised defence begins, they should retire.

It is enough to annoy the enemy and slow him up, it is not always necessary to organise a true ambush. Suitable forms of booby trap can be laid and left, with no risk to the patrol.

# Appendix D
# Auxiliary Unit Training Tests

*Coleshill devised competitions to find the best AU patrol.*

EFFICIENCY TESTS FOR AUXILIERS (Secret)

1. *EXPLOSIVES*
Practical. Each man to make up the following charges.
a. To set alight a dump of 2 gallon petrol drums.
b. To destroy an aircraft (description of where to be placed).
c. To cut down a tree.
d. To de-rail a train.
e. To put a tank out of action.
f. To destroy a lorry full of stores.
g. Unit charge as shown in calendar.
h. Make up an anti-personnel mine.
5 points each. *Total 40.*

2. *MAP READING*
a. Each man to give correctly 3 map references.  6
b. Each man to point out on map a given landmark.  2
c. Each man to draw correctly 4 conventional signs (to be given by the examiner).  4
d. Each man to measure correctly distance between two given points on a map.  2
e. Each man to say from looking at a map whether two points are visible from each other.  3
*Total 17.*

3. *WEAPONS*
a. Each man to load correctly a Sten gun and prepare it for firing with dark glasses.  3
b. Each man to fire six rounds with a revolver at a figure target 20 yards away.  6
c. Each man to throw 5 grenades into a pit 10ft square from 20 yards.  5
*Total 14.*

4. *BOOBY TRAPS* – Verbal
   a. What weight is required to set off a pull switch? 3
   b. What pressure is required to set off a pressure switch? 3
   c. What safety precautions have been laid down for practice with pull switches? 3
   d. When setting booby traps would you put a switch on the door of a room? 1
   *Total 10.*

5. *FUSES AND TIME PENCILS*
   a. How long would a piece of Bickford 2'6" long take to burn? 2
   b. What safety precautions must be applied when using Bickford? 2
   c. How can you distinguish between a 7 sec. and a 4 sec. grenade igniter set in the dark? 1
   d. How does a time pencil work? 2
   e. How does an 'L' delay pencil work? 2
   *Total 9.*

6. *GENERAL*
   a. What battn of the Home Guard do you belong to? 2
   b. What is the patrol code name? 2
   c. Give correct sequence of issuing order. P.L. only. 10
   d. What is the operational entitlement of Sten and .300 rifle ammunition? 5
   e. At what temperature would you consider your O.B. too hot? 5
   *Total 24*

Total possible 94; patrol leaders 114.
Standards: Special 90% and above
            Pass Above 60%
(A pencil note on the original document reads: *Lunnon* – Your Patrol code name is *HW2*)

*****

## SECOND HOME GUARD COLESHILL SHIELD COMPETITION

EVENT 1 – OBSERVATION
Five troops will be concealed on a frontage of approximately 200 yds at distances varying from 100 yds to 500 yds from the competing teams, which have 5 minutes to spot them.

The Judge will allot 1 point to each Auxilier of each Patrol for each 'enemy'.
TOTAL: 25 points per Patrol.

EVENT 2 – NIGHT PATROL
The Patrol is given one numbered magnet per Auxilier, who has 2½ hrs in which to penetrate the defence (2 sentries at least 20 yds away from target, and 3 trip wires up to 15 yds in length, at least 20 yds from the target), place his magnet on the target and return to his starting point. Distance from starting point to target is approximately 1,000 yds. Patrols will proceed fully equipped and armed.
SCORING: For each magnet on the target – 10 points. For each Auxilier back at the starting point, having successfully placed his magnet on the target – 10 more points.
For each Trip wire set off – DEDUCT 10 points.
TOTAL: 100 points.

EVENT 3 – MILLS BOMB
Six throws per man: 3 standing at 30 yds; 3 kneeling at 20 yds.
Target to be an enclosure or pit, 10 ft side, out of and into which the bomb will *NOT* roll.
SCORING: 1 point per bomb in enclosure or pit.
TOTAL: 30 points.

EVENT 4 – EFFICIENCY RACE
The quickest team will score 30 points, and each successive losing team 5 points loss.
a. on whistle blast first man adjusts his respirator;
b. loads 3 rounds into Tommy gun magazine;
c. runs forward 50 yds to firing point;
d. loads, and fires at figure target 20 yds away. If target is missed, he will reload with 3 rounds and fire again until target *is* hit by each man in turn;
e. clears gun correctly;
f. removes respirator, and returns to starting point;
g. hands over Tommy gun to next Auxilier, who adjusts his respirator as soon as he takes over the gun.
TOTAL: 30 points to winner, 25 points to runner-up, down to 5 points for 6th; 0 points for 7th and onwards.

EVENT 5 – EXPLOSIVES

A different one of the following events will be allotted to each Patrol to perform correctly.

*10 points* (a) Set a trip wire attached to a shrapnel mine to be made up by the Auxilier.

*5 points* (b) Set a charge so as to fell a tree in a given direction.

*10 points* (c) Set a combination of Mills Bomb and Incendiary to be actuated by a Lead delay pencil.

*10 points* (d) Make use of Primacord or Cordtex to lay a combined charge of H.E. and A.W. bottle.

*5 points* (e) Sabotage telephone wire by removing wire without leaving any trace of the wire having been tampered with (i.e. remove inner wire, leaving insulation apparently intact).

TOTAL: 40 points.

### HIGHEST POSSIBLE AGGREGATE POINTS – 225

# Appendix E
# Royal Observer Corps posts in the Mendip area

CLUTTON GR 642600.
Opened June 1953 – rebuilt underground June 1959 – controlled by ROC Lt Roger Wilsdon until final stand-down 30th September 1991.

FROME GR 765485.
Opened January 1938 – underground May 1962 – in use until final stand-down 30th September 1991.

GLASTONBURY GR 497381.
Opened September 1938 – resited to GR 493382 January 1944 – rebuilt underground September 1959 – closed October 1968.

RADSTOCK GR 686549.
Opened January 1938 – resited to GR 688544 – rebuilt underground May 1959 – closed October 1968.

SHEPTON MALLET GR 625432.
Opened January 1938 – resited to GR 605428 – rebuilt underground May 1959 – in use until final stand-down 30th September 1991.

WESTBURY-SUB-MENDIP GR 507507.
Opened January 1938 – resited to GR 500508 – rebuilt underground November 1961 – closed October 1968.

WEST HARPTREE GR 560565.
Opened January 1938 – resited to GR 546561 – rebuilt underground November 1961 – in use until final stand-down 30th September 1991.

WESTON-SUPER-MARE GR 318615.

Opened sea-front January 1938 – resited to Uphill Tower GR 317582 July 1942 – resited to Bleadon GR 345578 May 1957 – rebuilt underground April 1959 – in use until final stand-down 30th September 1991.

WINSCOMBE GR 426577.

Opened January 1938 – resited to GR 540570 – rebuilt underground July 1960 – closed October 1968.

# ACKNOWLEDGEMENTS

The Mendip Ranger Service providing unstinting practical support and encouragement in the research for this book.

Very many people gave generously of their time, energy and memories to provide material for this book. Others supplied helpful leads to follow. Warmest thanks go to them all, with apologies to any not included here, and also to Graham Max and Noel Hetherington who worked wonders to restore some foggy wartime photographs.

Jim Adams; Andrew Addicott; Mrs Valerie Alderton; Brian Alford; Jane Allwood; Philip Ashley; John D. Baker; Mrs Megan Baker; Ken Banwell; Tina Bath; Bill Bent; Verdon Besley; Mrs Phil Blackwell; Miss Helen Boileau; Mandy Brading; David Bromwich; Frank Browning; Frank Buckley; Tom Bush; Mrs Dorothy Chalker; Freddy Chapman; John Chapman; Jack Chew; Mike Chipperfield; Mrs Claire Clark; Kenneth Cleary; Brian Coombs; B.S. Counsell; Michael Crowe; Les Davies; Roger Davis; Syd Davis; Ron Dawson, North Somerset Library; Preb Ronald Denman; Bill Dunkerton; Dennis Dyke; Mrs Gladys Dyke; Mrs Sheila Dyke; Andrew Eddy; Howard Edwards; Tom Elkin; Major E.R. Emery; Henry Esain; John Fear; Eion Fraser; Albert E.C. Frost; Brigadier Alastair I.H. Fyfe; Alan Gallop; Sam Gilling; Horace Godfrey; Bryan Green; Fran Gregory; Mrs H.B.S. Gunn; Mrs Judy Harrill; Ken Hartry; John Hayes; John Hellis; Ron Hicks; Mrs Jill R. Hines; Michael Hodges; Mrs Rosemary Hodges; Geoff Holburd; Jim Hooper; Charles Howe; James Hunt; David Ingrams; Philip Irwin; Tony Jarrett; Dom Philip Jebb; Harry

Jelley; Mrs Janet Johnson; Mrs Margaret Jordan; R.J. Keel; Robert King; Mrs Terry King; Wally King; Don Kinsey; John and Rachel Kuzemka; Harold Lane; Mark Lane; Mr Lane; Francis Laver; Mrs M. Lees; Jeremy Lock; Don Lovett; Jim Loxton; Mrs Kitty Loxton; Tony Loxton; Mrs Marion Loxton; Mrs Joan Lyons; Julie Mansfield; Terry Matthews; Mrs Pam M.W. May; Col I.H. McCausland; Elaine Mellor; Jim Morris; Mrs Joyce Morris; Keith New: R.F. Newbery; D.S.S. Nicholson; Mr Nunzio; John Nurse; Mike Parfitt; David Parker; Arthur Parsons; Bernard Parsons; Edward Parsons; John Penny; Roy Phillips; Pam Pockson; Ann Porter; Mervyn Powney; Frederick R. Reed; Geoff Revell; Roy Rice; Chris Richards; Archie John Roberts; Peter Roche; Vince E.J. Russett; Keith Salter; Norman Salvidge; Fred Sawyer; Somerset Studies Library; Mrs Audrey Sealy; John Sealy; Miss L. Simmons; John Small; Mrs Enid Smith; Mrs Mary Smith; Cmdr J.A.F. Somerville; Roddy Southwell; Dr William J. Stanton; Professor Peter Stewart; Mike Stone; Francis Stott; Mrs Daisy Targett; David Thurlow; Mrs. Nora Trego; Henry C. Trego; Peter Trott; Keith Trussler; Mrs Gloria Tyson; Hugh Tyson; Fred Villis; Ralph Vowles; John Wall; Arthur Walton; Charles Wainwright; Dr William Ward; Chris Webster; Harry Western; Bert White; Mike Willett; Jeremy Williams; Sir John Wills; Roger Wilsdon; Peter Wise; Robert Wood; Adrian Woodall.

# BIBLIOGRAPHY

*Bombs on Axbridge*, W.J. Egan, Chief Fire Officer, Axbridge RDC.
*Bristol Air Raids 1940-44*, A.M. Patterson, Bristol Waterworks Company.
*Bristol Evening Post* 22/06/94.
*Britain's Modern Army Illustrated*, Odhams Press.
*Burrington Church and Village*, C. Marsden-Smedley.
*Chew Magna and Chew Valley*, Ian and Mary Durham.
*Churchill, a brief history*, Michael Hodges.
*Churchill Parish and World War II*, M.A. Hodges, 1996.
*Community at War*, John Wroughton, Lansdown Press 1992.
*Congresbury at War*, Derrick Holmes, Congresbury History Group, 1991, 1994.
*Deception in World War II*, Charles Cruickshank, OUP 1979.
*Defence Lines*, Defence of Britain Project Newsletter.
*Engineer's Annual Report 1944*, Bristol Waterworks Company.
*Green Velvet Dress*, Kathleen Young, Tallis Press 1989.
*Heart of Mendip*, Francis A. Knight, Dent 1915.
*History of Somerset Territorial Units*, W.G. Fisher, Phoenix Press, Taunton 1924.
*Home Guard*, S.P. Mackenzie, OUP 1996.
*Home Guard of Britain*, Charles Graves, Hutchinson 1943.
*Invasion 1940*, Peter Fleming, Rupert Hart-Davis 1957.
*Isle of Wedmore News* May 1995 No 186, Hazel Hudson.
*Last Ditch*, David Lampe, Cassell 1968.
*Mars and Minerva*, SAS magazine, December 1995.
*Mendips*, Coysh, Mason & Waite, Robert Hale.
*Military Archaeology*, Terry Gander, PSL 1979.
*Operation Bolero, the Americans in Bristol and the West Country 1942-45*, Ken Wakefield, Crécy Books 1994.
*Report on Blackdown Decoy*, English Heritage.

*Secret War 1939-1945*, Gerald Pawle.
*Secret War, the Story of SOE*, Nigel West, Hodder & Stoughton 1992.
*Sedgemoor and the Bloody Assize*, C.D. Curtis, Simpkin Marshall 1930.
*Seeing It Through, Wells at War*, Wells NHAS 1995.
*Shadow to Shadow, A History of the Bristol Aeroplane Shadow Factory 1940-1991*, BAJ Coatings Ltd, Banwell, Weston-super-Mare 1993.
*Shipham's War 1939-1945*, Shipham History Society Nov 1995.
*Somerset at War, 1939-1945*, Mac Hawkins, Dovecote Press 1988.
*Somerset Within Living Memory*, Somerset Federation of Women's Institutes, Countryside Books 1992.
*Steep Holm at War*, Rodney Legg, Wincanton Press 1991.
*Steep Holm, the story of a small island*, Stan & Joan Rendell, Alan Sutton 1993.
*Story of Brean and Berrow*, Rev William St J. Kenn, pub Bill Kenn, Berrow, Somerset.
*Story of Bristol Waterworks Company 1939-1991*, A. Hodgson 1991.
*Story of Compton Bishop and Cross*, Margaret Jordan, R & M Jordan 1994.
*Story of Priddy*, Alan Thomas, Oakhill Press 1989.
*Story of RAF Lulsgate Bottom*, Ian James, Redcliffe Press 1989.
*10.24pm, 4th September 1940*, James Hunt, Banwell.
*The Times.*
*Twentieth Century Defences in Britain*, ed. Bernard Lowry, Council for British Archaeology 1995.
*Uphill Village Society Magazine.*
*Wedmore Past*, Hazel Hudson.
*Wells Journal.*
*Western Airways, the West Country Airline*, Graham M. Simons, Redcliffe Press 1988.
*Weston Mercury.*
*Weston-super-Mare and District ARP Organization & Services*, pub. Ed J. Burrow & Co Ltd.
*Winscombe Victory Carnival*, booklet lent by Mrs Pam May.
*Yeo Valley Gazette.*
*Yesterday in Easton*, ed. Ann & Richard Porter, Easton Ladies Guild March 1980.

# Index

Addicott, Pte L.C. (Weston) 46
Air Raid Wardens (ARP) 9, 20, 147, 150, 158, 161
Air raids 46, 146-161, 182
Airborne Div, 1st 194
Airborne Div, 101st 198
Airborne, 9th Field Coy 194
Aircraft crashes, Allied 161-164; German 179, 183-188
Alderton, Mrs Valerie (Wells) 37
Alexander, Rt Hon Albert Victor 32
Allen, Mrs (Dalleston) 18
Amesbury, Mr (Bleadon) 177
Amos, Mr (Compton Bishop) 156
Angwin, Mr (Shepton Mallet) 179
Anti-aircraft batteries 31, 46, 152, 201
Anti-invasion measures 32-37
Armoured Division, 3rd (US) 196
Army Group, 21st, VRD 198
Arnold, Arnold 206
Ashby, H. (Cross) 161
Ashwick Coy, Home Guard 216
Atkins, CSM F. (Weston) 48
Attwell, Mr (Congresbury) 228

Australian army 194
Auxiliary Units 65-115, 199, 200-202, 208, 221-237; arms 89-98; operational bases 75-88; recruitment 68-74; training 81, 99-111; uniform 68, 112 (see also under place-names)
Aves, Capt L.A. (Bath) 222, 223
Avonmouth 137, 188, 198
Axbridge 15, 84, 118, 119, 162; ARP 161; AU 222; Fire Service 147, 150; Home Guard 17, 39, 50, 51; MIC 17

Backwell 205
Bailey, Gladys 123
Bailey, Henry (Compton Dando) 226
Bailey, Len (Chilcompton) 225
Bailey, PC (Blagdon) 184
Baird, Capt T.A. (Bridgwater) 222
Baker, Charlie (Uphill) 214
Baker, Lt (Cheddar) 55
Ball, Frederick (Butleigh) 223, 228
Baltonsborough AU 222-223

# INDEX

Banner, Cliff (Winscombe) 70, 101, 226
Banwell 121, 153, 154, 155, 188, 205; Fire Service 150, 210; Searchlight HQ 152
Banwell, Ken (Wedmore) 98, 108, 187
Banwell, Cpl Francis (Wedmore) 65, 85, 227
Barber, Reg (Westbury) 115, 227, 228
Barnes, Charles (Ebbor) 225, 228
Barrage balloons 155, 201
Bartlett, Johnny (Churchill) 196
Barton Camp 121
Bason Bridge 37
Bath 36, 37, 41, 155; AU 222, 223
Bathampton AU 223
Battle, A. (Wells) 227, 228
Bazley, John (Wells) 227, 228
Beaufighter 85, 188
Beddoes, Mike 165
Bell, Mr (Wells) 37
Ben Knowle, Worth 56
Bennett, Frank (Redhill) 228
Bent, Lt C.R. 'Bill' (Wellington) 112, 113
Bent, Lt J.S. (Taunton) 222
Besley, Verdon (Winscombe) 49, 70, 101, 202
Bethell, Ernest 65, 227
Binegar 17, 18, 20
Binning, Charles 65, 227
*Birnbeck*, HMS 22

Bisgrove, Hughie (Wells) 227, 228
Bishop's Lydeard AU 221
Bissett, Jock (Wells) 37
Black out 9, 21
Blackdown 32-33, 58, 165-177, 196
Blacker Bombard 50
Blagdon 184, 194, 196; ARP 158; AU 67, 71, 85, 223; Fire Service 147; Home Guard 50, 58; Reservoir 32
Bleadon 109, 110, 156, 177
Blue Anchor AU 222
Boileau, Helen (Rackley) 15, 17, 51, 76, 119, 121, 127, 161
Brean beach 32
Brean Down 22-23, 24, 25, 28, 30, 31, 50, 212
Brent Knoll 34, 36
Bridgwater 205; AU HQ 67, 221, 222
Bridgwater Bay 29, 179
Brigade, 77, HQ 194
Bright, AC2 C.F.M. 176
Brinson, Arthur (Compton Bishop) 224
Bristol 12, 13, 32, 33, 58, 114, 119, 125, 155, 160, 161, 165, 166, 167, 171, 174
Bristol Aircraft shadow factory 46, 85
Bristol Channel 22-31, 212
Bristol Outer Defence Line 37
Bristol Waterworks Company 15, 32, 41, 126, 151

British Resistance Organisation 64, 65, 75, 112, 208 (see also Auxiliary Units)
Brock, Sgt Bob (Blagdon) 223
Brockley 205
Brooks, Dennis (Churchill) 196
Brown, E. 228
Browning, Bob (Uphill) 164
Brue, River 37
Bruton AU 222, 223
Bryce, Cholie 142
Buckett, Bill (Longleat) 225
Buckingham, Rev Cecil (Easton) 53, 54
Burnham 36, 37, 39
Burrington 212
Burrington Combe 50, 85, 198, 223
Burrough, Robert (Butleigh) 223, 228
Bush, Tom (Midsomer Norton) 202, 225
Butcher, Lt (Cheddar) 55, 73
Butleigh AU 223

Carter, Sgt (Binegar) 58
Carver, Boxer (Easton) 53
Casualties, treating of 15, 20
Catell, Brian 140
Celestra, Gaetano 205, 206
Chalker, Dorothy (Street) 138-141
Chambers, Capt B. (Washford) 222
Champion, Hugh (Baltonsborough) 223

Channon, Kenneth (Axbridge) 224
Chapel, Leslie (Chewton Mendip) 146
Chapman, Freddy (Cranmore) 67, 75, 106, 107, 200, 201, 222
Chapman, John (Banwell) 121
Chard, Dennis (Temple Cloud) 225
Charterhouse 20, 114, 125, 127, 179, 183; Home Guard 56; School 58
Cheddar 121, 125, 127, 136, 156, 157, 194, 196, 213; ARP 147, 179; AU 67, 76, 84, 95, 99, 100, 109, 224; Fire Service 150; Home Guard 55, 73, 104, 110, 216; Reservoir 32, 150, 151
Chew, Jack (Cheddar) 55, 73, 84, 92, 100, 108, 109, 110, 132, 208, 224
Chew Magna 168, 175, 176, 212; AU 224
Chew Stoke 123
Chewton Mendip 136, 194, 196, 203, 214, 218; AU 67, 77, 227; Home Guard 61, 62, 217; Special Constables 146
Chilcompton 37, 101
Christon 119, 163
Church bells 42, 55, 84
Church, Charlie (Chewton Mendip) 146, 147
Churchill 116, 119, 196, 227; Home Guard 49-50, 126

Churchill, Winston 11, 14, 15, 21, 38, 64, 89, 92, 127, 170
Clark, Charlie (Wells) 41, 73, 224, 228
Clark, Ron (Banwell) 153
Clark, Roy (Weston) 226
Clarke, Stanley 65, 227
Cleary, Ken (Bath) 89
Cleeve Head House 50, 52
Clutton, ROC 178, 179, 238
Cobb, 2/Lt G. (Chilcompton) 17
Coldstream Guards 108-109
Coleshill House 103, 106, 221
Compton Bishop 127, 156; AU 67, 76-77, 213, 224
Compton Martin 156
Congresbury 35, 156; Home Guard 188
Consford, Connie (Shipham) 17
Cook, Clifford (Hewish) 132
Cooke, Capt Jim (Yoxter) 193
Coombs, LT Cliff (Weston) 86, 87, 95, 100, 226
Counsell, B.S. 176
Countryman's Diary 105, 106
Coxley 37, 127, 136, 169
Coxwell-Rogers, Capt C. 221
Cranmore 11, 67, 75, 77, 106, 107, 108, 201, 221
Crick, Alan 67
Croker, Lew (Compton Bishop) 76, 224
Croker, Ted 142
Cross 70, 127, 156; Home Guard 50
Crossman, Bert & Francis (Longleat) 225
Crow, Lewis (Chelwood) 226
Crown Jewels 125

Davis, Marion (N. Wootton) 141
Dawson, SMI Ron (Yoxter) 193
Day, Arthur (Blagdon) 140
De Cremer, Lt (Horrington) 60
De Latour, Lt Robert 203
Dead, disposal of 15, 20
Decoy targets 165-177
Dept of Miscellaneous Weapons Development 22
Denman, Preb Ronald (Cheddar) 196
Derrick, Stanley 123
Dietrich, Heinz 207
Dinder 34, 35, 37; AU 67, 73, 81, 99, 104, 108, 224-225
Division Rhyne 37
Dolata, Uffz Hans 179
Dolebury 50, 97
Domesday Book 125
Dornier *Do 17* 185, 186
Douglas, Lt (Nedge) 61
Doulting 171
Down, Sidney (Dinder) 73, 224, 228
Down, 2/Lt T.H. (Watchet) 222
Downside Abbey School 161, 162-163

Drake, Bill (Blagdon) 158
Draycott 213
Duckett, Sgt Arthur (Wedmore) 65, 227
Duddon, Stanley 140
Dulcote Hill 36, 73, 81, 224
Dunball WLA hostel 143
Dunkerton, Bill (Baltonsborough) 223
Dunkirk 10-11
Durnford, Lt Col N.S.M. (Wells) 43
Dyke, Dennis (Dinder) 81, 99, 104, 205, 225, 228

E boats 31
Easton 214; Home Guard 53, 73, 198
Ebbor 206; AU 67, 70, 76, 80-81, 99, 108, 225
Edmonds, Iris 122
Edson, Sgt (Cheddar) 55
Edwards, Howard 165, 169, 171, 205
Egan, W.J. (Axbridge) 150
Eisentrager, Alec 206
Elephant shelters 78, 80
Ellis, Christopher (Compton Bishop) 224
Emborough 17, 20
Emery, A.R. (Gurney Slade) 20
Emery, Major E.R. (Yoxter) 193
Esain, Henry (Gurney Slade) 185, 187

Evacuees 9-10, 119-123, 156
Evercreech 124
EY grenade launcher 58

Fairhurst, Steve (Wrington) 111, 228
Farley, Irving (Ebbor) 225, 228
Farley, Jack (Ebbor) 225
Farming 127, 130, 132-145
Farrington Gurney 127, 164, 214; Home Guard 216
Fear, John (Burrington) 165
Fenwick, Capt Ian 66, 67, 68, 71, 199, 200-201, 221
Filton 146
Finn, Dr (Oakhill) 20
Fire guard 20, 50, 150
Fire Service 147, 210 (see also place-names)
First aid 146, 150, 151, 160
Fixed Defences Severn Line 24, 31
Flat Holm 24, 31
Food stocks, emergency 18, 20, 127
Ford, Charlie (Chewton Mendip) 77, 227, 228
Fraser, Eion (Blagdon) 71, 85, 107, 194, 223
Freshford 37
Fricker, Kenneth (Longleat) 225
Frome 9; ROC 178, 238
Frost, Albert (Langford) 50, 126, 127
Fund raising 118, 119

Garnham, Sgt Ron (Cranmore) 67, 200, 201, 222
Gas attacks 9, 19, 20
GHQ Stop-line Green 37, 55
GHQ Stop-line Yellow 36
Gilbertson, Moyna 122
Gill, Sgt R. (Gurney Slade) 17
Gillard, Queenie 160
Gilling, Frank (Burrington) 49
Gilling, Sam (Rickford) 49, 69, 85, 95, 97, 111, 116, 124, 127, 130, 132, 134, 137, 143, 146, 160, 201, 206, 226
Glastonbury 55, 196; ROC 178, 179, 238
Gloucestershire Post Office Battalion, 15th, Home Guard 41
Gloucestershire Regiment TA 184, 191, 193
Goathurst 221
Godfrey, Horace (Wells) 73, 81, 92, 97, 99, 108, 141, 206, 224, 228
Godwin, Mr (Blagdon) 150
Gough, Lt V.A. 221
Gould, Sgt Edwin (Baltonsborough) 222
Gracey, Pte 222
Great Oone's Hole 84, 224
Green, Bryan (Chewton Mendip) 39-40, 42, 58, 61-63, 71, 77, 95, 102, 111, 114, 132, 136, 143, 147, 161, 194, 227, 228

Green Ore 60, 61, 198, 216; AU 67, 77, 78, 227; ROC 238
Griffiths, Pte 222
Guards Armoured Division School 190
Gubbins, Major Colin 64, 65, 92, 106, 200, 221
Gurney Slade 17, 20

Haimes, Sgt Leonard (Butleigh) 223, 228
Ham, R. 20
Harding, Mr (Pensford) 226
Harding, W. (Butleigh) 223, 228
Harrison, Lt E.A. (Wells) 70, 71, 72, 73, 222, 228
Harrison, Jonathan (Ebbor) 225, 228
Harston, Major W.W. 221
Hartry, Sgt Ken (Street) 225
Harvard 162
Hawes, G.W.F. 228
Hayter, Fred (Sandford) 226
Heal, Terry (Cheddar) 119, 147, 156, 194
Heath, Lewis 49
Heinkel *He 111* 179, 183, 188
Hepper, Sgt F.M. (Blue Anchor) 222
Hewish 130, 188
Hewlett, John (Cheddar) 74, 224
Hicks, Ron (Bristol) 97
Higgins, Stanley (Butleigh) 223, 228

Higgs, Andrew 65
Higgs, Austin (Theale) 227
Highbridge 171, 188
Hillier, Jack (Oakhill) 58
Hodges, Alf (Cheddar) 140
Hodges, Rosemary (Blagdon) 156
Holberton, Capt John 221
Holder, CSM Hector (Yoxter) 193
Hollier, Reg (Blagdon) 158
Home Guard 12, 17, 24, 32, 34, 36, 38-63, 111, 112, 126, 183, 190, 201, 209, 216-220; arming 40, 41, 50, 53, 55, 58, 60; Bomb Disposal Unit 46; recruitment 39, 40; training 50, 55, 56; transport 43; uniform 62; Women Auxiliaries 51 (and see under place names)
Hook, C/Sgt S.F. (Weston) 46
Hooper, Jim (Pensford) 69, 71, 94, 110, 112, 114, 226
Hooper, Joyce (Cheddar) 119, 184
Hornett, Lt W.R. (Bath) 222, 223
Horrington Home Guard 60, 217
Horsa glider 162
Housewives Scheme 20
Howe, Charles (Uphill) 214, 215
Howell, Mrs (Compton Bishop) 156
Hull, Percy (Dinder) 73, 109, 225, 228
Hunt, James (Banwell) 155
Hunt, Capt Richard (Bruton) 222, 223

Hurricane 161, 162
Hutton 110

Identity cards 35
Invasion Committees 15, 17, 18, 65, 202; War Books 17, 20

Jacobs, Bertie (Shepton Mallet) 179
James, E.A. 218
Jebb, Dom Philip 162
Jefferies, Arthur (Bleadon) 177
Jelley, Harry (Bristol) 12-13
Jones, Lt (Churchill) 50
Jones, Stanley (Chewton Mendip) 146, 147
Junkers *Ju 52* 12; *88* 187

Keel, Mr R.J. 123
Keynsham 111
Kidd, Cpl Jock 174
King, Leslie (Banwell) 152
King, Cpl Robert 168, 169, 175, 205
King, Wally (Sandford) 196
Kingston Seymour 169
Kitts, Pte 222

Lane, Harold (Wells) 40-41, 70, 80, 107, 225, 228
Lane, Mr (Wookey Hole) 37
Lanning, Charlie (Midsomer Norton) 69, 225
Lansdown 179, 223

Lattimer, Henry (Compton Bishop) 224
Lavernock Point 24, 31
Lee, Frank (Compton Bishop) 224
Leigh-on-Mendip 156
Leigh, Philip (Cheddar) 74, 224
Lewis, Sam & Trixie (Banwell) 155
Light, George (Blagdon) 158
Light, Wilfie (Blagdon) 223
Littleton 152
Litton Home Guard 216
Local Defence Volunteers (see Home Guard)
Lock, Jack (Shipham) 116
Locking airfield 36, 111, 155, 161, 196
Locking, Teddy 146
Loder, Lt E.E.G. (Yeovil) 222
Long Ashton Research Station 137
Longleat House AU 225
Lovell, Arthur (Temple Cloud) 226
Lovell, Arthur (Shipham) 226
Loxton, Jim (Easton) 53, 56, 198
Loxton, Tony (Easton) 53, 70, 81, 95, 99, 102, 103, 104, 115, 136, 206, 225, 228
Lulsgate 169, 187, 198, 205
Lunnon, Lt Jack (Easton) 70, 71, 81, 104, 225, 228
Lyme Regis 12, 36
Lyons, Arthur (Blagdon) 158
Lyons, Oliver (Blagdon) 184

Maesbury Ring 37, 184, 196, 204
Maps 18, 22, 35, 148
Marsh, Henry (Butleigh) 223, 228
Marston Park 108
Martin, Capt J.M. 221
Martin, Sidney (Axbridge) 224
Masters, Pte Philip (Weston) 46
Matthews, Harry (Binegar) 17
Matthews, Jack (Gurney Slade) 20
Maybee, Arthur (Blagdon) 158
McCue, Lt John 67, 75, 221
McDonnell, Lt Col J. (Wells) 40, 43, 45, 53, 61, 70, 122
Meacons 171
Mells 156
Mendip Coy, Home Guard 58-59, 61, 216-220
Messengers 17, 20
MI6 64
Midsomer Norton 127; AU 69, 89, 202, 222, 225; Home Guard 69
Military Information Committee 17
Miller, Derby (Shepton) 179
Milton 156
Moore, Henry (Westbury) 179
Morgan, Jack 65, 227
Morris, Clive 157
Morris, Cpl Jim 116, 157, 165, 173-175, 205
Moyle, William 140
Mullins, Dr (Wells) 41
Mullins, Kitty (Wells) 142

Nedge Home Guard 60, 61
Nicholson, Denis (Wells) 227, 228
Noble, Mr 37
Nordrach Hospital 21
North Somerset Yeomanry 191
Northover Projector 60
Nurse, John (Coxley) 37, 127
Nurse, Tom (Coxley) 136

Oakhill Home Guard 58
Oldmixon 46
Owens, Arthur (Weston) 46
Owens, Reginald (Weston) 46

Packer, Lt Arthur (Wookey Hole) 54
Painter, Bryan (Cheddar) 110, 224
Palmer, Daisy 139
Parfitt, 'Coffee' (Shepton Mallet) 227
Parfitt, L/Obs Mike (Wells) 178
Parsons, Arthur (Cheddar) 11, 55, 67, 73, 74, 84, 97, 99, 103, 104, 110, 111, 114, 115, 224
Parsons, Arthur (Midsomer Norton) 225
Parsons, Bernard (Cheddar) 121, 127, 130, 133, 198
Parsons, Ted (Doulting) 184
Paul, Wilf (Wells) 225, 228
Pavey, Sgt Arthur (Cheddar) 74, 84, 97, 100, 110, 224
Payne, Maurice (Chewton Mendip) 146, 147

Payne, Mr W. (Binegar) 18
Peacock, Dr (Blagdon) 184
Pearce, Edward (Exeter) 226
Penleigh POW Camp 204, 207
Pensford AU 67, 69, 71, 110, 114, 222, 226
Philips, Roy (Wells) 185
Pike, Lt (Sandford) 73, 222
Pillboxes 36, 37
Pimm, Hubert 130
Pole, Bill (Charterhouse) 57
Porter, Sgt W.H. (Wrington) 228
Portishead 24, 198
Poulsford, John (Shipham) 50
Powney, Mervyn (Midsomer Norton) 225
Price, Audrey 160
Price, William (Wrington) 228
Priddy Home Guard 217; WLA hostel 138, 141
Prisoners of War, English 210; German 206; Italian 145, 205-206, 210
Puriton 124, 179
Purn Hill 36

Rackley 15
Radford, Capt H. (Axbridge) 65, 73, 89, 95, 101, 222
Radstock 101, 156, 178; ROC 238
Raines, Pte Jack (Worle) 48
Red Cross 20, 146, 150, 155, 160, 212

Redwood, Colin (Blagdon) 158
Reed, Frederick 159
Reid, Sgt Percy (Wells) 73, 95, 227, 228
Rendall, Reg 115
Reynolds, Bob (Green Ore) 60
Reynolds, Capt (Green Ore) 58, 61, 63, 71
Reynolds, Lt, GM 156
Ricketts, 2/Lt (Weston) 50
Riley, Frances (Blagdon) 158
Ritson, Elsie 143, 144
Roberts, Archie (Bruton) 223
Rodney Stoke Home Guard 179
Rogers, Col G.H. (Bath) 51
Rogers, RSM 'Skinny' 193
Rootes, Pte 222
Rose, Reg (Westbury) 95, 227, 228
Rowberrow 48, 126, 196
Royal Anglian Regiment 191
Royal Indian Army Service Corps 24, 29
Royal Observers Corps 178-179, 185, 201, 238-239

Saint, Ron (Blagdon) 223
Saint, PC Wilf (Blagdon) 21
St John Ambulance 146
St John, Walter (Chewton Mendip) 63, 146, 147
Salter, Lt Keith 67, 106-107, 108, 200, 201, 222
Salvidge, Edgar (Chewton Mendip) 115, 146

Sampson, Sammy (Blagdon) 223
Sandford 213; AU 67, 69, 95, 100, 102, 226; Levvy 82, 83, 85, 86, 87
Saunders, Wilf (Charterhouse) 21
Sawyer, Fred 191, 193
Schools 117, 119, 121, 128, 129, 156
Scott, Dr 15
Scott, M.G. 228
Scout Section, Cranmore 106, 107, 108, 201, 221
Sealy, John (Westbury) 54, 72, 73, 77, 94, 97, 101, 114, 140, 227, 228
Sealy, Margaret 142
Searchlight posts 31, 152, 155, 179
Seaton 36
Shackell, Capt Malcolm (Swainswick) 69, 222, 223
Sharcombe Park, Dinder 35
Shatwell, Sgt Fred 73, 224, 228
Shepherd, Scorcher 54
Shepston, Sid (Blagdon) 223
Shepton Mallet 10, 18, 124, 125, 127; AU 67, 226; Fire Service 147; Home Guard 41; ROC 178, 179, 238
Shipham Home Guard 50, 69; Quarry 107, 206
Sidcot School 150, 208
Slim, Mrs 120
Small, John (Charterhouse) 143, 156

Small, Mary (Tynings) 32-33, 34, 134, 139, 175
Smart, Ike (Blagdon) 158
Smith, Percy 175
Smith, Sgt Stanley 214
Snook, Mrs H. (Dalleston) 20
Somerset & Dorset Railway 37, 194
Somerset Light Infantry 12, 17, 40, 46, 67, 191
Somerset levels 36, 37
Spearman, Capt J.G. (Bath) 222, 223
Special Operations Executive (SOE) 64, 200
Spencer, Col (Southill House) 107, 108
Spies 13, 123-125
Spitfire 162, 183
Springfields Refinery 56, 183
Stanton, William 84
Star 13, 152, 208
Steanbow Farm 139, 141
Steep Holm 22, 23-24, 26, 27, 29, 30, 31, 206
Stevens, Lt Cecil (Chewton Mendip) 61, 62
Stickles, CSM Bob (Yoxter) 193
Stiles, Capt R.O. 37
Stoberry Park POW camp 204
Stoke Lane AU 227
Stokes, Joan (Blagdon) 158, 184
Stop-lines 36
Stott, Francis (Westbury) 73, 78, 95, 103, 104, 135, 152, 156, 161, 208, 227, 228
Strangman, Capt L. 221
Stratt, Alfie 37
Stubbs, Harry (Charterhouse) 57

Tank traps 34, 35
Targett, Ted (Compton Martin) 58, 140
Taunton AU 222
Taunton Stop-line 36
Taylor, Clifford (Coxley Wick) 73, 225, 228
Thomas, Edwin (Keynsham) 226
Thomson, Tommy (Cannington) 136
Thorner, Mr (Gurney Slade) 18, 20
Tiarks family 119, 120, 136
Time pencils 91, 92, 97
Townley, Driver (Cranmore) 106, 222
Trego, Sgt Cecil (Worle) 86, 90, 95, 100, 114, 202, 226
Trego, Henry (Worle) 48
Trego, Mrs Nora (Weston) 114, 115
Tricks family (Litton) 184
Trowbridge 37
Trussler, Capt Charles (Pensford) 71, 222, 226
Tucker, Albert (Wedmore) 227
Tunstall, John (Cheddar) 224
Turner, George 65

Tyley, G. (Westbury) 225, 228
Tynings Farm 139, 165, 175, 205
Tyson, Hugh (Cheddar) 33, 150, 158, 161, 170, 179
Tyson, Mr J.J. (Cheddar) 150

Ubley 10
Uphill 28, 36, 48, 169, 176, 206, 214; Home Guard 215
Upton, Sgt Cecil (Charterhouse) 57, 58, 183
US 9th Army 195, 196, 198, 212

Villis, Fred (Charterhouse) 58, 127, 136, 165, 183, 196
Vowells, William (Compton Bishop) 224
Vowles, Ralph (Shepton Mallet) 127, 161, 198

Wainwright, Charles (Shepton Mallet) 10, 35, 124, 125, 133, 147, 161, 163
Walker, Rev Hubert (Wookey) 55
Walters, Percy (Charterhouse) 58, 183
Walton, Arthur (Midsomer Norton) 69, 89, 101, 114, 202, 225
War Agricultural Committee 132-137
War memorials 48, 58, 62, 163, 196, 212- 215, 227
Warren, Mrs (Binegar) 18

Warren, Rev (Binegar) 17, 194
Washford AU 222
Watchet AU 222
Water, emergency supplies 15, 20
Watts, Cpl Ken (Shipham) 50, 69, 86, 87, 95, 100, 226
Watts, Wally 146
Weapons, secret testing of 22-23, 25
Weare 155
Webbington House 119
Webster, Sgt Tommy (Wells) 41, 67, 100, 160, 200, 201, 222
Wedmore 187; AU 65, 67, 85, 98, 108, 227
Weekes, Gwyneth 160
Wells 9, 35, 37, 133, 161, 186, 187, 195, 204, 205, 212, 228; AU 70, 222, 227; Red Cross 160, 212 Home Guard 40-41, 43, 53, 63, 70, 209, 216
Welton 69
West Harptree ROC 178, 238
Westbury-sub-Mendip 142, 152, 156, 208; Home Guard 54; ROC 178, 179, 238
Western, Henry (Wells) 227, 228
Westhay 37
Weston-super-Mare 10, 15, 32, 152, 155, 156, 158, 161, 176, 188, 196, 214; ARP 150; Home Guard 17, 24, 41, 46-52; ROC 178, 179, 238

Weymouth, Ken (Weston) 86, 100, 226
Whitchurch 169
White, Mortimer 67
Whitehead, H. (Butleigh) 223, 228
Wills, Sir John 114
Wills, Pte M.T. 48
Wilsdon, ROC Lt Roger 238
Wilson, Bill (Blagdon) 223
Wilson, George (Blagdon) 33
Winscombe 9, 17, 46, 101, 132, 156, 211, 213, 224; Home Guard 49; ROC 178, 238
Women's Institute 127

Women's Land Army 138-145
Women's Voluntary Service 15, 18, 116, 119, 121, 146, 198
Wookey Hole 54, 156
Worle 48
Wrington AU 111, 228

Yarrow, Thelma 160
Yatman, Col A.H. (Winscombe) 17, 46, 47, 49, 213
Yeovil AU 222
Yoxter 50, 103, 184, 189-193, 198
Young, Mrs Kathleen 121

Z-gun batteries 171, 173, 188